November [date]

To Judge Bellacosa:

I do hope you enjoy reading "I Rest My Case" as much as I have enjoyed writing it !!

All the Best
at St. John.

[signature]

I REST MY CASE

*MY LONG JOURNEY
FROM THE CASTLE ON THE HILL
TO
HOME*

a memoir
by
J. Stanley Shaw
with
Peter Golden

CHESTNUT STREET PRESS
Albany, New York

CHESTNUT STREET PRESS, INC.
Albany, New York
(888) 969-3614

Printed in the United States of America

ISBN 0-9677796-0-X

DEDICATION

To Doris Shaw, my friend and lover and the one person in the world who, with broad shoulders, stood by me, nurtured me, and took on the burdens of life so that I could follow my dreams.

To my daughter, Lisa, and her husband, Lon, my son, Jeffrey, and my beautiful grandchildren, Ashley-Lynn and Brittany-Lee.

The purpose of writing this memoir was to leave a legacy to my children, grandchildren, and their children. I want them to know that whatever you strive for can be reached if you are honest, clear thinking, and lucky enough to marry someone as brave and kind as my lovely wife, Doris.

AUTHOR'S NOTE

When I originally sat down with Peter Golden to write *I Rest My Case*, my intention was to create a book that would stand as a living legacy for my children, grandchildren, and their children to-be. I not only wanted to leave a written record of my memories, but more important, a history of life's lessons that future generations of my family might benefit from.

During the three and a half years that Peter and I worked on this memoir, a number of people asked about the subject matter. After I outlined it for them, they felt that the story of the Depression and the decisions made by families who could not afford to care for their children, the history of the Liberal Party between 1968 and 1974, and the enormous changes in bankruptcy law since the Bohack case in 1974 would make interesting reading for people outside of the Shaw family.

So upon reflection, I decided to publish this book for a wider audience. All proceeds from the sale of *I Rest My Case* will be donated to the Association for Adults and Children With Learning and Developmental Disabilities (ACLD) to support the mentally challenged like my son, Jeffrey, and his friends.

CONTENTS

CHAPTER 1

THE AUTHOR AS ORPHAN
OR
HOW I CAME TO WRITE MY MEMOIRS

The building was known as the Castle on the Hill, and I saw it from the back seat of my Aunt Shirley's sleek brown convertible on the first day I can remember, a cold, gray winter morning in 1933. I wasn't quite four years old, and the building, surrounded by a low wall of thick, neatly clipped hedges, seemed to rise up on Ralph Avenue like a medieval stone fortress with great towers and a high entranceway from which you half expected to see a drawbridge being lowered.

As my aunt drove around the red brick building, with my mother, Ida, seated beside her in the front seat, and my older brother Sol sitting next to me in back, I could see that it covered an entire city block, stretching back to Howard Avenue and bordered on either side by Pacific and Dean Streets.

Aunt Shirley was my mother's sister, her rich sister. She was married to Harry Miller, and they lived in a beautiful house with their son and daughter on Long Island, first in the town of Hewlett and then later, after three more sons were born, in Lawrence. I had a sense of the Millers' wealth as a child because every morning Uncle Harry was chauffeured to the Garment District in a black limousine. In the 1950s, when I became close to my uncle, I learned about his textile business, Miller Fabrics, which operated out of its own sixteen-story building on West Thirty-sixth Street in Manhattan. The company purchased material from the mills down south and then resold it to coat and suit manufacturers in the city, a profitable venture in the days when a good deal of clothing was still being manufactured in the Garment District.

Although I had no memories of living with my parents, I just knew it would be wonderful to grow up with my aunt and uncle. For some reason that nobody bothered explaining to me, my oldest brother, Eli, who was born in 1920, had been lucky enough to move out to Long Island to live with the Millers. Years later I understood that Aunt Shirley and Uncle Harry had taken in Eli to help ease my parents' financial and emotional burdens, and I wish they had taken me as well, but I guess with Eli living with them, and their own young son and a daughter who was severely learning disabled and required close supervision, my aunt and uncle had neither the room nor the energy to take in more children.

And so on that winter morning in 1933, I found myself wondering where I was going and why I was heading there. My destination continued to be unclear even after Aunt Shirley parked the car, and all of us walked into the enormous brick building. Sol was four and a half years my senior, but he was a quiet, frightened child, and he always stayed close to my side, as though I were the elder sibling.

Inside, we must have been met by someone, and there must have been other people around, talking, saying hello, going about their business, but I haven't been able to recall any of those details or even conjure up an accurate scene in my imagination. What I do remember is that it didn't seem like a very long time had passed before my mother and Aunt Shirley put on their coats to leave.

Mother was a short woman with dark, brown hair, merry brown eyes, and a smooth dark complexion. She did have a wonderful smile, but I doubt she was smiling that day, although I have no memory of her crying. I remember that after Sol hugged her, it was my turn. The instant she gathered me in her arms I began to cry and hugged her as if it had to last me forever. She kissed me and held me, and after a while, she tried to let me go. I clung to her and cried and begged her not to leave. Suddenly there were other arms around me, presumably belonging to my aunt and a social worker, and they were trying to separate me from my mother, and I was screaming and crying; my ears were filled with my own noise; and then I wasn't holding on to my mother anymore. I was standing there and watching her walk away with Aunt Shirley, the two women growing smaller as they moved down a hallway, and then a door closing behind them with what to a three-and-a-half-year-old boy must have been an incomprehensible finality.

Today, sixty-five years after the fact, imagining Mother walking out that heavy wooden door while I stood there with Sol standing silently beside me fills me with such helplessness and loss that I find it difficult to breathe, which leads me to conclude that the age-old assurance that time heals all wounds is not always true.

The name of that Castle on the Hill was the Brooklyn Hebrew Orphan Asylum, and I would be under the supervision of the BHOA from the winter of 1933 until the summer of 1939. I have spent tremendous energy during much of my life both embracing and fleeing from those six and a half years, simultaneously trying to remember and forget them, but invariably trying to solve the mystery of what brought me there.

I do not want to make more of this than it is. I suppose everyone's life, especially one's childhood, remains in some way hidden from view, lurking behind the overheated feelings and fantasies of children. And for all of us, childhood itself is a mystery that you solve as you become an adult, or rather, a mystery that you must solve in order to enter that psychological realm we refer to as adulthood.

At best, solving this mystery has been a bumpy journey for me, since I suspect that my early years were more mysterious than most. Not only were my circumstances unusual—and in that era, shameful—but as I grew up I was given no ordered narrative to carry into the future by my parents or foster parents or any of the counselors or social workers at the orphanage. No one wanted to discuss it, and taking my cue from the adults around me, I never bothered asking, at least not until the spring of 1996, as I approached my sixty-seventh birthday, and by then many of the significant players in my drama were gone.

Also by that year, I'd had a serious heart attack and a heart bypass operation, and I was the somewhat wary owner of a pacemaker. My experience has been that confronting your own mortality makes you want to remember things—in my case, nearly everything—as though by recalling your life you can convince yourself that you will be able to keep it.

I can't claim any particular dissatisfaction with my current situation; I consider myself lucky. The late journalist Walter Lippmann

defined success as having someone to love, something to do, and
something to look forward to, and I have all of these things in abundance.

Yet on more than a few occasions—some of them joyous, some
of them not—it has struck me that the individuals most responsible for my happiness, for my overcoming the confusion and sadness of my beginnings, know hardly anything about my past, and I
am guilty of keeping it from them.

I kept most of it from my wife, Doris. She is an astonishingly
practical, loving, and capable person who does not believe in looking backward. For Doris, looking over your shoulder is worse than
a waste of time; it is a sin against the promise of the future. But
then, Doris's childhood was far different from mine. At any moment she chooses, Doris can reflect on her generous, close-knit family, and a girlhood full of laughter and safety. Our son, Jeffrey, and
our daughter, Lisa, know even less of my life than Doris, and, perhaps sensing that I didn't care to discuss it, never peppered me
with questions about my boyhood.

Part of the reason for this memoir is that I have decided it is
incumbent on me to provide a story for my wife and son and daughter, and for my grandchildren, and for the children who follow them.
For years now I have carried a typed paragraph with me sealed in
plastic, and it reads, "Each of us has roots and the ability to trace
those roots. The highest and most powerful motivation in doing
that is not for ourselves only, but for our posterity. . . . As someone
once observed, 'There are only two lasting bequests we can give
our children—one is roots, the other wings.' "

I don't mean to suggest that I am an altruist. This memoir is a
gift that I am also giving to myself, so I can look back without fear
or too much regret.

I have struggled to piece the facts together, match them with
half-remembered images and emotions, and discover whether I am
truly remembering or being assaulted by feelings I'd stored in the
nether world where we assign our unpleasant memories.

What you have here is the written record, not all of it grim, of
that struggle, my efforts to meld the past with the present, to organize my life into chapters and finally to have what millions of people
grow up with and thus take for granted—

A whole story I can tell.

CHAPTER 2

FOSTER CHILD

Shortly before Thanksgiving of 1997, I contacted the Jewish Child Care Association of New York. As their name suggests, the JCCA is involved in caring for children who, for one reason or another, are facing difficult circumstances. My interest in the organization was because they also function as the overseer of the client records that the Brooklyn Hebrew Orphan Asylum had relinquished on June 30, 1939, when the facility on Ralph Avenue closed.

The JCCA is headquartered at 575 Lexington Avenue in Manhattan, and when I phoned I was directed to a kind, helpful woman, Leona M. Ferrer, who serves as the coordinator of quality assurance for the agency. Ms. Ferrer explained that although New York State social-service law prohibits direct access to case records by former wards of the BHOA, she would be happy to check the JCCA archives and provide me with a written summary if she found my file. Before hanging up, she warned me that she received numerous requests from former residents and wards of the BHOA, and she was often unable to recover any significant information.

I was tempted to tell Ms. Ferrer that since I lacked any information that I could fully trust, anything she dug up that might explain why Sol and I came under the protective wing of the Brooklyn Hebrew Orphan Asylum would be considered significant by me. She probably knew that and was preparing me for the disappointment that many people who call her must feel when she, through no fault of her own, fails to solve their personal mysteries.

During the few weeks that I waited to hear from the JCCA, I was excited about what I would learn and apprehensive about learning it, because I suspected that the early history of my parents' marriage would be unpleasant. In the first memories that I have of them together—and by then I was past the age of ten—they are fighting bitterly until my father retreats from my mother's invective.

The letter from Leona Ferrer arrived in mid-December. She hadn't located my entire file, but she did come upon an admission form and a page or two of narrative. The summary provided by Ms. Ferrer states that I was born on May 4, 1929, at Israel Zion Hospital in Brooklyn. My father, Louis Shaw, whose occupation was listed as "waiter," had been born in Russia in 1898, and he arrived in New York City with his mother, Sarah, when he was two years old. (His father, Samuel, had already emigrated from Kiev. My grandfather, I am told, had originally changed his last name from Sharetzsky to Shore. He revised it to Shaw because a distant cousin had become a medical doctor, and this cousin had felt that Shore was still too Jewish, and he decided to change it to Shaw. The whole family followed suit, believing that in America it was smart to have the same last name as the one relative who was a doctor.)

My mother, Ida Gross Shaw, had also been born in Europe, in Romania, in 1901, and she came to New York City with her parents, Dora and Abraham, in 1904. There is no mention of her occupation, but I know my maternal grandmother, whom everyone called "Dubbi," was a seamstress, and I believe that my mother worked with her when she wasn't busy with Eli, Sol, and me.

My brother Sol and I were admitted to the Brooklyn Hebrew Orphan Asylum on February 23, 1933. The reason given for our admission was that Ida and Louie were separated. I wasn't surprised by their marital status: I have no memory of residing in one place with both my parents—and almost no recollection of my father—before I was ten years old. In January of 1998, when I shared the JCCA letter with Sol, he told me that for several weeks before we went to the orphanage, we had been living with my mother's brother Willie Gross and his wife, somewhere in Brooklyn, but to this day I have no memory of it or even any idea of the address.

Perhaps this explains my tendency not to forget any of the numerous street or house numbers where I've lived as an adult. Now, whenever anybody asks me the location of a former residence, I don't respond with the borough or street: I give them the whole *schmeer*—numbers, cross streets, apartment or private house, basement or top floor.

One fact in the JCCA summary that startled me was that my parents didn't just hand two of their sons over to the BHOA. Sol and I had been remanded there by a judge because we had been neglected. I'm unsure as to what constituted neglect during the worst part of the Depression. Family court as we know it today did not exist in the 1930s, but I contacted John D. Coakley, a division supervisor of records at the New York State Family Court, and he checked the archives and found a file on the case.

The brief record indicates that my mother and I and my two brothers were living at 8201 Bay Parkway in Brooklyn. My father's address isn't mentioned, so apparently he wasn't living with us. On December 18, 1930, Louie was brought before Magistrate Steers and arraigned for nonsupport of his family. Then, on January 30, 1931, he was ordered to pay my mother eight dollars a week in child support. Evidently, Louie wasn't reliable about making the payments, because on November 22, 1932, Magistrate Brill put him on probation and ordered him to pay twelve dollars a week in order to make up for the missed payments.

Louie didn't comply regularly enough to suit the magistrate and eventually not at all, because he was ruled to have abandoned his family. My mother wasn't earning much, if anything. Consequently, she couldn't afford the rent on our apartment or to buy groceries. I assume we went hungry and were about to be put out on the street, and so her sole option was to allow the court to arrange for us to be taken in by the Brooklyn Hebrew Orphan Asylum.

My oldest brother, Eli, wasn't mentioned in the JCCA summary, but his name was on the court record. My cousin, Eddie Miller, one of Shirley and Harry's sons, told me that his family moved to the house in Hewlett in September of 1932. If Sol and I were in the BHOA by February of 1933, it's clear that at some point during those five months Eli had moved out to Long Island with the Millers, and the court was satisfied with the arrangement.

I don't know who brought our predicament to the attention of the authorities. It could've been my mother pursuing my father for child support. My late Uncle Frank, my father's youngest brother by eighteen years, didn't know if that was how it happened. But Uncle Frank suggested that the Shaw family, especially my grand-

mother, Sarah, and her daughter, Esther, were relentlessly critical
of my parents and may well have reported the situation to someone.

This was nothing new. Sarah and Esther had started criticiz-
ing Louie long before he married my mother—not without reason—
and I suppose this is as good a spot as any to mention some of what
I've recently learned of my parents' past, for it has been in looking
back at their lives that I have come to understand how it worked
out that a court deemed them unable to care for their sons.

Louis Shaw grew up in the Williamsburg section of Brooklyn, and
it must have been crowded in his family's apartment. There were
six children, three boys and three girls. Samuel and Sarah operated several restaurants, which is probably too grand a description
since these were the sort of joints that used to be known as coffee
shops or luncheonettes.

With Sarah working, her eldest daughter, Esther, was put in
charge of the household, a lucky break for the other children because even as a youngster Esther proved to be an adept, loving
caretaker, the quintessential Jewish momma. Her skills ultimately
served her husband and children well when she grew up, married,
and had her own family. It would also explain why she would become so critical of Louie and my mother in the future.

Louie dropped out of school after the sixth grade, and he worked
in the family business, as did all of his brothers and most of his
sisters when they were old enough. According to the stories I later
heard, my father was wild, staying out late, coming home just to
sleep for a few hours and to change his clothes, but even Louie's
harshest critics couldn't accuse him of laziness. No matter how late
he was out the night before, he managed to drag himself off to
work.

A year or so prior to his death, Uncle Frank mentioned that
Louie was their mother's favorite, her eldest son and one of her
two children, along with Esther, who had been born in Europe. But
Sarah constantly reprimanded Louie for developing what she viewed
as extravagant and frivolous American ways. His behavior and his
mother's reprimands grew worse as Louie got older. During World

War I, he was drafted. At the time, Louie was running a coffee shop for his father on Church Avenue in Brooklyn. After basic training, the Army made him a mess sergeant and stationed him at Camp Upton on Long Island.

On weekends, Louie would frequently visit Brooklyn, and now, unexplainably, he was flush with cash. He bought his mother and sisters fancy coats with fur collars. He bought a car and treated his brothers and sisters to days at Coney Island—hot dogs, French fries, tall cups of iced orangeade, and endless rides on the Ferris wheel. By today's standards, this would be considered a modest treat. Yet given that the Shaw family was hard-pressed to come up with an extra dollar or two, Louie's free-spending ways must have made him seem like J. P. Morgan to his parents and siblings.

Louie accounted for the rise in his financial status by saying that he had earned the money providing Army officers with special dinners, or procuring foods for them that were hard to find due to the wartime shortages. It soon became apparent, though, that Louie was gambling heavily and the money had been won during a rare streak of good luck at various poker tables, pool halls and betting parlors, and the crap game he was running at Camp Upton.

On one of his weekend leaves from his base, Louie was riding the subway into Manhattan when he noticed a petite young woman, dark and pretty, sitting in the train. A man was standing by her seat, trying to strike up a conversation, and she kept asking him to leave her alone. My father, for all of his faults, was a generous man with an inbred dislike for seeing anyone pushed around, especially a young woman, and one who was good-looking to boot.

Louie ambled to her end of the car and told the would-be Romeo to take a hike. Pictures of Louie from these years show a trim, muscular, broad-shouldered man with a hard, keen gaze, and I presume that it was the intensity in his eyes, along with his snugly tailored Army uniform and his obvious strength, that convinced the fellow to move on without a fight.

It was also his gaze, and maybe the snazzy dress uniform, that impressed the young woman. She thanked him, and Louie introduced himself. She said her name was Ida Gross. She lived with her brothers and sisters and parents in Brooklyn. Louie sat down beside her. She smiled, glad to have him close by. Ida had a wonderful smile, sunny and sudden, full of girlish mischief and womanly promise. The subway clicked along the tracks, and apparently, so did Louie and Ida.

Conjuring up this scene brings to mind the magnificent short story by Delmore Schwartz "In Dreams Begin Responsibilities." In the story, a young man, the narrator, sits in a darkened theater and watches his parents courtship unfold in the silent movie that rolls across the screen. He sees his father walking the Brooklyn streets and picking up his mother for a date and their trip to Coney Island, where they stand on the boardwalk and breathe in the salt air. Then they eat dinner in a restaurant; a marriage proposal is made and accepted. Since the narrator of the story knows how difficult life will turn out for his mother and father once he is born, and the suffering he will undergo due to their difficulties, he shouts at them in the darkened theater, "Don't do it. It's not too late to change your minds." At last, the narrator wakes up from his dream to face the bleak winter morning of his twenty-first birthday.

I don't regret being born, but I empathize with that boy in the theater. Mother and Louie were doomed to their private desperation and collective misery. Both were extremely stubborn. They had their own unshakeable ideas about how things should and should not be done, and they were temperamentally unsuited to each other. Mother was gregarious; she liked to laugh and dance and play. Louie, however, was a somber man, puffing on a cigar and keeping his nose to the grindstone; he even gambled as if it was work.

Louie dated my mother during his weekends in the city, and after the Armistice, he returned to Brooklyn and found a job as a waiter. My Uncle Frank was convinced that his vocation proved to be his downfall, transforming a bad habit into an addiction. Waiters have plenty of free time and tip money in their pockets. Louie apparently couldn't tolerate boredom (a trait that I share with him), so he filled the empty hours with gambling. Uncle Frank claimed that he would bet on any game or sport, including two cockroaches crossing the street.

I suppose that while Louie was courting my mother and they became engaged to marry, he hid the extent of his wagering from her, not that my mother was innocent or had grown up under the best of circumstances. Her brother Phil Gross was a runner for various bookmakers, including his brother Willie, who ran his own bookmaking operation out of a candy store on Mermaid Avenue in Coney Island. Willie was a generous and considerate bookie. On Saturday nights, he used to treat his players to dinners and drinks at a nearby restaurant. But as kids, the Gross children didn't have much in the way of financial or emotional security. Making the rent was a constant struggle, and their father, Abe, and their mother, Dubbi, were separated well before my tenth birthday.

From the details I could pick up listening to the grownups gossip, it would appear that Dubbi despised Abe because he was a *shikker*, which is Yiddish for "drunkard." Although I only met my maternal grandfather once when I was ten, I didn't think this description of him was completely fair. Dubbi liked to drink, too—scotch, rye, and from her ever-present bottle of schnapps. I can't say she was an alcoholic, but she was rarely without that glowing, red-cheeked animation common to heavy drinkers, whether she was playing *tablanette*, a card game similar to gin rummy, with my mother, or primping herself to go out on the town.

Dubbi enjoyed a party and spent her Friday and Saturday nights kicking up her heels in wine cellars. She had a suitor, Mr. Grossman, who visited her regularly and brought her pickles, pickled watermelon, bottles of wine, and skirt steaks, the small, round Romanian cuts of meat that Dubbi and my mother loved. Dubbi stayed with Mr. Grossman for years, but she didn't legally divorce Abe.

I believe Louie and Ida were married in 1919, and they resided somewhere in Brooklyn, Bay Parkway, I think. Eli was born in 1920; Sol in 1924; and I came along in 1929, named Stanley to honor the memory of my father's father, Samuel, who had died two years before. My parents' personality clashes aside, the major strain in their marriage was Louie's gambling. My Uncle Frank recalled that when Louie was winning, life was a new bowl of ripe cherries. Louie would show up at his parents' house after a big score and hand his mother four or five hundred dollars and instruct her not to give it to him under any conditions. Then Louie's luck would go south, and he'd be back demanding his money. Sarah would argue with him, pointing out that he had to take care of his wife and children. Louie would assure her that he had his responsibilities covered, and she'd give him his money. He'd lose it in a matter of hours and return to beg his mother to loan him thirty bucks so he could pay the rent.

Even before I was born, Uncle Frank said, Louie's gambling had careened out of control, taking center stage in his life. With his continually heavy losses, Louie had nearly exhausted the generosity of his friends and family, and with nowhere else to turn, Louie began to cover his losses by borrowing from the shylocks. Uncle Frank remembered these guys as real bonebreakers—one of them, Johnny Bad Beach, was a made man with one of the Mafia families. Louie, it seems, owed Mr. Bad Beach more than he could pay, and Johnny, accompanied by a nasty quartet of his musclemen, started pestering my aunts and uncles to cover their brother's debts, insinuating that Louie would find it challenging to work as a waiter if his legs were broken.

His siblings anted up, but his close call didn't tame Louie's addiction, and he soon became desperate enough to run a series of scams on his family. For example, once, during a wedding dinner, he suggested to his brothers and sisters that they each give ten dollars apiece to help out their mother with her bills. They agreed, and Louie collected the fifty bucks and wrote Sarah a check for sixty, the extra ten covering his contribution. On Monday morning, Sarah went to the bank to cash the check, and it bounced; Louie had lost the cash in a card game.

Louie was ashamed of his habit and of being chronically broke. Uncle Frank said that when his brother hit these low points, he would disappear for days—and occasionally weeks—at a clip. Then one day he took a powder for good. My mother, I am told, was frantic. She went to Sarah for assistance, but my grandmother, a widow now, had enough trouble taking care of herself, and there was nothing she could do.

My mother arranged for Eli to live with her sister Shirley in Hewlett, and the court ordered her other two sons to the Brooklyn Hebrew Orphan Asylum. My father's sister Esther was appalled. Uncle Frank reported that when Esther heard the news she confronted my mother, saying, "How could you? Even a cat knows to take care of her kittens."

My mother wasn't one to mince words, and her response went straight to the heart of the problem: "With me," she replied, "my boys will starve."

So Sol and I were delivered to the BHOA in the winter of 1933, and Ida moved in with her mother.

History tends to soften the past, bathe it in the muted gold light of nostalgia. For so long, I have read and listened to the inspirational tales of those long-ago Jewish immigrants who reared their children with unending love and devotion until those cherished sons and daughters grew up to sprout the gilded American wings that their parents had dreamed of when they were trapped in the despair and poverty of the old country. There was enough truth in these tales to keep them alive for over a century. However, despite the social and financial success I have achieved as an adult, my childhood is proof of a darker side of that American fairy tale.

Looking back, what strikes me is not that in the good old days this country had orphanages. It is that so many children who entered institutions like the Brooklyn Hebrew Orphan Asylum were not motherless and fatherless. Like me, they carried more complicated baggage and had become the responsibility of the state due to, euphemistically speaking, profound social dislocation. Even though my life demonstrated this truth, it was a vision so at odds with the pictures painted by historical mythmakers, that over the last sixty years I have tended to discount my experience. Thus, in December of 1997, right after I received the summary from the JCCA, I sent a researcher to the American Jewish Historical Archives. I wanted him to sift through the BHOA papers that had been donated to the society by the estates of former wards of the orphanage. I was told that among these papers were several informal histories of the institution which would prove that I was not as unique as some nostalgia addicts might have you believe.

I was delighted by my researcher's findings. As far back as 1878, when the BHOA opened its doors at 384 McDonough Street, the city was awash with children who couldn't be cared for at home. The problem was created by waves of impoverished, uneducated immigrants from eastern Europe. In fact, the BHOA was founded because the New York Orphan Asylum, which had previously handled Brooklyn's displaced children, had run out of room.

The Brooklyn Hebrew Orphan Asylum soon filled its beds. By 1892, it desperately needed to expand and they moved to Ralph Avenue and the Castle on the Hill. With funding from the city, state, Jewish charities and their annual ball, the BHOA steadily increased the number of children it took in, and still, when Sol and I showed up forty-one years later, the Castle was packed to capacity: they had 362 children living in the institution, and oversaw another 738 residing with foster-care parents.

Sol and I, it would seem, had a fair amount of company.

Yet regardless of how obsessively I dig into my memory, the details of my stay at the Brooklyn Hebrew Orphan Asylum are hazy. We slept in a dormitory, I think, and ate our meals at long wooden tables in a crowded dining hall. I remember that once I was locked in a closet by one of the counselors for some form of misbehavior. It was standard punishment at the BHOA, as were spankings. I was frightened, but I didn't feel brutalized by it, perhaps because it was common and the children constantly chattered about it, as though it were a game.

I also recall playing outside on a screened-in rooftop. Through the steel mesh, you could see a three-dimensional patchwork of snow-covered Brooklyn rooftops running out to the horizon, but the lasting impression I have of playing in that elevated cage is being enthralled by a young girl riding a bicycle. I will never forget standing there and staring at her as she pedaled in circles. She seemed to go around and around in slow motion, like an angel moving through a dream, and I remember thinking that she was as beautiful and mysterious as a storybook princess.

Although I can't recall her face or the sound of her laughter or if I even spoke to her, I still feel a pang of longing when I imagine that little girl gliding through the bright winter sunshine. And I was mesmerized by her ability to ride a bike, as well as the handlebars and seat and wheels and pedals of the bicycle itself. I never would own one or learn to ride, as I would never own or wear roller skates. I was dimly aware of these deprivations as a child, barely comprehending that I was missing things other children had—possessions and, by extension, a home that I could consider my own. I am certainly aware of it now.

One aspect of my stay at the orphanage that was cleared up by my 1997 letter from the JCCA was that I'd always believed Sol and I had been at the BHOA for a minimum of a year. This perception proved to be impressionistic, a measure of my reaction to being separated from my mother. The truth is that we were there for less than five weeks—from February 23 until March 27. Then we were sent to the Greenbergs, who lived at 261 New Jersey Avenue in Brooklyn.

In the 1930s, the prevailing wisdom regarding child care among social workers conveniently dovetailed with the economic upheaval of the Depression. The social workers had determined that the majority of very young children would not flourish under the collective parenting and among the large peer group of an institution. Instead, they needed the more focused care provided by living with one mother and father and a small circle of quasi-siblings. Meanwhile, the Depression was making it tough for families to survive, even if the father and mother were employed. The BHOA paid families a fifty-dollar-a-month stipend to take in children. They also distributed clothing a couple of times a year from their annex and provided free medical care at their infirmary, where I had my tonsils removed.

The BHOA administrators must have been anxious to place their wards because on Sundays we had to dress up and put on a dog-and-pony show for the prospective foster parents. We would line up and smile at them and answer their questions. It sounds humiliating, a step up from the slave market, but the truth is that the closest I ever came to the idyll which is supposed to be your childhood was the three years that Sol and I spent in the home of Max and Jennie Greenberg.

The Greenbergs lived in a spacious upstairs apartment over a Bohack supermarket. (Ironically, in the 1970s, the Bohack bankruptcy would play a pivotal role in my life.) Max was a gentle, quiet man who had a job cutting linings for men's caps, and Jennie was a housewife. They had four children of their own—three daughters, Rita, Pauline, and Frieda, and a son, Sammy, who worked at Bohack.

All of the Greenberg children were teenagers or in their early twenties, finishing high school or working.

Sol and I were doted on by the family. It was my first experience of being treated like a special little boy. Sol and I were given our own bedroom, had the run of the house and ate our meals at the dining room table with the Greenbergs. Because Sol was painfully shy and a bit slow intellectually, I became the main focus of my foster family's attention.

The Greenberg children and their friends spent hours playing with me. It was easy to see that they had inherited their generous spirits from their mother, Jennie, who had more love for youngsters than she knew what to do with. Jennie was an old-fashioned Jewish lady, with more of eastern Europe in her than America. She wore house dresses and her hair in a bun, she spoke Yiddish to me, and there were lots of hugs to go around. Some of my fondest memories are of the summers, when Sol and I would go with the Greenbergs to the beach at Coney Island, and I fell in love with the sand and the sun and the sea, and the fact that I had my own locker to hang up my clothes. That first fall with the Greenbergs, I started attending P.S. 96, and school bolstered my spirits even higher. With my inborn confidence and the affection that flowed to me from my foster parents and siblings, I was confident enough to speak up in class and develop a wide circle of playmates.

Now according to the JCCA summary I was sent in 1997, it was noted in the Brooklyn Hebrew Orphan Asylum records that while I was in foster care "both your mother and father were actively interested in you and visited together regularly." Sol and I are convinced that this observation represents wishful thinking on the part of the BHOA social workers. My mother did come to see us a couple of times a month, but she always came alone. And Sol and I have a single vague memory of visiting with Louie while we were with the Greenbergs. He took us to his furnished room for the weekend, and we slept on mattresses on the floor and ate at the diner across the street, where Louie had a job as a counterman.

Despite the abundance of joy in my foster home and the loving attention I received from the Greenbergs, I was confused, probably hurt, and definitely obsessed with why I wasn't residing with my real family. I suppose my confusion and wounded feelings were inevitable, and the issue gained new force and meaning for me once I entered school and realized that my classmates didn't share my dislocation.

The obsession took an interesting form. Every weekday evening without fail, while Max and Jennie sat in the living room, I stretched out nearby on the rug and listened to the staccato-voiced radio commentator H. V. Kaltenborn as he broadcast his reports on the trial of Bruno Richard Hauptmann, the German immigrant accused of participating in the kidnapping and murder of Charles A. Lindbergh Jr., the infant son of the famous aviator. If I'm not mistaken, I also heard parts of the trial on the radio, because I remember my fascination with the moral indignation of the prosecutor, David Wilentz, and how artfully he grilled Hauptmann on the witness stand. It is my first conscious memory of being attracted to the profession I would pursue, but I believe that it was the actual kidnapping that drew me to the story.

Perhaps it was a way for me to understand my own dilemma. After all, I had also been taken from my mother against my will and, at some barely perceived level, I was at least as indignant about it as David Wilentz was about the kidnapping. Then, too, it may have been that imagining another child torn away from his family made me feel less odd and less alone, less responsible for my own predicament, as though a better, more lovable child wouldn't have been given up by his mother and father. Such is the malignant reasoning of four-year-old boys in foster care.

I do know that Mrs. Greenberg was curious about my listening to Kaltenborn, because one night she asked me why I stretched myself out on the carpet every night without moving.

I'll never forget my reply: "This is my pleasure," I said.

My answer made her laugh.

In April of 1936, after three years with the Greenbergs, Sol and I were informed that we would be relocated to a second foster home.

I was stunned and frightened. It seemed unimaginable to me that having already been taken from my mother, I would now be dragged away from the foster family I'd come to trust and love.

The 1997 JCCA summary claimed that the reason for the move was "insufficient room." This was a complete fabrication. I asked for an explanation at the time from Mrs. Greenberg, and again, decades later, when I was grown. Sol and I weren't the first foster children that Mrs. Greenberg had accepted, and she was well acquainted with the foster-care philosophy of the BHOA administrators. Mrs. Greenberg told me that the people running the foster-care program at the orphanage believed that three years was the maximum a child should spend in one household. Otherwise, they reasoned, he or she would become too attached to the foster family and be unable to migrate back to their original home.

This would be laughable if it weren't so heartbreaking and insensitive. Too attached? Take it from me: When a child enters foster care he is so needy that any reliable kindness offered over a relatively short period forms a bond that the child carries with him forever. Yet I don't believe that the BHOA philosophy was the product of institutional cruelty or represented an absence of concern for its wards. Rather, it was ignorance.

Although a substantial amount of Freud's psychoanalytic writings had been translated and published in English by the 1930s, my understanding is that most of the scientific research exploring childhood attachment was done following the Second World War. Thus, the BHOA policy wasn't informed by studies that demonstrated the rapid and profound attachments a child makes to parental objects. Instead, the policy reflected the accepted thinking of the day.

I can only speculate as to why a social worker in 1936 attributed our relocation to a lack of space. Mrs. Greenberg did mention that the three-year rule was an unwritten policy of the BHOA, and my researcher supports her observation. He uncovered no evidence of the policy in the cache of asylum papers or informal histories that he examined at the American Jewish Historical Archives.

My guess is that the BHOA policymakers were attempting to avoid alarming the children being placed in foster care or the parents who were placing them. After all, if a youngster knew from the beginning of his placement that his stay would be circumscribed, he might choose to withdraw, refusing as best as he could to form an attachment to his foster family (and making a meaningful bond is key to a successful placement). And even if an attachment did develop, then it would seem logical that as the three-year limit approached, the child's anxiety would mount and he would become either unmanageable or inconsolable or both.

Biological parents would also suffer by an awareness of the limits, since the uncertainty of who would care for their sons or daughters wouldn't be settled over the long haul, and one can imagine how worrying about this issue would heighten the problems that had sent the children into a foster home in the first place. Finally, I suspect that the policy was hidden in order to pay homage to the prevailing cultural norms. This was the 1930s, when one's parents, regardless of their skills or lack thereof, were considered sacred, a step below the Divine. An institution would never suggest openly that your biological mother and father weren't qualified to care for you.

I have no recollection of packing my few belongings to leave the Greenbergs. Nor do I have any memories of tearful good-byes or glancing around at the apartment for a last look at the surroundings where I had been happy. Though I don't remember the details of the move, I can vaguely recall that I had the same feeling of desolation as when I'd arrived at the orphanage with my mother and Aunt Shirley.

The pain of leaving the Greenbergs could have been lessened had Sol and I transferred into an equally warm environment at our new foster home. That wasn't the case. Far from it, actually, because while we were living with Mrs. Bella Wind and her family at 1967 Seventy-third Street in the Bensonhurst section of Brooklyn, we had an experience that was as close as I ever hope to come to being a boy in a Charles Dickens novel.

Mrs. Wind didn't shove us out into the streets to pick pockets, but looking back at our years in her care it is clear that her prime motivation for taking in foster children was to earn the monthly fifty-dollar stipend from the BHOA. Almost every nickel of that stipend must have been pure profit for the Winds because Sol and I lived like prisoners.

Every afternoon when we returned from school, Mrs. Wind ordered us to go to our room, a cramped, dreary space that I recall as perpetually dark with a single, bare light bulb in a ceiling socket.

There was no such thing as snacks, and we were told to remain in our room until we were called for supper. In fact, Sol and I weren't permitted to leave our bedroom for any other purpose than to use the toilet or take a bath; and we couldn't venture into any other area of the apartment except for meals.

Each day for lunch we were given a boiled egg and a glass of milk. Our breakfasts and dinners were equally Spartan, and we did not sit with the family when they ate in the dining room, but at a side table in the kitchen. On Saturdays, we were sent to the movies with an extra penny for candy. Mrs. Wind rarely spoke to us, unless she was barking out orders, and the only socializing Sol and I did was with each other, and occasionally with Mrs. Wind's son, Wally. He was much older than us, a strange boy who appeared to have no friends, and he was so weird when he came to visit us that I wished he would leave us alone.

What especially gave me the creeps about living with the Winds was that the mattresses that Sol and I slept on were overrun with bed bugs. Yet as grim as my situation was, it presented me with an extraordinary opportunity that would serve me well as an adult and, to some degree, help shape my career. Instead of being overcome with sadness at the Winds' and sinking inward, I became hyper-responsible, burying my despair by tending to my little world and doing everything in my limited power to improve it. I can even remember feeling this awesome weight of responsibility resting on my small shoulders, and my response to it was alluded to in the reports of the BHOA social workers, who referred to me as a "bright, self-reliant and attractive child."

Today, I am able to recognize that taking on these "burdens" was my way of convincing myself that I had some control over my life, which invariably seemed to spin beyond my grasp. Of course, even then I knew that I had far less control than I imagined, but it beat sitting around and doing nothing.

As I mentioned, Sol was slow intellectually and very shy, often refusing to speak to anyone but me. He needed an advocate in the schoolyard and with Mrs. Wind; and I played that role for him. Furthermore, I launched an advocacy campaign with my mother the moment we arrived at the Winds', and she came for a visit. I didn't scream or cry; I just simply made my case, as if I were addressing a judge or a jury, telling her about being kept in our room and pointing out the bugs. Sol and I wanted to leave, I told her. She either had to persuade the BHOA to assign us to another family or, better yet, she could take us back herself or with Louie.

I can't remember any of Mother's specific replies to my pushing, but I had the distinct impression, as children sometimes do, that I was both making her feel guilty and impressing upon her how badly Sol and I were being treated. The bed bugs provided me with a real cause, and I hammered away at Mother, saying at least she could find us clean mattresses. She complained to the people at BHOA, who had the mattresses cleaned, and my victory fed my confidence that I could persuade my mother and, ultimately, Louie, to save us.

Perhaps my parents would not have given their marriage another shot if I hadn't tried so hard to close the deal. They must have been lonely—adults casually dating was socially unacceptable in the 1930s unless you were a movie star, and even then you had to hide the sexual nature of the relationship.

Also, to some degree, Ida and Louie were condemned by their respective families for farming out Eli to the Millers and allowing their other two sons to reside with strangers. My Uncle Frank told me that the Shaws felt quite free to criticize Louie about his failure as a husband and father.

I do know that I never let up pressing my parents to bring their three sons home. My mother was visiting us several times a month; Louie was still coming to visit by himself, but he was showing up more frequently; and I persisted in asking my parents what arrangements had been made for all of us to live together. It was my only topic of conversation. What were they going to do about us? My approach prefigured the obsessive pose I would one day assume as a lawyer working on a case or negotiating a deal.

My parents never mentioned or discussed with their sons the confluence of events and emotions that brought them together again, and it wasn't until December of 1997, when I read the JCCA summary of my file, that I had the slightest notion as to how they went about giving their marriage another try.

The summary suggests that Ida and Louie made the decision to reconcile in the summer of 1938, when Sol and I had already

been at the Winds' for over two years. The summary doesn't explain the background of their reconciliation.

I wonder if my parents felt that it was now or never for us as a
family. Given that they must have had some inkling of the unwritten BHOA policy of three-year limits on foster-care placement, they
knew that at the latest Sol and I would be moved again by the
following April. If two of their sons passed another three years in
placement, and their oldest, Eli, stayed on with the Millers, by the
time our next placement was finished, Eli and Sol would be fully
grown, and I'd be a teenager. We would be related by blood and not
by the common experience of sharing a mother and father during
the course of an actual home life.

According to the JCCA summary, "In September 1938, very soon
after their reconciliation, your parents rented a four-room apartment at 2879 West Fifth Street in Brooklyn for $35 a month and
furnished it on the installment plan. . . . Your father was employed
as a counterman in various restaurants and was earning about $20
a week. Your mother was employed as a dress finisher earning $15
a week. They were most eager to have you and Solomon back. However, BHOA staff wanted to make sure the home was stable."

It is here, in the summary, that we learn about the crux of the
battle that had been raging between Ida and Louie. Although Louie's
gambling isn't mentioned, the effects of it are obvious. The summary states: "Your mother seems to have been better at handling
the family finances, which your father apparently now conceded.
Comment is made that your mother showed 'a great deal of stamina
and planfulness [*sic*] during this period and proved herself capable
of assuming many added responsibilities.' "

The BHOA staff waited until Louie and Ida had been living
together for close to a year before discharging Sol and me to their
care on July 15, 1939, six weeks before Hitler invaded Poland and
launched the Second World War. The four rooms Louie and Mother
had rented were inside one of the bungalows that used to line the
streets of Coney Island before they fell to the wrecking ball of urban renewal and were replaced by concrete high-rise projects.

I was just two months past my tenth birthday when I left the
Winds', and I felt as though I'd been paroled from prison. There
were rats galore in the bungalow, but Louie used to set traps to

catch them, and I didn't mind since I was now with my real family. I was also free to wander our apartment, and I walked from room to room for the sheer pleasure of it, reveling in my freedom.

One day, I remember standing in the kitchen and facing the icebox. I stared at it. I wasn't hungry, but I was dying to see what was inside. Slowly, I reached toward the handle to open it, but then memory took over, and I retracted my hand, scared that I'd get in trouble for opening the door.

I hadn't realized that Mother was standing behind me until I heard her say, "Go ahead, Stanley. It's all right. You can open the icebox."

I turned and looked at her. "I can, really?" I said. "Sol and I weren't allowed to at the Winds'."

"Well, you can here," my mother said. And I will never forget the tears that I saw in her eyes when she said it.

That was the only time, up until she died in 1976, that my mother ever alluded to the fact that I had been a foster child.

CHAPTER 3

A FAMILY

Regardless of the happiness and sense of security that I initially felt at being reunited with my parents and brothers, the emotional confusion and personality rifts that had torn my family apart in the late winter of 1933 were still present, only now I would be trapped in the middle of them. I was blissfully unaware of that psychological peril in 1939, so I went about the business of exploring my new neighborhood and becoming acquainted with Louie and my older brother Eli, both of whom were essentially strangers to me.

And it's funny how things work out. To this day, I'm not sure that I ever truly got to know them.

My Uncle Frank Shaw once recalled that he'd never heard me, as a youngster or an adult, reproach my father for his gambling and failure to provide for his wife and children. Uncle Frank also noted that he had never heard me refer to my father as "Dad" or "Pop."

Uncle Frank had an accurate memory for the salient detail. I didn't reproach my father mainly because I was raised in an era when sons were not—shall we say—encouraged to offer a running commentary on the weaknesses of their parents. My criticism was more subtle. I called my father Louie. I suspect that he understood my reasoning because he didn't ask me about it or try to make me use a more endearing expression.

My earliest solid recollection of Louie dates to a summer Sunday morning. After breakfast my mother asked Louie if he would go see if her father, Abe, was all right, and she suggested that he take me along. Louie agreed, and we rode the trolley down to the other end of Coney Island.

Even if Louie could have afforded to own a car, it wouldn't have done him any good, because he no longer drove. At some point he told me that back when he was in the Army, he had been home on leave and was driving around New York City and a little boy darted out in front of his car, and Louie ran him down. I don't know if Louie killed the child or even seriously injured him, but my father never recovered from the terror of the experience and he quit driving.

Separated from Grandma Dubbi and without a companion to replace her, Grandpa Abe lived by himself in a tiny furnished room on Surf Avenue in Coney Island. It was a rundown place, sort of a last stop en route to oblivion. I recall climbing up a long musty stairway, and that the door to my grandfather's room was open, and Louie and I walked in.

Grandpa Abe was lying on his bed, staring at the ceiling. He had worked as a house painter, but on this Sunday morning I had the impression that he didn't work much anymore. For a moment, I thought he might be dead, but then Louie asked him if he needed anything, and my grandfather turned his head toward us and replied, "Cigarettes."

Louie handed me a dollar bill and sent me to the candy store. I bought a pack of Old Golds, ran back upstairs and gave the cigarettes to Grandpa Abe. Because he looked so old and tired and broke, I also gave him the change from the dollar, an act of generosity of which Louie seemed to approve.

Abe didn't have anything to say, nor did Louie or I, so after we stood around for a few minutes watching him smoke a cigarette, we said good-bye to him. I felt sad, as if we were leaving him alone in some kind of adult orphanage. When we were outside I discovered how generous Louie could be. That dollar was all the money he had in the world; the change from the cigarettes was our trolley fare home; and it took us three hours to walk back to 2879 West Fifth Street.

That summer, Louie's gambling was under control, which didn't necessarily mean that he was betting less, but that he was probably breaking even. He had neither a fat bankroll to encourage him to bet until he was broke or the devastating losses that sent him scurrying from his wife and children.

Louie was working twelve or thirteen hours a day in Manhattan as a counterman at Christy's, one of those old-fashioned metal diners on Twelfth Avenue by the docks. The longshoreman were decent tippers, and Louie used to say that he made out all right because he had good feet; they never hurt him at the end of his shift and he could get around fast behind the counter. Yet just when things were going okay for him, the owner of Christy's announced that the diner was closing so he could haul it to Chicago for repairs to its exterior.

Louie was out of a job, but I have to hand it to him: Instead of unwrapping a fresh cigar and taking up residence at one of the bookie joints or sitting down at a marathon poker game, Louie became an entrepreneur. There was a big vacant lot on the site where the diner had been, and Louie opened up a stand in the middle of it to feed the longshoreman. Presumably this violated every ordinance ever passed by the New York City Board of Health but Louie, bless his heart, was a hustler, and odds are he greased an inspector's palm here and there.

The longshoremen weren't about to complain: eating at Louie's was better than going hungry. Louie cut deals with Christy's former suppliers of milk, soda, bread, eggs, meat, coffee and doughnuts. Naturally, the suppliers hated to lose the business when the diner was hauled off to Chicago, and they were thrilled to have it again when Louie set up his stand on the barren spot. Some of the suppliers even fronted Louie food until he got up and going, and several kicked in with equipment, notably an old gasoline stove.

At night, Louie would lock up his stand and return to Coney Island to buy gasoline to replenish the stove. He would fill up a huge can and then bring it back to the bungalow on the subway, which was not only perfectly illegal but dangerous as well, since back then passengers routinely lit up cigarettes or pipes or cigars and smoked in the subway cars. Louie would leave for work the next day at four-thirty in the morning, again riding the subway with his gasoline can.

When my oldest bother, Eli, wasn't in school, he used to accompany Louie to help set up the stand and serve the customers. Eli was an intelligent, quiet teenager, very meticulous about everything. He had been a top student when he had lived out on Long

Island with the Millers, and he spoke about wanting to go to college and then becoming a dentist. Eli didn't complain about having to help Louie, but I had the impression that he wasn't particularly pleased to be reunited with his parents and younger brothers. The only time Eli seemed to be at peace was when he was playing his trumpet. "Stardust" was either his favorite song or the only one he knew, and he played it over and over while I stood near him and watched him. I was taken with the music, but even more fascinated by the fact that Eli could produce it with his trumpet. My fascination must have been obvious to Eli, because one night he stopped playing and showed me how to blow through the mouthpiece and play notes. It was the only moment I remember feeling as though I had a big brother.

When I was older and thought about it, I couldn't blame Eli for his mounting frustration. He'd had an awfully nice deal at the Millers. He had his own attic bedroom in a beautiful house in Lawrence, one of the swanky Five Towns on Long Island. He had lots of friends at a terrific high school, money for the movies, and I believe my aunt and uncle had sent him to summer camp. Now, he was sharing a bedroom with two brothers. He was a senior at Abraham Lincoln High School in Brooklyn, where he didn't know a soul in his class. Throughout the summer and frequently on Saturdays during the school year, he had to get up well before dawn to ride into Manhattan to assist a father who didn't have two words to say to him if he wasn't telling him to do something.

It worked out fine and dandy for Louie. In the evening, he would walk into the kitchen and pile the day's receipts, a shining mountain of silver with cash stuffed among the coins, on the table. Everyone sat around and counted the money. With Mother keeping her eye on him, Louie set aside some of it to pay his suppliers. He put some away to take care of the rent on our bungalow apartment. He even saved a few bucks so he could chase his dream— opening a real indoor luncheonette. I'm not sure that he had any profit left over to pay Eli. Along with his abrupt drop in status, maybe that explains why Eli finally exploded.

The events leading to the explosion aren't clear to me now, but I remember that even as a ten-year-old I could feel the tension between Eli and Louie. Eli wasn't himself, at least not the teenager he had been while he was living with Aunt Shirley and Uncle Harry. The most noticeable change in my brother was that, without saying a word to anyone, he suddenly stopped going to school. The principal contacted my parents and told them. Mother asked Eli to explain his truancy. Eli had no answer for her. Despite the ease with which he handled his schoolwork, Eli simply quit attending classes at Lincoln. Mother met with the principal, and she implored Eli to return to high school so he could get his diploma, but he refused.

Louie didn't involve himself in this mother-son struggle. I guess he had enough on his plate, making it to his food stand every day and not donating his earnings to the bookies. One evening, I heard Eli talking to Louie in our bedroom. I didn't hear the whole conversation, but the way I remember it is that Eli was asking Louie for money. Whether my brother was asking for wages that he felt were owed him for his work at the stand, or whether he wanted money for the movies, I can't say. All I'm certain of is that Louie said no, and their voices became progressively louder until they were screaming at each another.

Mother went to calm them, and that was when the shouting stopped, their raised voices replaced by the thwack and splintering of crashing furniture and men rolling around on a wooden floor. Mother ran out of the bedroom. It was odd to see her run. I'd never imagined my mother running. Then Eli and Louie were screaming again, wrestling and swinging away. I didn't want to look. Mother grabbed the phone, and I heard her frantic call to the police.

Suddenly the apartment was silent, and it felt like a long and dangerous time before a cop was knocking on our door, a strapping guy in a dark blue brass-buttoned uniform with a visored cap and a pistol on his hip. He went into the bedroom while Mother, Sol, and I waited outside. Then somebody called for an ambulance, either the cop or my mother. I thought Eli and Louie had been seriously hurt; from the bedroom, it had sounded like one of those barroom brawls that I recalled from my Saturday afternoons watching cowboy movies.

But when the ambulance attendants came into the bungalow, Louie shuffled out of the bedroom, more embarrassed than angry. His hair and his clothes were messed up; I think his shirt was

ripped. Otherwise, he was fine, no blood, no black eyes. The attendants carried out Eli, who was strapped to a stretcher. Eli was
crying now and trying to talk, but the words were incomprehensible. He wasn't bloody or noticeably bruised, and I felt sorry for
him, this stranger, my brother.

Eli was taken to Kings County Hospital and admitted to a psychiatric ward. He was depressed, the doctors said. Eli was treated
as an inpatient for almost a year. During his hospitalization, he
attended sessions with psychiatrists and received several courses
of shock treatment. I went to visit him, but I was too young to enter
the ward, so I stood outside a window, and he waved to me. I don't
think he was permitted to play his trumpet in the hospital, but he
was less agitated than he had been in the days before he had fought
with Louie. He didn't talk much. Mostly, the way I heard it from
my mother, Eli nodded in answer to questions, which were limited
to asking him how he was doing and if Mother or Louie could bring
him anything.

Many years later, I would, now and then, feel guilty that I had
pushed Mother and Louie to take us to a home of our own. Being a
boy, I hadn't considered anyone's situation but my own, and I would
have cut off my arm to escape the Winds. But it didn't turn out well
for Eli. He would have been better off had he remained in Lawrence,
in the gilded suburban haven that Aunt Shirley and Uncle Harry
had provided for him. I don't believe Eli ever recovered from his
move back to Brooklyn. Being older now, I understand how little I
had to do with what happened. The guilt, however, has stayed with
me, and a lingering sadness for Eli.

Mother eventually saw to it that Lincoln High School awarded
my brother his diploma. Upon being discharged from Kings County
Hospital, Eli returned to our apartment on West Fifth Street for a
very brief period and then one day he went off to one of the camps
run by the Civilian Conservation Corps. The CCC was established
by the Roosevelt administration in 1933 to provide meaningful jobs
to young men during the Depression. I read somewhere that overall the CCC had about two million men working around the country, housed in fifteen hundred camps, all of them deeply involved
in useful conservation work—reforesting, building roads, and con-
structing dams for flood control.

After about a year, around the time that the war was about to start, Eli came back to Brooklyn from Georgia and heard they were hiring in the factories in Bridgeport, Connecticut, and he packed his things into a battered suitcase and moved away.

It would be misleading if I left the impression that my home life was unrelentingly grim. It had more than a few bright moments, although admittedly the majority of them were not when all of us were together.

During summer vacation, Mother and Louie were at their jobs all day, so Sol and I had plenty of freedom to sample the local playgrounds and wander the busy Coney Island streets. At the suggestion of his sister, Louie had joined the Society of Jewish War Veterans in Brighton Beach, and Sol and I, being his sons, were recruited into the group. We were given blue uniforms with blue shirts and yellow ties, and we marched in a variety of parades around New York City. I have a vivid memory of marching down Fifth Avenue in Manhattan one Memorial Day. Because of the trumpet lessons Eli had given me, I was able to play the bugle, and I played it proudly as I marched past the throngs of spectators lining the sidewalks.

My uncle Harry Miller was a supporter of the University Settlement House on the Lower East Side. It was a kind of community center for poor kids from all around the city, and Uncle Harry arranged for Sol and me to spend some time at the settlement house overnight camp, which was located in upstate New York, along the elegantly curved, tree-lined shore of a lake. I had originally been sent to the camp for a week or two of fresh air, a supposed cure-all for city boys, helping them get the grit out of their lungs and off their souls. My bugle playing earned me an extra month at the camp. They had a regular bugler, a teenager who played reveille in the morning, taps at night, and summoned us to meals and activities in between. He used to stand on a high hill above the campers. I wasn't as talented as this boy, but I was a lot more coordinated. One night, after playing taps, he was ambling down the hill and tripped over his own two feet and broke his ankle. Thus, I was his replacement for the rest of the summer, my stay extended from July through August.

The most enjoyable and reliable family ritual that we shared while we lived in the bungalow on West Fifth Street began after supper on Saturdays. Six days a week my parents worked, and Mother didn't get back to Coney Island until five or six o'clock, when she would cook something for Sol and me. Louie would eat at his stand before coming home, so we rarely sat around the table together. On Sunday, my mother would serve a special late-afternoon dinner, and it was on Saturday evenings that all of us would go out to buy Sunday's main course.

We would take a long, leisurely stroll down Brighton Beach Avenue, which would come alive as the sun set. Finished with celebrating the Sabbath, religious Jews would pour out of the synagogues and their houses and apartments to join everyone who was already outside chasing a good time, talking with their friends and family and neighbors, and even perfect strangers, anybody who would listen or had something to say. You could talk about the weather or the Depression or the war in Europe—it didn't matter, for this was Saturday night on Brighton Beach Avenue. Lights glimmered in the stores and restaurants and bars and pool rooms, and you could hear laughter and music seeping out into the street from the makeshift dance halls that dotted the avenue, and all around you the giddy night air seemed to be swollen with party sounds, and for a young boy it felt as though the carnival had come to town.

My family's destination on Saturday nights was the kosher butcher shop, Glick Brothers. (Coincidentally, the great grandson of one of the Glick brothers would one day be employed as an associate in my law firm.) Inside, Mother would purchase half a pound of chopped meat and receive an added bonus for free—beef bones, which she used to make her delicious Sunday soup. And then, with Louie carrying the package, we would stroll back past the shoppers and revelers.

On this particular Saturday night, Mother, Louie, and I were returning from the butcher shop, when, a block away, we noticed that a fight was taking place on the corner of Brighton Beach and Coney Island Avenues. A crowd had gathered on the busy corner, and people were running toward the commotion, waving for their friends to follow and yelling for the cops.

My mother, referring to her two brothers, said, "I've got a feeling Phil's over there fighting with Willie."

Louie handed her the package of chopped meat and soup bones and ran over to take a look. Mother and I weren't far behind him, and when we reached the corner we saw that Uncle Phil was indeed in the midst of a fistfight, but not with my Uncle Willie. Three guys were holding Phil, and somebody was hitting him. You would need a minimum of a half-dozen arms to hold Phil. He was strong as an ox, and he would punch your lights out in a New York minute if he thought you were screwing around with him.

"You're hittin' the wrong guy!" Uncle Phil was shouting.

My uncle's friends finally broke up the brawl. The fight had started when Uncle Phil was driving his car down the avenue with his pregnant wife, Ethel, and his adopted daughter. Ethel had been a twenty-six-year-old widow with a young daughter, Helene, and when Uncle Phil married Ethel, he adopted the little girl, and now Ethel was in her ninth month with their new baby.

The fight started when Uncle Phil pulled up to a crosswalk, and a guy crossing the street said something nasty to him. Uncle Phil being Uncle Phil, he jumped out of the car and said something equally nasty to the guy. Ethel and their daughter also got out of the car, and by then Phil and the guy were in each other's faces, and the guy threw a punch at my uncle. Being a pretty good boxer, Uncle Phil easily ducked out of the way of the punch, and that was how Ethel got hit. Uncle Phil began pounding the guy for hitting his wife, and the people running over had thought my uncle had instigated the fight so they grabbed him. Meanwhile, the other guy took advantage of his lucky break to even up the score with my uncle.

Just another Saturday night on Brighton Beach Avenue.

I was glad that Uncle Phil was okay, but being ten years old I hadn't believed that there was a man alive who could take my uncle in a fight. I idolized him for as long as I can remember. He was the toughest man I ever knew, and before he had married Ethel, a real ladies' man, girls hanging around him like he was Errol Flynn. Sure, my Uncle Phil chauffeured mobsters around town, and he was a runner for bookies and had served a year in jail at some point for taking part in a gambling operation. All of that was irrelevant to me. And I have to give him—and my Uncle Willie—their due: they refused to handle any of Louie's action, a testament to their practical natures and the abounding love they had for their sister, Ida.

My Uncle Phil also gave me the only gift I can ever recall receiving during my childhood, a stylish white bathing suit. He gave it to me when I was in foster care, and I treasured it, wore it to the beach at Coney Island and probably, on occasion, to bed. I wore it until it unraveled.

The nicest part of all was that I would one day get a chance to repay my idol many times over, long after he had stopped serving that function for me.

In our family, the biggest news event in the wake of the Japanese attack on Pearl Harbor and America's entry into the Second World War was that the repairs on Christy's had been completed in Chicago, and the shining metal diner had been hauled back to New York and repositioned on the location where Louie had stationed his food stand.

By then, Louie had saved three or four hundred bucks, and he said to my mother that he ought to open his own restaurant. Mother suggested that he go talk to William Biren, a lawyer who lived on Ocean Parkway not far from my Grandma Dubbi. Louie stopped by to see him and asked if he could assist him in buying a restaurant. Mr. Biren hadn't been involved in this type of deal before, but Louie had his fee for him, maybe thirty or forty dollars. Biren wasn't exactly overloaded with cases, so that very morning he and Louie got on the subway and went to a broker in Manhattan. The broker said that he had the perfect setup for Louie over in the Garment District, a small coffee shop on Thirty-sixth Street off of Sixth Avenue.

The three men hurried over to inspect the place. It was a little hole-in-the-wall with ten stools at a long counter. Dirty dishes could be lowered below on a dumbwaiter for washing and drying in the basement, which also had a big old stove and plenty of space for storage. The single necessity that the restaurant lacked was a certificate from the Board of Health because it was one of the great roach palaces of the Western world. But Louie either wasn't paying attention or didn't care, and he forked over a twenty-five-dollar down payment for a three-year lease on his lifelong dream, Shaw's Luncheonette.

With World War II under way and our soldiers fighting and dying in Europe and the Pacific, Mother and Louie were worried that my brother Eli would be called upon to serve. Furthermore, in conversation, Eli had exhibited the patriotic fervor that was sweeping across the country, and so it wasn't a complete surprise that one day Eli took a train from Bridgeport down to New York, stopped by a recruiting station, and tried to enlist. When my mother got wind of it she went down to our local draft board and informed them about Eli's stay at Kings County, and he was rejected on the grounds that he had been an inpatient in a psychiatric ward.

Mother and Louie were relieved, feeling that once Eli was safe, their sons would be out of harm's way. I was too young for the war, and my parents weren't overly concerned about the draft status of Sol, because they couldn't believe that he would be cleared for military service.

Sol had barely earned passing grades in his classes at a vocational high school. Although he hadn't been diagnosed with a specific psychological disorder, Sol apparently suffered more than his share of emotional difficulties. He rarely spoke, except to me and some of my friends, and he seemed jittery when he was around people. On the day that Sol announced he was going to Whitehall Street in Manhattan because he had been drafted by the Army, Mother and Louie didn't worry since they assumed he would be rejected for service. However, that evening, when Sol strode into the apartment with a sheath of official documents and told us that he would be leaving for basic training at Camp Grant, Illinois, in ten days, I could see that Mother and Louie were in shock. After they offered him their tentative congratulations, they calmed down. At worst, they later said, the Army would station Sol in the States, assigning him a military occupation that wouldn't stress his intellectual and emotional resources.

But the Army had other plans. Sol went off to Camp Grant. He was as thin as a rail and weighed exactly 113 pounds. No one understood how he could possibly survive boot camp, but he did, and then he went on to further training as a litter bearer for the infantry. When he returned to Brooklyn before shipping out, Sol was up to 148 pounds, all of it muscle. After his furlough, Sol spent twenty-three days on a boat to Casablanca, and then he hit the beach at Anzio, Italy, picking up the wounded and dead soldiers in some of the most vicious battles in the European theater. From there, he was sent to participate in the fighting around St. Tropez, France.

In all, Sol would spend twenty-seven months overseas. He would not, as the saying goes, have a very good war.

Beginning in 1942, the manufacturing shops in the Garment Center seemed to be open around the clock, turning out goods for our boys, and Shaw's Luncheonette was packing them in, customers lining up four and five deep at the counter.

The sudden fortuitous change in Louie's financial situation enabled us to move "uptown" to Brighton Beach, where we rented a sunnier, roomier, cockroach-free apartment at 238 Neptune Avenue. But success, as it invariably does, brought Louie an unforeseen headache.

With men either rushing to enlist in the military or being drafted, there was an acute labor shortage around New York City; so numerous businesses were providing well-paid employment for the previously unemployed survivors of the Depression. With high steady wages available, it was extremely hard for Louie to hire anyone willing to accept the meager salary he could afford to pay a helper at the luncheonette. He had an older Polish guy, Al, who came in once in a while. And he had a series of semi-sober denizens of Bowery doorways and benches, who would stand in the basement washing dishes until they had sufficient pocket change to buy a bottle and leave for a permanent vacation, sending one of their thirsty pals to fill in for him.

Louie's sole option was to ask Mother to pitch in at the store. She agreed, and so both of them were now behind the counter, which turned out to be a lot like having Muhammad Ali and Joe Frazier in the same ring.

When school was out, I would go to the luncheonette with my parents. I was too short to man a station behind the counter; I could barely see over it; but I quickly learned to operate the cash register, take the checks, and make change. Louie cooked the hot food; the soups and stews, hamburgers, chickens, turkeys, and roast beef. Mother slapped together the takeout sandwiches and served the customers who sat on the stools. She was not a patient person. Hungry people who were in a rush to get back to their jobs were queued up to fill each empty seat, and my mother did her level best to empty those seats as fast as possible.

If you were drinking coffee, the instant you picked up your cup to take your first sip, Mother would snatch away the saucer, like Pee Wee Reese nimbly fielding a grounder, and then she would call for the next person in line to sit down and order. The same was true if you were chewing the last bite of your tuna fish sandwich—your plate would suddenly disappear and a bill would be in front of you. Louie frequently used to cringe about the way Mother treated the customers, but he didn't dare criticize her or offer her any suggestions because she wasn't any more patient with him.

When Louie didn't bring out the orders quick enough to suit her—which was frequently, since given the rush in the morning and at noon it would have been humanly impossible for Louie to fill every order immediately—she would scream at him and pick up one of the washrags that she used to wipe the counter and fling it in his general direction. She had a pretty good arm, too, and one of my favorite childhood games was standing behind the register and counting the number of times that Mother threw a rag at Louie.

Despite their battles, I knew that Mother worried about Louie, and nowhere was this more evident than at the luncheonette when the dumbwaiter's rope fell off the pulleys and had to be reattached. The dumbwaiter was key to the success of the operation. When it wasn't functioning, you couldn't send dirty dishes to the basement for washing and you couldn't send up clean plates from below. So when the rope slipped off, Louie had to hunch up and back into the dumbwaiter and stand there, perched precariously on it and tying the rope to the pulley, while my mother and I watched him, scared to death that the rope would slip again, and Louie would go crashing to his death in the basement. Fortunately, he was quite handy, and he never even had a close call.

My most indelible memories of Shaw's Luncheonette are of my parents going at it hammer and tongs. Not that it wasn't occasionally funny, which leads me to my all-time favorite moment as a spectator at the Ida and Louie Show. On Fridays, Louie would put two soups on the lunchtime menu instead of one. And on this Friday, he had made chicken soup and pea soup. Mother and Louie were just a few feet from each other behind the counter when a customer who had asked for chicken soup changed his order to pea soup, and my mother, with what seemed like every ounce of strength in her body, screamed, "Louie, hold the chicken and make it pea!"

I don't know if the customers laughed, but I certainly did. Fifty-seven years later, I'm laughing still.

About two o'clock in the afternoon, the rush at Shaw's Luncheonette would slow down. Louie would go to a bar on Sixth Avenue for a beer and to check on the scores of the games to see how he'd done with his bets, and Mother would be cleaning up, waiting for Louie to return for the late-afternoon crowd and to spray the roaches into eternity and then finally to lock up.

With all that time on my hands, I was looking for something to do, so I decided to go into business for myself. I figured the folks in the Garment Center would get thirsty so I delivered them sodas. It was a dime a bottle. Louie would make four cents a bottle, and I would make tips, usually a nickel. I'd sell at least a case, often more, because I was working in the summer before air conditioning, and people were dying for an ice-cold Coke. My soft-drink concession led me to another idea. Phones were scarce in the Garment Center, so right before noon I started walking over there and taking lunch orders. I'd run them back to Louie; he'd fill the orders; then I'd deliver them, earning another nickel in tips. It was a useful lesson. I would eventually open up my own takeout business and sandwich shop, using my earnings to put myself through two years of the Junior College of Connecticut (the predecessor of the University of Bridgeport), and two years of Columbia University.

Louie was scared of success, or maybe it was the numbing routine of running a luncheonette, or that he was sad about the state of his marriage or just that he was, as my Uncle Frank Shaw claimed, a hopelessly addicted gambler, but by the time I was entering ninth grade at Lincoln High School, Louie was betting heavily again and I knew the effect that it had on our daily existence.

A bookmaker kept phoning us at home in the evenings, asking for Louie and saying that my father owed him a thousand dollars, which sounded like a fortune to me back in the 1940s. No doubt it must have been a fortune to Louie, because whenever the phone rang he nearly jumped out of his chair and then sat there, listening to it ring and refusing to answer it. My mother was alarmed. Although I wasn't aware of it at the time, for her it must have been like Johnny Bad Beach all over again, and she was probably worried that now nobody was around who would bail him out and the bookie would have Louie's legs broken. Since no teenage boy likes to see his mother scared, I decided to take matters into my own hands.

I had a distant cousin, Eli, who ran a bar somewhere on Kings Highway. Eli was acquainted with a wide circle of real wise guys and the typical assortment of street mice who got their kicks and earned beer-and-cigarette money by hanging around the outskirts of the rackets. During the war, a lot of mobsters invested their racket money in bars. It was a good place to hide their cash or sell their hijacked liquor, and the profits were enormous. Since most mobsters invariably had rap sheets, they couldn't get liquor licenses in their names, so they were forced to hire other guys as fronts to acquire the licenses and oversee their investment. That, I believe, was Eli's situation.

I hadn't been to his bar, and I asked my Uncle Phil to find me the telephone number. It took him a couple of days to track down Eli, and then Uncle Phil gave me his number, asking if I needed him to act as an intermediary with Eli. Naturally, I was scared, and I considered asking my uncle to help me out, but the year before I had celebrated my bar mitzvah at the Ocean Parkway Jewish Center. My parents put together a nice little dinner afterward, and invited all of our relatives, whose gifts were used to pay for the reception. My total take was a check for $3.50 from the women's auxiliary of the center. That was the day, according to Jewish law, that I supposedly became a man. Like most thirteen-year-old boys I didn't feel like a man on that Saturday. Now, I figured, it was my time, and I told Uncle Phil that I would take care of this on my own.

I phoned my cousin Eli, and asked him if he knew the bookie who was pressuring Louie for his money.

"He comes in the bar," Eli said.

"Can you set up a meeting for me with him?"

Eli said, "I could reach out to him and see."

"Would you do that for me, Eli?"

"I'll give it a shot."

I sweated it out until Eli called me back several days later.

"Stanley," he said. "I spoke to the guy, he says he'll sit down with you. Be here tonight at eight. But wait off to the side. You're too young to be at the bar. I don't want no trouble."

That evening, at eight o'clock sharp, I walked in and stood around until Eli waved me over.

"He's in the back room," he said. "The guy sitting by himself at the table against the wall."

It was a dimly lit room, loud and smoky and packed with hoods, who were sitting around drinking and laughing. No one paid attention to me, and I walked over to the bookie and introduced myself.

He nodded and said, "How ya doin', kid. Have yourself a seat."

"I'm okay," I replied, sitting across from him.

I couldn't tell if the guy was annoyed or amused by my presence, but he had no plans to go out of his way to make me feel comfortable.

I said, "My father owes you a thousand dollars, and he can't pay. You keep calling the house and you're scaring my mother. I have a job after school. I don't make much, a few bucks a week, but I could give it to you. Then in the summer I'll work full time and pay you more. And I promise that I'll keep paying you until you have your thousand dollars. But please, stop calling."

The bookie studied me for a moment. I can't remember what his face looked like or how he was dressed, but I recall being scared, something about the dark flatness in his eyes, which made me understand that even though he didn't personally bear any ill will toward Louie, he would knock the hell out of him if that was what he was forced to do to collect his money.

The bookie said, "You're a helluva son. Tell your old man to forget the debt. But you also tell him that he can't bet with us. Make sure he understands, you got it? He shouldn't call us no more."

"I promise, I'll tell him," I said, and after thanking the guy three or four times, I beat it out onto Kings Highway, too relieved to think of anything but that I'd gotten Louie off the hook.

That explains why it didn't occur to me, until I started working on this memoir in the spring of 1996, that not every fourteen-year-old has to straighten out his father's debts with a bookie.

In the last week of April 1943, soon after I met with Louie's bookie, I attended a play with my mother at the Royale Theatre on Broadway and decided to become a lawyer. I'm sure of the date and the theater because I saved the playbill from the performance. The play was *Counsellor-at-Law*, a comedy, written by Elmer Rice and starring Paul Muni as the attorney George Simon. Mother and I must have gone to a Saturday or Sunday matinee, because the tickets would have been cheaper, and we rarely had money to spare for Broadway shows.

I can't say that the play was exquisitely staged or riveting or hysterically funny—that my life's path was determined by a brush with high artistry. Rather, it was studying the fictionalized specifics of Paul Muni's role. George Simon was a wealthy, debonair attorney with a fondness for glen plaid suits, snazzy ties, gorgeous shirts with French cuffs, sharp cufflinks, and elegant wristwatches. He was smart and he was glib. And this I have never forgotten: He was always trying to demonstrate to his mother that he had arrived, so to speak, and he made certain that she had everything she needed to be comfortable. She was safe because he was a lawyer and he could protect her with his money and his craft. She was terribly proud of his helping her, and she didn't worry about gambling debts, and she didn't stand behind the counter of a roach-infested luncheonette, screaming at his father.

That was the reason I chose to become a lawyer. So my mother—and I—would, at last, be safe.

The sole sense of normalcy I found living with my mother and Louie while I was in high school was when I left our apartment and went to the schoolyard with my friends. I wasn't tall or strong enough to play organized sports at Lincoln High School, but I did win a letter for being the manager of the basketball team. In the schoolyard, though, I played everything, and my friends and I went at it every day we could until we had to go in for supper.

In school, I was a decent student. I did my homework, went to class, didn't make trouble, earned Bs and Cs with the occasional A, played the tuba in the orchestra, and even had a steady girlfriend. I also belonged to the Boy Scouts, and one of the proudest accomplishments of my childhood was becoming an Explorer Scout. I knew that to be a lawyer, I had to go to college, but I was more concerned about the money than handling my courses. I saved what I earned working with Louie, which took up much of my free time since he had sold his lease on the Thirty-sixth Street place and opened another Shaw's Luncheonette on Fourteenth Street and Eighth Avenue.

It was a seven-day-a-week, twenty-four-hour-a-day operation. The new location had the advantage of being roomy enough to seat seventy, and it was close to the United Parcel Service building, which provided droves of hungry customers around the clock. The disadvantages were that it was in a rough neighborhood, and it was right next door to another, similar restaurant, a diner owned by a Greek family.

Louie worked incessantly, but Mother didn't go with him to his new luncheonette. Perhaps Louie was earning enough that she didn't have to, or they simply couldn't stand the battles behind the counter. On Saturday nights, when Louie was at his restaurant, Mother, accompanied by Grandma Dubbi, used to go to an upstairs

Romanian dance hall in Coney Island known as *Shtiggies*, which is
Yiddish for "steps." Mother had a friend she would meet there, a
Mr. Costello. I do not know the extent of their relationship, nor do
I care to reflect on it. She was, after all, with Dubbi, so it could be
that Mother and Mr. Costello were innocent dancing partners.

I was the one who helped Louie at his luncheonette. I would
take the midnight shift on Saturdays and school vacations and stay
there until Louie's chef showed up at seven in the morning. If the
chef didn't show, I filled in for him, and I used to turn out a fair
roast beef. The worst aspect of the job was dealing with the drunks
who wandered in after midnight. One of them threw a salt shaker
at my head and another hurled a sugar bowl through the front
window. When I wasn't busy ducking, I could glance outside and
report any number of muggings and robberies to the police. If it
hadn't been my father's restaurant, and if I hadn't needed the money,
I'm certain that I could have discovered more pleasant ways to
spend my Saturday nights.

My brother Sol brought the war home with him in early 1946. He
weighed 148 pounds when he had completed basic training at Camp
Grant, but he was at least twenty or thirty pounds lighter now. He
had contracted dysentery in Casablanca and had suffered with it
on and off for a while. He was quieter than usual, almost withdrawn, and he told me that he had atrocious nightmares, memories of the dead and horribly wounded that he had carried on his
stretcher during twenty-seven months of combat.

The news when he checked into our apartment on Neptune
Avenue didn't lighten his burden. While he was in the Army, Sol
had religiously sent his paycheck home every month. Our parents
were supposed to hold it for him. Louie, though, figured out that he
could make a real killing with the extra cash if he could just pick
some winners in the World Series or at the track. Then he could
pay back Sol and have a nice bankroll for himself. Except it didn't
work out that way. Louie lost every cent of my brother's savings to
the bookies.

Sol was hurt when he learned about it, though I doubt that he
was shocked. That was Louie and his gambling sickness, and Sol

didn't pursue the matter with him, didn't say word one. Like most children of our era, we were raised with the ethos that a child honors his father and mother regardless of their behavior. This meant that you didn't yell at them or criticize their actions.

As I recount this story, I can easily see how, given the nature of our childhood and the manner in which Louie treated Sol (and later, me), that it would seem as though obeying this rule against speaking up to your parents would appear to be bordering on the insane. Yet a cultural injunction is not robbed of its force merely because it is thoroughly irrational, and the three Shaw brothers were unmistakably children of their times.

Sol complained to our Uncle Frank, telling him that Louie was constantly gabbing about himself, talking about what he wanted and what he needed. When, Sol asked, would any of his sons get a turn? But however personally troubled or limited Sol might have been, he knew the answer to that question, and when he learned about his missing savings, he shrugged and kept his mouth shut.

Like every veteran, Sol was anxious to get on with his civilian life. It must have seemed that everyone in America had been off at a party while he was away fighting the war, and now he attended a round of dances at the clubs in Brighton Beach, searching for a girlfriend. During the war, he had been a pen pal with a young woman who lived with her parents in the Bronx, and Sol couldn't stop talking about her. He did manage to arrange a date with her, but when the appointed evening rolled around, he was too nervous to pick her up. So I went with him to her parents' apartment. It was clear when we arrived that the young woman wasn't interested in Sol, and we spent an uncomfortable hour or two chatting in the living room and then I went back to Brooklyn with my heartbroken brother.

Before he had been stateside for very long Sol had a nervous breakdown, and he spent nine months in the psychiatric ward of the Fort Hamilton Veteran's Hospital. His depression was treated with insulin injections, a treatment that produces convulsions similar to electroshock therapy. When he was discharged, he went to work in the Brooklyn Navy Yard, and he married a woman, Evelyn Pines, who, unfortunately, shared some of Sol's emotional problems. Mother and Louie tried to persuade him not to marry Evelyn.

I also spoke to Sol about it, but he went ahead with it, and I understood why: his loneliness was palpable, and he was grabbing for the closest life raft in his vicinity.

The consequences would be tragic.

CHAPTER 4

SHAPING A FUTURE

In the fall of 1947, I began my freshman year at the Junior College of Connecticut in Bridgeport. I knew my courses wouldn't challenge me beyond what I'd been taking in high school for my last couple of years, but the tuition was low. I could pay my own way out of my savings from working at the luncheonette. Over the summer, I'd also worked as a children's waiter at Pollack's Hotel in Ferndale, New York, one of the Borscht Belt hotels scattered around the Catskill Mountains, where my Uncle Frank had a job as the social director.

I had already lined up an inexpensive place to live in Bridgeport. My brother Eli had married a wonderful, friendly girl, Ruth Platzek. Eli and Ruth were renting a small apartment in one of the low-income housing projects that dotted the Bridgeport skyline. Ruth's mother, who was a widow, lived in a three-bedroom apartment in the same project, with a son who was mentally challenged, and I helped Mrs. Platzek with her son and the rent.

I could have attended one of the excellent New York City public colleges. I considered that option during my last months of high school, but then I would have been trapped on Neptune Avenue with my parents while they fought their ongoing battles. Without ever consciously considering it, I realized that it would be best for me to escape from the constant hostility that flared up between Mother and Louie.

It was a lonely year in Bridgeport, and I remember the weather as cold and rainy. I suspect that if I were to go to a library and check the local newspapers from September of 1947 to May of 1948, I would learn that the days were no colder or wetter than usual. Yet recalling those months now, I see myself shivering on the way to class with my coat collar turned up. The sky is as gray as the

ships in the Brooklyn Navy Yard; and I watch the rain falling outside the classroom windows.

Without much to distract me, I managed to socialize more with
Eli and become closer to him. It was good to see my brother away
from Louie. He was calmer without our father around, and he was
progressing nicely in his job at the General Electric plant. His wife
was a warm person, kind and generous and patient. However, Eli
and Ruth weren't people I could be friendly with on a daily basis,
and the truth was that hanging around Mrs. Platzek's was a bit
grim. My studies weren't challenging and didn't occupy me for long,
and I promised myself to apply to a better college as soon as I could
afford to pay the higher tuition.

Ruth had met Eli at one of the socials at the Bridgeport Jewish
Community Center, and she suggested that if I wanted to make
some friends maybe I could get involved in some of the activities
there. During the evenings, I began playing basketball for the team
at the JCC, a move that had an unforeseen and not unpleasant
side effect on my social life. Here I was, a new Jewish boy in town,
young, going to school, if not a perfect catch then at least someone
who would ultimately be transformed by time and a diploma into
an eligible bachelor. I suspect the Jewish matrons couldn't help
themselves—some of them had to have daughters in need of a
date—and the next thing I knew I was being introduced to a nice
young woman, Marion, whose parents owned a liquor store.

Marion and I attended a number of dances around Bridgeport.
I recall that I enjoyed talking with her, but sadly my lasting and
less-than-noble impression of Marion is that she had a bad tooth. I
believe it was in the front of her mouth, though I can't exactly
remember which tooth it was. Over the last fifty years I have occasionally wondered whether if I'd been in New Haven attending
Yale the Jewish matrons of that city would have found me a date
who had been born with straighter teeth than Marion, or had perhaps been treated by an orthodontist, but I understand that these
are idle and narcissistic speculations.

Marion certainly worked out better than the date I'd recently
had back in New York. I had invited a gorgeous young woman from
the Bronx to accompany me to a party for my Uncle Harry. We
laughed and danced and had a wonderful time, and when I es-

corted her back to the Bronx and we entered her apartment, I saw that her parents weren't home. We sat on the couch, and I figured this was my chance to make my big move, but before I could make the move to kiss her, she explained to me that she was a lesbian with no interest in anything beyond Platonic friendship with men. At least Marion and I played in the same ballpark. She was a sweet person, but I couldn't stop feeling lonely. I even invited my old high-school girlfriend, Mona, to visit for a long weekend, so I could escort her to the Sweetheart Dance at the college. She stayed with Eli and Ruth and slept on their living-room couch, and after the dance Mona managed to fall off the couch in the middle of the night and wake up everyone. I remember that Mona and I laughed about it later, and so end my memories of my first year in Bridgeport.

That summer, I worked at Shaw's Luncheonette on Fourteenth Street and Eighth Avenue, which despite Louie's best effort, was slowly going broke. It was that summer, quite by accident, that I took my maiden voyage into the complexities of our legal system. Louie had signed a note in order to open up this luncheonette, to pay for the fixtures and some essential equipment. He had borrowed the money from a Mr. Silverman, his accountant. Mr. Silverman could not have known my father very well or been a particularly shrewd investor, because if you spent an afternoon with Louie, including his stops by his bookie and a high-stakes poker or dice game, it quickly became clear that lending him money was as solid an investment as using a hundred-dollar bill to light a cigar.

Since the luncheonette was going bust, Louie was unable to make his monthly payments to Silverman. Understandably the accountant wanted his money back, with interest, and he concocted a creative and patently illegal method for collecting it, and thereby became the first person (but not nearly the last) to sue me. Silverman claimed that I was fully responsible for Louie's debts, and he had the physical evidence to prove it. He moved for summary judgment, meaning that the court should award him the amount he was asking for because the evidence was overwhelmingly in his favor and there was no issue of fact that needed to be determined at a trial. The moment I was served with the papers I went to see Louie's lawyer, William Biren. I was outraged when I reviewed

Silverman's evidence, a piece of paper with my signature on it, and above my name were the words "I hereby assume the obligations of my father."

I recognized the paper. I had been doodling on the page while I was working the counter at the luncheonette, signing my name over and over again for the hell of it, giving the letters the flourish that I assumed a wealthy, important man would use when signing his big-time deals and million-dollar checks. I suppose it was my way of fantasizing about a future far away from a sweltering, debt-ridden luncheonette. Silverman had taken the paper, snipped off all the signatures but one and inked in the sentence about my assuming Louie's debts.

I would one day sign more notes than were healthy for me and spend years meeting the immense financial burden that came with that mistake, but even at the tender age of nineteen I knew that it would be nuts to sign a note for Louie. The funniest thing about the evidence was that Silverman didn't even produce a middling forgery. The words he had penned in above my signature were obviously not written by the same person who had signed his name.

I showed the paper to Mr. Biren and explained what had happened. He shook his head and commented: "Ridiculous."

"Can Silverman win with this garbage?" I asked. Even back then I sensed what every decent trial lawyer soon learns—a courtroom can be a capricious place and the good guys don't always win.

"Ridiculous," Biren said again, and I was overjoyed when the judge agreed with him. He ruled against Silverman's motion for a summary judgment and instructed him that he would have to present a case if he wanted his money. Months passed. Silverman didn't pursue the matter, and I thought the suit was behind me. This was not the last time I was wrong about a case.

My sophomore year at the Junior College of Connecticut proved to be the polar opposite of my first, and this fortunate turn of events was set in motion by Billy Wolk, another student at the college who came from Brookline, Massachusetts.

Billy was a big man on campus by virtue of the facts that he had a sizzling, outsized personality—imagine Bugsy Siegel without the murder in his heart—and he owned a car. Billy felt that residing in a dormitory cramped his style, so after we started to hang around together, he suggested that we move into other quarters. I thought that was a terrific idea. Mrs. Platzek had been friendly to me, but her apartment was small, and it was a strain living around her son, who was so needy and, at times, difficult to manage.

Naturally, Billy had a place lined up, a large old house on Park Avenue in Bridgeport. The house was owned by an elderly Jewish widow who lived alone, and almost immediately I nicknamed her "Queenie." I can't recall why I gave her that name other than it seemed to suit both her oddly casual and regal manner. One thing I won't forget: next to my foster mother Mrs. Greenberg, Queenie was the kindest person I had ever met, a classic variety of Jewish mother—funny, infinitely patient when it came to listening to us, and a first-rate cook, who fed us breakfast every morning and made certain that we ate a good dinner every night by preparing nearly every Jewish food you could name, all of it delicious and served in portions that made it a challenge to clean your plate.

I don't recall how much rent Queenie charged us each month, surely less than we should have paid her given the splendid dinners that she served us, and I think that having young people around her house was more important to her than collecting the money. Still, I wanted to do my fair share, and so on the occasional weekends that I visited Mother and Louie in Brooklyn, I would stop by the luncheonette before hitchhiking to Bridgeport, or taking the train back from Grand Central, and stock up on canned goods that I could give to Queenie. The free cans of food were about the only gift I could afford, and she invariably seemed pleased to receive them, but I suspect all she ever wanted was the company.

In the evenings Billy, a fourteen-carat ladies' man, was generally out painting the town every color of the rainbow, and I stayed in my room to study. Almost without fail, Queenie would brew me a cup of tea and serve me homemade cookies while I worked. Afterward, I would sit in the kitchen with her, and she would listen to my trials and tribulations, and she became a wonderful sounding board for me, offering advice when she could but mainly encouraging me to pursue my dreams by assuring me that things would work out for the best.

Most weekends, Billy Wolk and I used to go to his house in Brookline, and other than my rare visit to Aunt Shirley and Uncle Harry's home in Lawrence, I had never seen a prosperous suburb up close. Mr. Wolk, Billy's father, had died before Billy had gone off to school, but he had left Mrs. Wolk a substantial estate, or perhaps she had family money of her own, because their house was a gorgeous, stately Victorian, and Billy had money to burn. He dressed beautifully in smartly tailored blue or herringbone blazers, gray flannel slacks, and shined loafers, and his car was new, an unheard of luxury for a college boy back in my Brooklyn neighborhood.

Fortunately for me, Billy was quite happy to let me use his car. In fact, he taught me to drive, and I owe my driver's license to him, since he took me for my road test in Bridgeport, and in those days there was reciprocity between Connecticut and New York. Billy also had a nice-looking kid sister that I dated on weekends, and we passed our Saturday nights exploring the delightful side of genteel Boston, seeing the sights and even attending the opera.

My lasting impression of my visits to the Wolks' revolve around a man named Bob, who lived with Billy's mother off and on. Bob was a gambler, and I understand that in light of my family life it is no great mystery why another man who shared my father's compulsion would stick in my memory fifty years later. However, Bob wasn't Louie's kind of gambler. He was a high roller, from his meticulously barbered hair right down to the glossy polished cordovan leather of his shoes, and he either won a lot more than he lost or maybe it was that he could afford to pay his losses, because I didn't get the idea that this guy had bookies and loan sharks calling him at every hour of the day and night to settle up with them.

Bob not only dressed immaculately, he had a manner that was as smooth as his silk shirts and ties. I could never really describe him properly to other people, to catch his happy-go-lucky, high-living attitude and his apparently inexhaustible fund of street wisdom until the 1960s when I saw the film *Funny Girl,* and I recognized Bob in the character of Nicky Arnstein, the role played by

Omar Sharif, another fellow who, from what I've read, is acquainted with the vicissitudes of the gambling passion.

Bob had that city-slick snap in his walk and an unlimited supply of glib patter, and he would bet on everything—horses, cards, sports. One Saturday, Bob came into the house with a portable dice table, and he set it up in the living room for a game he was going to run for his friends. I was fascinated by the numbers and boxes on the baize-topped table, and when Bob offered to teach me how to play craps, I couldn't resist. I was half a wise guy anyway, and I had seventeen bucks in my pocket that Mother had given me to buy a new pair of shoes.. I must have won a few rolls, and now I was really excited, figuring I'd discovered one sweet shortcut to wealth and happiness. But about two minutes later I lost the roll and then bet against Bob, and my seventeen dollars disappeared into his wallet.

Later, I said to Billy, "Something stinks about that guy."

"What d'you mean?" Billy asked.

"He must have been using shaved dice, and he was practicing on me so he could use the dice tonight on his friends."

"You're kidding," Billy said.

My conviction that Bob cheated me at the dice table has not changed since that evening in 1948, although the truth is that I have no proof beyond my sense of Bob's dishonesty. However, he did teach me a crucial lesson about craps: Always bet with the house, a bit of wisdom that I now never fail to heed when I visit Atlantic City with my dear friend Joe Ferrara.

As I was completing my course work at the Junior College of Connecticut, I applied for admission to Columbia University, and I was accepted for the following fall. My financial situation was definitely on the anemic side. In order to attend Columbia, I would have to move into Mother and Louie's place on Neptune Avenue and commute back and forth by taking two trains to 116th Street and Broadway in Manhattan. I calculated that an Ivy League degree would be well worth the trouble, especially when it came time to apply for admission to law school. Now my only problem was how to pay the university's steep tuition.

I solved that dilemma during the summer. Louie heard about a promising lead on another luncheonette, this one at Forty-eighth Street and Madison Avenue, right in the heart of Manhattan. It was a small, ten-stool operation with an upstairs where orders could be prepared. The one stumbling block was that the luncheonette was located in a building owned by Longchamps, the tony restaurant people. They weren't willing to sign a long-term lease, so I negotiated a deal for my father. He would give the owners a thousand dollars in cash, and two thousand more over the next three years. However, if Longchamps asked him to move, his payments would stop. The deal was signed, and Louie had himself a terrific spot to do business.

With the luncheonette's easy access to the Time-Life Building, Rockefeller Center, and the other thousands of offices clustered in Midtown, I saw an opportunity to develop an enormous takeout lunchtime business. I had stacks of menus printed up with our phone number, and I made the rounds at the offices, handing out the menus and sweet-talking the secretaries into convincing their bosses and coworkers to order from me. The luncheonette specialized in triple-decker sandwiches, the salty, cholesterol-laden deli meats that everyone loved and no one worried about dying from in the 1940s and 1950s. Before the summer was over, I had to hire a dozen people to keep up with the orders. I had three sandwich makers, four people answering the phones, and five runners to deliver the food and drinks.

By then, Louie had signed over the ownership of the luncheonette to me in order to protect his assets, since his other place was in trouble. In September, when classes began at Columbia, Louie was back working at his other luncheonette, and I had to take on a manager to keep the business going. The guy I hired was a short, squat, wisecracking fellow who was rarely without a cigar stub jammed in the side of this mouth.

I told him: "Look, I know you're gonna steal from me when I'm not around. But try to be reasonable."

"Okay," he said. "I smoke cigars."

I handed him a box of his brand and said, "Here's your cigars. Maybe they'll keep your hands out of the register."

The guy stole anyway, but he wasn't a pig about it, and the operation ran pretty smoothly. All I had to do to keep it going was to stop by for a few hours every day after classes and then put in a full day on Saturdays. I was a political-science major and was doing quite well in my courses. I also took a number of rhetoric classes and found that I enjoyed giving speeches. The truth is that I loved every minute of Columbia, and even now I am still enthralled by my good luck at having been accepted at the top school in New York City and putting together a business that could pay for it. Living with Mother and Louie wasn't as trying as I'd expected, because they seemed to have forged a separate peace with each other, and because I was older now and could simply leave if one of their minor earthquakes suddenly arrived.

Then, as if to complete my new life, I found a girlfriend.

Her name was Harriet. She was the first and only Gentile woman that I ever dated. She was very natural-looking with an easygoing manner, lovely smile, and long light brown hair. I met her in the Columbia library while we were both studying. The moment I spotted her my attention shifted from the pages of my book to the shape of her legs, and she noticed me staring, and I smiled at her, and we struck up a conversation.

Harriet was a graduate student, a couple of years older than I, and she had come to New York from Florida. She was living in one of the big rooming houses that bordered the Columbia campus. It had a common kitchen and bathroom, but more peace and quiet and privacy than if you lived in a dorm. Like me, Harriet was working her way through college, only she had a far more exotic job: Harriet was a nude model for art majors at Columbia and other artists around the city. This information had a salubrious effect on my hormones, and within a very short period Harriet and I were going steady, and I was spending the weekends at her rooming house, where, with Harriet's assistance, I learned how to draw nudes with charcoals and pastels.

The policy of the house was that men were not permitted to spend the night. It was a policy that was completely and happily ignored. The late 1940s and early 1950s were an interesting era in New York City. The public relaxation of traditional morality that would arrive in the 1960s hadn't shown up yet, but those societal changes had their roots in those giddy, prosperous years immediately following the Second World War. Since the 1920s, Greenwich Village had owned the reputation as the local Bohemia, but it was spreading uptown, and coffeehouses, sidewalk artists, beatniks, and couples living together without the benefit of marriage became common around the Columbia University campus.

My mother was one of those people whose attitude was "if you're a friend of Stanley's then you're a friend of mine," so even though she knew I was living part-time with Harriet, I didn't feel the slightest embarrassment about bringing Harriet to Brooklyn to meet her. I was so proud of Harriet's beauty and her free spirit, but I did think she was naive about her profession. She considered herself part of the artistic process, while I suspected that she was, on occasion, working for pornographers. In those days, you could buy those tiny viewers from one of the sex shops lining Forty-second Street. The viewers were the small plastic kind they used to put family pictures in at the Catskill hotels. You would hold them up to the light and the color photos would come alive. Only the pictures they sold on Forty-second Street were of women, sometimes just posing nude, other times in positions straight out of the *Kama Sutra*.

One morning, Harriet said to me, "I've got a new job, and it's for the most money I've ever made."

"Where is it?" I asked.

"Some studio on Forty-fourth Street between Sixth and Seventh Avenue."

Beginning to feel nervous for her and a bit jealous for myself, I said, "I don't think this is right. I don't know who you're with or what this is about."

"Stan," she said, "don't worry. I'm going there tonight, and I'll tell you about it when I'm done."

"If it's okay with you," I said, "maybe I could meet you there, and we could go out for dinner afterward."

"That would be fine, Stan."

I made it over to the studio where she was working, but a pretty big guy was blocking the door and wouldn't let me inside.

"Harriet is expecting me," I said, doing my best to sound as tough as my Uncle Phil and every Brooklyn wise guy I'd ever heard speak.

The guy finally jerked his thumb in the direction of the stairs, and I went into the studio. There was Harriet bending and stretching in a variety of nude poses while a photographer snapped pictures of her.

I said, "Harriet, put your clothes on. We're getting out of here. What you're doing is illegal. This is a porno shop."

Two guys, not as big as the doorman but big enough to scare me, suddenly appeared, and one of them said, "What the hell do you mean by breaking in here and busting up our shoot."

Harriet was staring at me as if I had slipped loose from the bonds of sanity. I replied, "Hey, you're not dealing from the top of the deck here. I know what you're doing. You're taking these pictures and selling them. Last I heard, pornography was against the law."

Neither fellow appeared impressed by my ability to cite legal statutes. Actually, they were downright aggravated by it, and one of them swung high and hit me in my face, and the next thing I knew I was stretched out on the floor. Although I didn't know it then, he had managed to break my nose, and to this day I have a deviated septum.

Looking up at the guy from the hardwood planks, I said, "Hit me again and I'll get the cops up here, and then we'll have some real fun."

They let me go, Harriet got dressed, and I took her to dinner. She was shocked that she'd been posing for porn shots, not eternal art, but she needed the money, and I could see that she was worried about losing the income from the job. I fixed that by bringing her to work with me in the luncheonette on Saturdays. We got her a nice waitress uniform, and she was a big hit with the customers behind the counter. She made money, and it was a wonderful arrangement because when we were through for the day, I'd lock up and we'd go out on the town.

Although I understood that the most painful and confusing moments of my childhood were due to my parents' problems, it was almost impossible not to believe that the root cause was their persistent lack of cash, some of it due to Louie's gambling and some of it because he hadn't developed the skills to earn a better living. Thus, when I went off to college, I was an overly pragmatic young man with an enormous desire to make money, and lots of it, at least enough so my future—and the future of my wife and children— would be more secure than my past.

Dating Harriet for two years provided me with a whole new perspective. Although she could be a bit unsophisticated about the darker motives of people, she was an erudite woman who spent most of her time with her head buried in books about philosophy and art. She also seemed to take great pleasure in the simplest things, preparing a meal, spending a weekend exploring the back roads of Virginia or dairy farms or trails the led across the Blue Ridge Mountains.

Then in the winter of my senior year at Columbia I was accepted at New York University Law School for the following September. Nothing changed on the surface of my relationship with Harriet, but I knew that our time together was coming to a close. NYU Law, I was sure, would be my passport to a gilded life, my chance to become as suave and debonair and successful as George Simon, the Paul Muni character in *Counsellor-at-Law*. I wasn't in a rush to marry, and the truth was that because Harriet wasn't Jewish I probably would not have married her anyway. I know that for Jews times have changed with respect to intermarriage, and my parents proved that marrying within your religion is no guarantee of happiness, but it was the way I was raised, and I never considered doing otherwise.

As I prepared to enter law school, Louie finally was forced to close his luncheonette on Fourteenth Street and Eighth Avenue, and he went to take over my business at Forty-eighth Street and Madison. It dried up my income, but he had no other opportunities, and my parents were broke enough even when Louie had a job.

I began NYU Law after Labor Day in 1951, and from the moment I arrived I knew I was surrounded by nearly two hundred intelligent, highly motivated and competitive students that possessed George-Simon fantasies of their own. Early on I was unnerved by the fact that the dean herded our class into an auditorium and gave us what is now known as the Harvard Law School entering-class speech: He instructed us to look to our right and our left, and then he promised that the odds were relatively high that one out of three of us wouldn't have the grades to return for his or her second year. Having already started my classes, it was easy to believe the dean. Like almost all beginning law students, I was overwhelmed with the sheer volume and complexity of the work our professors assigned us. I had always been a relatively diligent student, but to get through that first year required a Herculean effort on my part.

It didn't help that by October I was dating one of the only two women in my law-school class. Her name was Debbie and to this day I have no idea why she was the least bit interested in me.

Debbie was a graceful, strapping athletic woman with dirty blonde hair and a pretty face. We came from completely opposite worlds, and she was as different from Harriet as two women could possibly be. Debbie was Jewish and quite sophisticated. Her father was a renowned physician, and the family lived in Newport, Rhode Island. They were obviously quite wealthy and provided me with my first glimpse of the luxury I had long aspired to. At that time, Debbie was only person I'd ever met who had traveled through Europe without being born in a *shtetl* or being shipped there in an American uniform to fight a war. Debbie dressed like a fashion queen. She had a beautifully furnished apartment in Greenwich Village, and we used to meet her parents for dinner in a suite at the Waldorf-Astoria Hotel. She kept her string of polo ponies in Newport, but on occasion her father would see to it that Debbie's favorite horse was flown down to New York so his daughter could go riding.

Debbie was awfully bright and earned decent grades in our courses, but while she was at NYU, learning the law wasn't her top priority. Clearly, she wasn't going to need the work after she graduated. Debbie turned out to be a headstrong woman, and I shouldn't have been surprised. She was evidently used to getting whatever she wanted. Her main interest, it seemed, was exploring the ritziest aspects of Manhattan nightlife, and she had no intention of doing it alone. She wanted to be escorted by her own true love, and I was selected to play that role.

Initially, it was exciting. Debbie and I went out to dinner or on the town almost every night. Of course, with paying my NYU tuition I didn't have a nickel to my name, but Debbie didn't let my poverty get in her way. She simply paid the bill. If she didn't like the sports jacket I was wearing, we would stop at Paul Stuart's or Brooks Brothers en route to the restaurant or nightclub and she would buy me another one. It was the closest I've come in my life to living as a kept man, and while it had a few glittering moments and some distinct economic advantages, I can't say that I enjoyed it. Besides, I've always felt capable of picking out my own clothes.

My nonstop social life cut into my studying, and by the end of that year at NYU my grades were borderline, and I was right on the edge of being told not to return. Debbie wasn't fazed by it. Even though I hadn't given her an engagement ring, she considered us engaged and was eagerly anticipating our perfect future. I, on the other hand, was starting to feel like a pawn on a chessboard. That summer I needed to make some fast money since Louie had now taken over my luncheonette, and so I decided to escape the city by visiting one of the employment agencies that sent waiters to the Catskill hotels for the season. They had an opening at the Riverside Hotel in Divine Corners, New York, and I jumped at the job, packed up my green Plymouth, said good-bye to Debbie and headed north on Route 17.

I didn't know it yet, but as it worked out I had just made the most important decision, and best move, of my young life. It was the type of decision that I often refer to as Divine Intervention, proof that no matter how difficult my life has been, at the more crucial moments somebody up there is watching over me—frequently testing my resolve but also rewarding my efforts.

Five minutes after I drove up to the Riverside Hotel, I met the social director. He was the size of a middle linebacker, with the rabid personality to match. He tapped me on the shoulder, pointed to an attractive young woman, and said, "Stay away from her. She's my girl. You got it?"

"Sure," I said. "Listen, I've got a girlfriend. Believe me, the last thing I need is another one."

A young, blonde teenage girl herded a group of toddlers past us, and he said, "That's Doris Meyerowitz. She's a counselor for the little ones. Her cousins Shirley and Hyman Benskie own this place."

"Thanks for all the help," I said, and proceeded to go about my business. Between waiting on tables three meals a day and cleaning your own silverware, a requirement of the job, and keeping your uniform washed and ironed, I didn't have much free time. In addition, I was going to have to return to New York one weekend in order to take my last law-school exam for my course in equity, so whatever time I could steal I spent with my head in a law book.

Fortunately, the waiters did have some help. The girl counselors used to troll the waiter cabins for boyfriends. In these days before Women's Lib, they not only depended on their charm and looks to attract guys, but they demonstrated their domestic skills by assisting us with our laundry and sometimes remaining in the dining room after meals and giving us a hand with the silverware.

The girl who seemed intent on selecting me was Doris Meyerowitz. She constantly offered to do whatever she could for me, and I appreciated it, although I couldn't really take the whole thing seriously since I was twenty-three and she was about to turn sixteen. We used to talk, though, and I told her about law school and Debbie and my family. I have never been one to open up immediately to people, but Doris was easy to talk to.

The day came when I had to go to New York for my equity exam. I got in my car at about six in the morning and took off. I was driving down the highway when I suddenly heard a voice in the back seat say, "Hi, Stanley."

Startled, I pumped the brake pedal, gripped the steering wheel tight, and turned around. Doris was sitting there, smiling at me. Apparently, she had been sitting in the back seat since before dawn.

"What're you doing here?" I asked, returning my eyes to the road and glancing at her in the rearview mirror.

"I wanted to go visit my family," she replied. "We live at 302 East Forty-eighth in East Flatbush. You know where it is?"

I nodded. "Doris, how did you know I was going to the city?"

She shrugged, but I saw her smiling at me in the mirror. Years later I learned that Carl, one of the busboys I worked with at the hotel who also happened to be my roommate, was a friend of Doris's from school. Carl overheard me say that I was going home and passed on the information to Doris.

It was making me nervous having her in my car. She was a beautiful sixteen-year-old blonde, which legally made her jail bait. One day, long after our ride down Route 17, I would tell Doris that I knew her when she didn't need a top to her bathing suit. However, at the moment, I was only half kidding when I said to her, "Hey, you know we're crossing state lines on this trip. If I get pulled over by a cop, he could get the wrong idea and I could wind up in jail."

"Can I come sit up front?" Doris asked, thus demonstrating her single-minded resolve for the first time, a quality that I would come to appreciate over and over again for the next forty-seven years.

I delivered Doris to her door and met her parents, Betty and Dave Meyerowitz. Her father owned a plumbing business, and they lived in a single-family house on a comfortable street. They didn't seem to think there was anything unusual about my bringing Doris home, but truthfully, I was a little relieved to have their daughter out of the car.

I went into the city and managed to pass my equity exam by the skin of my teeth. Then I stopped by Debbie's apartment to talk with her. I suppose I always knew that the relationship wouldn't work out. I wasn't born to be a kept man who followed orders. Nor was I eager to start my second year at NYU Law. The classes were too competitive and stressful, and I couldn't imagine getting through successfully while I was involved with Debbie.

I also had my Army obligation hanging over my head. My draft board had already notified me that my country was eager to fit me for a uniform, and I was attending school through the grace of a student deferment. I figured my smartest move was to drop out of law school, complete my military service, and then pick up where I left off after my discharge, with some financial aid from the GI Bill and without Debbie and her fastidious plans for me.

Debbie didn't bat an eye when I told her my decision. I guess she believed, not without reason, that she could find someone to fill my role. I drove back to the Riverside Hotel, and the summer passed uneventfully. Doris was around, and we kibitzed quite a bit, but I considered her too young for anything serious, or even casual. She did come into the hotel bar one night and saw me talking with a married woman who was spending the summer at the Riverside while her husband came up on weekends. The woman cheated on him constantly, much to the delight of the waiters and the gossips by the swimming pool. When Doris spotted us, she burst into tears and said to me, "And I thought you were a nice boy."

I never had an affair with the married woman, and I was surprised by the intensity of Doris's feelings and felt bad that I'd hurt her, but as I said, she was too young for girlfriend material. Yet my mother sensed something unique about Doris. I had saved some money to bring Ida and Louie up to the Riverside for a brief vacation. One evening, Mother told me that she wanted to do my laundry. Doris overheard her, and immediately volunteered to lend my mother the box of Duz Soap that she kept in her room. It would be almost another year before I discovered Mother's opinion of Doris. By then it was clear that she had been taken with the energetic teenage blonde at the Riverside Hotel and convinced that Doris would be a wonderful wife for me, proving once again that it often pays to listen to your mother.

I took my Army physical at the draft board on Whitehall Street in Manhattan. I had suffered from diplopia—double vision—since college, and the doctor wanted me to be evaluated by the Army specialists on Governors Island. I was reexamined, and the ophthalmologists declared that I should be reevaluated after completing basic training.

I did basic at Camp Gordon, Georgia, and was pleased to discover that after all those years in school, I liked the mindless repetition of the Army training. I was in the best physical shape of my life, and being older than a lot of the guys in my unit, I didn't take the hazing of our drill instructor to heart. He was an abusive gnome of a man from Tennessee, and I recall that one day he woke us up at four in the morning and had us standing outside for what seemed like forever with full packs and rifles. He asked for somebody to come up and read the duty roster, and before I had a chance to think, I heard myself blurting out, "Hey, this ignorant SOB can't

even read," and then I broke the cardinal rule of the Army by tossing my rifle up in the air.

Everyone started to laugh, and yours truly became acquainted
with the rigors of KP. I did make a close friend in basic, Dick Warren. He was in my barracks, and I met him one night while I was
trying to sleep and heard sobbing coming from one of the lower
bunks. I climbed down from my upper bunk and went toward the
crying. I saw Dick curled up with his hands over his eyes.

"What's wrong?" I asked.

He calmed down enough to whisper: "We got a lot of colored
here, you know?"

"Yeah," I said. "They're nice guys."

"I'm from Dunne, North Carolina," Dick whispered. "And we
don't live with colored."

"You'll learn," I said. "And I'm Jewish. You got any of us in
Dunne, North Carolina?"

"Not any I know of," Dick said, smiling. Then he added: "I
thought y'all were supposed to have horns."

I eventually met Dick's family, and I was the best man at his
wedding. He never did have a problem with any of the black soldiers in our unit; in fact, he became friendly with a few of them. I
guess President Truman knew what he was doing when he ordered
the integration of the armed services.

When I came home on leave after basic training, I checked in at my
parents' house and made a date with Harriet. I hadn't seen her for
a while, and she was still living near Columbia and taking graduate courses. Mother handed me a postcard from Florida. It said:
"Wish you were here. Love, Doris."

"Very nice," I said, dropping the postcard on the kitchen table.

Mother asked, "Stanley, that's the little blonde who gave me
the Duz Soap at the hotel?"

"Yep."

"You should call her," my mother said.

"Ma, I got a hot date with Harriet. I'm gonna get more lessons
sketching nudes."

"You forget about hot sketching," Mother said. "You call that nice girl who gave me the Duz Soap."

I got the number from the phone book and called. Mrs. Meyerowitz answered the phone. I had waited on her table at the Riverside. I reminded her that I'd met her and her husband last summer and asked if Doris was home.

"She's around the corner at the beauty parlor," Mrs. Meyerowitz said.

"Well please tell her I called to say thank you for the postcard."

"You hold on," said Mrs. Meyerowitz. "I'll have somebody get her."

I thought that was odd, but it would have been rude to hang up, so I held on for ten minutes until Doris came on the line and asked me how I was. I said fine and tried to get off the phone, but she asked me what I was doing that night. I couldn't really share my artistic aspirations with her, so I said I was busy later on, nothing too important.

"Come on over," she said.

And so before going to the Upper West Side to see Harriet, I drove to East Flatbush wearing my uniform and spent the evening with Doris, her parents, her brother, Lenny, and his new wife, Sandi. I sat with them in the kitchen, and we ate and drank and talked and laughed, and I was a bit stunned and overwhelmed by the joy that seemed to bounce off the walls. Frankly, I was intimidated by it and found myself hanging back from the conversation. I had never seen such warmth in a family, an almost palpable happiness and pleasure they took in each other's company. I stayed very late. I didn't see Harriet that night. I never saw her again.

I was sent to Camp Pickett, Virginia, and my military occupational specialty was signal supply clerk. Before I completed my MOS schooling, I was told by my lieutenant that my diplopia appeared to qualify me for an early discharge. All I had to do was go talk to a board of eight doctors. I spoke to them at Camp Pickett and thought I'd made a convincing case for my discharge until the doctor at the end of the table, a short man with glasses, said that he had a question. He said my records indicated that I had graduated college and finished a year of law school. How was it possible, he asked, for me to study with double vision?

I answered, "I closed one eye."

"Good," the doctor said. "Then you can close one eye here and stay in the Army."

To this day, I suffer from diplopia. Whenever I focus my vision on anything within a foot of me, I see double. In fact, when I speak to people in close quarters, I have to take a step back to see them. (I suspect the cause is genetic, since my granddaughter Ashley-Lynn has the same problem.)

As it worked out, I really didn't mind staying on in the military to do the standard hitch. Once I had completed my advanced training, the Army asked me to teach at the school, but I thought they would keep me forever if I agreed, so they gave me a top-secret clearance and set me to work overseeing the signal-supply warehouses. I ran an office with mainly civilian workers. I became especially close to Helen Dyson, an older woman who lived on a farm and used to take me home to have dinner with her husband and children. Just as Queenie had been, Helen was like a surrogate mother to me and would freely criticize my casualness about government forms in triplicate, saying, "Stanley, you're so sloppy you could mess up a livery stable."

I even got to continue my minor assaults on authority. At one point, there was an outbreak of German measles. A lieutenant came around and made the soldiers take off our shirts, stating he needed to see which one of his sissies got a case of it. This lieutenant didn't like me. He had offered to recommend me for Officer Candidate School, and I had turned him down because I didn't want to spend more time in the Army than the standard hitch.

He did a fast inspection of his troops, and a couple of guys turned out to have a case of the German measles and were sent to the hospital. Then the L-T disappeared for a week, and I found out that the lieutenant himself was in the hospital with a case, and I sent him flowers with a card that said: "To one sissy from all the others."

He knew I was the one who had sent the greetings, but he could never prove it and no one turned me in.

* * *

On weekends I used to fill up my green Plymouth with five soldiers and drive to Washington, D.C. I would charge each soldier for the round-trip ride, so I had money to spend on a hotel and good restaurants. While I was at Camp Pickett the focus of my social life had become Doris. We constantly wrote each other, and because of my job I had a phone by my bed, and since all the operators knew me they would put me through to Brooklyn for free, and I spoke to Doris for hours at night. Whenever I had the time, I would go to New York on leave and see her. That little blonde I remembered from the Riverside Hotel was turning into a gorgeous young woman. Sometimes I would meet Doris in Washington, D.C. She would come down on the train with an escort, and we would spend the days seeing the sights.

The worst fight I have ever had with her occurred while I was courting her. One weekend when I was in New York, I had borrowed eight dollars from Doris to get back to Camp Pickett. A couple of weeks later, I met her in D.C., and she stepped off the train and said, "You didn't pay me back yet. Where's my money?"

"Eight bucks?" I said, annoyed and a little hurt that she would dun me for such a piddling sum.

"Yes," she replied. "The eight dollars you owe me."

"We talk about getting married and you worry about eight bucks so much?" I said, furious now. "Let me put you back on the train and you can go to Brooklyn and worry about your money."

Doris didn't back off on her demand, and she returned to New York. By the time I got back to the base, I had calmed down enough to call her. We made up, and she eventually got her money, but it was clear that she watched a buck, not a bad quality for someone like me to have in a wife.

I might never have gotten the opportunity to marry, or even to continue living, if the general at Camp Pickett didn't save me from what surely would have been a dangerous stay in Korea. According to the newspapers, the war was winding down over there, but I saw soldiers leaving for it on a regular basis. Then my orders came to go. I was frightened, but this was the era when young men did as they were told. I packed my gear and went to say good-bye to the general, a kindly fellow with a gray buzz cut whom I'd met because

I was making some extra money working as a waiter in the Officer's Mess and had been assigned to his table.

"Where you going, Shaw?" the general asked me after I'd entered his office.

"Korea, sir," I said.

"No you're not," replied the general. "I'll take care of your orders. And I'll see you tonight at dinner."

The general also later rescinded the orders I received for Saudi Arabia. Part of me was disappointed about my missing a government-paid world tour, but given the casualties in Korea I prefer to think of the general as another case of Divine Intervention. The same holds true about going to Saudi Arabia. I played a lot of craps and poker in the Army, and developed a fondness for bourbon, and with the severe Islamic prohibitions against both, I probably would have wound up getting my hand—and maybe my head—chopped off.

Mother and Louie were getting by while I was in the Army. One Friday, I had to travel to New York because someone had made Louie an offer to buy the luncheonette. I went up to iron out the details. Louie received about ten grand for it, seven more than I had originally paid. I let him keep the money, but made sure that he invested some of it in another luncheonette—a small, busy place on Third Avenue—and that he took the balance of his payments in notes. Otherwise, the sale would have been nothing but a big payday for Louie's bookie.

In August 1954, I was informed that I would be mustered out in early September. By then, I had made some plans. I wasn't going to enroll again at NYU Law. I didn't want that kind of pressure, and I needed to work besides going to school, and at NYU I wouldn't have the time. So I applied and was accepted to New York Law School. A number of their students were older and had jobs. Classes were held in the mornings, and your afternoons were free. All I had to do when I got there was find a place to work. The GI Bill, a government educational-scholarship program, would cover tuition and books, but I was going to need to earn some real money now because Doris and I had decided to get married and planned a wedding for the spring of 1955. I was going to buy her an engagement ring as soon as I hit New York with the money I'd been sending to my parents to save.

My last official order from the Army was to make certain that the signal-supply warehouses at Camp Pickett were emptied. There were four warehouses, each of them about 300,000 square feet. I only had thirty days to do it. No way it was going to happen, because with the Korean War over so many of the troops had been mustered out. I was told that my discharge would be delayed until the job was completed. My rough estimate was that it would take me and my small crew until Christmas to finish the task. I cut a deal with my colonel, requesting that he lend me the prisoners from the stockade. If the men held up their end, then they could win a one-third reduction in their sentences. The colonel took my idea to my old friend, the general, who agreed to handle the details. We cleaned out the warehouses in short order, and I was, once again, a civilian.

Betty Meyerowitz, my mother-in-law, was one of the most remarkable people it has been my privilege to know. We used to call her "Betty Books" because she managed all the money for both her immediate and extended family (a role that her daughter, Doris, would assume after her mother passed away.) Betty spent much of her life making everyone else's life easier, and she claimed to derive enormous pleasure from it. She was inordinately generous, and my first indication of her generosity was shortly after I asked Doris to marry me.

Like my brother Sol before me, I had been sending my Army money to my parents to put aside for when I was discharged. And like the money that Sol had mailed to Brooklyn during the war, there wasn't a penny left when I came home. Mother said she wasn't sure what had happened to it, but we both knew that Louie had gambled my savings away.

Louie never apologized or explained, and I never reproached him for it. Had Louie suffered a medical calamity and needed an operation, I would have paid for it, and that was the way I regarded his obsessive betting. Decades prior to psychologists declaring gambling a genuine addiction, I was acquainted with the perniciousness of its symptoms, and in my family we dealt with it as if it were an illness.

However, now that I was getting married I had to buy an engagement ring, and all I had was the four hundred dollars the Army gave me when I mustered out, not nearly enough to buy the ring that I wanted.

Enter Betty Books: She told me she had a cousin in the diamond business who would do the right thing for exactly what I had in my pocket. I knew the diamond would cost more than I had and that didn't include the setting. But Betty offered to lend me the money for the setting and said that when I had the money, I could pay her back.

This was the main reason I considered Betty so remarkable. She was not just generous, but inordinately sensitive. She realized that a young man would have his vanity to protect and feel uncomfortable that he was starting off his engagement unable to afford the ring. Betty made sure that I got the engagement ring that Doris would want while at the same time leaving me with my pride. Quite a feat.

That was the first time Betty helped me. It was far from the last.

CHAPTER 5

ON MY WAY TO WHERE?

I loved New York Law School from the day I arrived. My professors were first-rate, two of them becoming famous—Roy Cohn and William Kunstler. I was studying like mad now, and my grades were excellent. I was one of the founders of the school's *Law Review*. But I needed to earn some money, and I got a break one day when I checked out the student bulletin board and saw a help-wanted ad for a law clerk at the Manhattan firm of Smith and Steibel.

I ran to a pay phone, called the firm, and made an appointment to meet Bernard Smith in his office at 460 Park Avenue. Smith was an astute Jewish guy aspiring to WASP-hood with the affected speech and manners to match. (I didn't discover that he was Jewish until years later when I wrote his mother's will and saw her last name was Cohen.) Smith was the resident rainmaker and damn good at it. The firm represented several popular television quiz shows as well as the advertising agencies who produced the television commercial spots for them. Smith was also the honorary legal advisor to the British government, meaning that the firm handled the estate work for the British Consulate.

After grilling me for a half-hour, Smith brushed the lint off the pants of his Brooks Brothers suit, raised his eyes in contemplation, communing, perhaps, with the Almighty, and then hired me at a salary of $18.40 a week.

Every Friday night after I finished up at the firm, I would go to Doris's family for dinner and proudly endorse my check and hand it over to Betty, who would place it carefully in her money pot underneath her sink and then give me my salary in cash so Doris and I could go to the movies.

The first lawyer I became close to at Smith and Steibel was Michael Alexander, a Harvard-trained attorney who was about my age. Mike handled the actual legal details for the TV shows and ad agencies. Today, this assignment would not have any serious political overtones, but in the mid-1950s Senator Joseph McCarthy of Wisconsin was terrorizing the nation by publicly labeling people Communists during his televised witch hunt. The ad agencies would phone Mike and give him the names of people on the show. Mike would then give me the list and I would have to check it against the index of names that McCarthy generated from the transcripts of his hearings. I was appalled, and so was Mike, and neither of us was able to locate any actors or contestants who posed a threat to our national security.

Most of Mike Alexander's billable hours were dedicated to representing beneficiaries of estates, people who generally lived outside the United States and whose next of kin had died here and left them an interest, either full or partial, in an estate. My role was to assemble the information that would give a clear picture to the potential beneficiary of his position.

To do this I had to dig into mountains of official paperwork—for example, birth and death certificates, or marriage licenses. Frequently, I also had to interview witnesses or other family members and take their statements. At Smith and Steibel, I did almost a hundred kinship hearings and never lost one. The goal of these hearings was to establish who was the rightful heir or heirs. You got there through a process of elimination. Was there a wife or two? Children? I used to draw family trees. That was the trick, along with countless hours of research, and all we had for overseas documents were cables, not fax machines.

There was another lawyer who rented space from Smith. His name was Franklin Desser. Frank was basically of counsel to the firm, and he handled the litigation. He was my idol. He knew the law front and back; he had that special ability to make his clients' problems his own; and he was a marvel in the courtroom. I could learn more in an hour watching Frank in court than I could in a semester's worth of classes at law school. As much research as my clerking demanded, I always knew that I wanted to do what Frank did, stand up before a judge or jury and persuade them to see things in my clients' best interest.

With Frank as an example and hoping that Smith and Steibel would offer me a permanent position after I graduated law school and passed the bar exam, I figured it was time to show some initiative beyond the call of duty. One day, I found an old file in a cabinet. The name on it was Rudolph Fluege. It was an odd name, and I began to read through the papers.

Rudolph Fluege was a German national who had $35,000-worth of his property in the United States confiscated during the Second World War. I was cocky enough to think I could solve the issue for Mr. Fluege, so I took the file to Bernard Smith, showed it to him, and asked if he minded my giving the case a try.

"No problem, Stanley," he said. "I'd forgotten about it. You go ahead and give it a whirl."

I phoned Mr. Fluege and invited him to my office, which was about the size of small storage closet. Mr. Fluege came by. He discussed his case with me in a heavy German accent.

"Mr. Fluege," I said. "You have to come to Washington with me to testify that this property is yours. Will you do that?"

He nodded and shook my hand.

I filed the papers. A few months later Mr. Fluege and I flew to Washington so he could swear before a hearing administrator that he had owned the property prior to the war. Then we flew home. Shortly afterward, I received a call at the office and learned that Mr. Fluege had prevailed. The government was going to refund his $35,000. I was ecstatic. It was the first case I won on my own. I phoned Mr. Fluege to relay the happy news.

"You keep it," he said. "You earned it."

I said, "No, Mr. Fluege, you don't understand. I represent you. These are your funds and you're entitled to them. You can do what you want once I give it to you, donate it to charity or whatever. But until then, it's your money."

He finally agreed. Then he invited me to attend a dinner party at his home with my wife. Without thinking, I accepted, and then I realized that Mr. Fluege hadn't extended an invitation to the firm's senior partner, Bernard Smith. Worried that I could be putting my future in jeopardy by accepting the invitation, I went over to Smith's office and told him about the dinner. He encouraged me to go.

Doris and I attended the dinner party, and we were rewarded with our first, closeup look at New York high society. Mr. Fluege lived with his wife in a magnificent fifteen-room apartment on Park Avenue, with high ceilings and ornate woodwork and furniture that looked like it belonged in a Sotheby's auction. On the walls were paintings by Rembrandt and Van Gogh, and probably a bunch of equally valuable masters whose names I didn't know.

To say the least, Doris and I were impressed; a little over-whelmed is probably more accurate. I don't recall much about the evening; I guess I was too busy looking around at the sights, but I do recall being introduced to the head of Memorial Sloan-Kettering Hospital, and that after the meal was served all of the men went into the library to smoke cigars and drink brandy.

I must not have made a fool of myself because a couple of weeks after the party Mr. Fluege phoned me at the office. He said that he had appreciated my efforts on his case, and he now had more legal work for me.

"I need a will," he said.

I explained the procedure to him, that we would have to go through Federal Estate Form 706 together as if he had died. Then, once we had an idea of the nature of his total assets, we would be able to make a plan that would keep the profits from a lifetime of work out of the government's greedy hands.

A few days later, Mr. Fluege wedged himself into a chair in my tiny office. I sat behind my desk with a pen and legal pad and asked him if he had any bonds.

He said, "I have about ten million dollars in bonds."

Given the location and size of his apartment, I shouldn't have been so surprised, but I couldn't help it. I was stunned and didn't know whether to raise my head and look at him or just take notes as though every day somebody with his kind of net worth was in my office making out his will. I opted to go the professional route and kept asking my questions and writing down his answers.

"Mr. Fluege, do you have any stocks?"

He said, "I have approximately five million dollars in stock."

Our conversation continued for a few more minutes until I determined that Mr. Fluege had over $20 million in assets, about $150 million in today's dollars. No wonder the thirty-five grand I'd recovered for him had seemed like pocket change. I also discovered that he had been an investment banker and that he and his wife had no logical heirs because neither of them had any immediate family—no children, siblings or parents.

It was then that our conversation took a truly astounding turn. I asked him who he would like to name as the executor and/or trustee of his estate, and he replied that it should be me.

"No, no, Mr. Fluege, that would be inappropriate," I said, even as I wistfully calculated that my fees for handling such a big estate would easily run over a million bucks.

I told him that I would have to discuss the matter with Bernard Smith. We said good-bye, and I promised to be in touch.

After he left, I walked over to Smith's secretary. As a rule, Smith kept his door closed. Even if you worked for his firm, you had to schedule an appointment to see him. His secretary guarded his office like a German shepherd, and when I told her that I needed to discuss an urgent matter with Mr. Smith, she replied, "He's on the phone and can't see you."

I said, "Oh, he'll see me now," and walked right in.

Smith looked kind of annoyed by my transgression, but after he hung up the phone and I recapped my meeting with Mr. Fluege, Smith said, "Stanley, why don't you sit down and go over everything again."

When I was finished, Smith got back on the phone and invited Mr. Fluege to lunch at the Drake Hotel. And during that lunch, Bernard Smith was named executor of the Fluege estate. I continued to handle his work, though, and in the process of outlining Mr. Fluege's family tree, I did find out that he was a first cousin of Wernher von Braun, the German-born American rocket engineer who had been instrumental in helping Nazi Germany develop the V-2 rocket, and who later came to the United States to direct the Redstone program, which launched the first U.S. satellite, Explorer I, in 1958.

The Fluege will was over forty pages long. The paintings, I believe, were left to the Metropolitan Museum of Art, and after Mr.

and Mrs. Fluege passed away, the trusts I had set up for them enriched a number of worthy causes. Of course, the firm of Smith and Steibel made a couple of million dollars in fees. By then, however, I was no longer working there.

Four months before Doris and I were married, Ida and Louie, who had managed not to pass along every nickel of his profit in the luncheonette sale to his bookie, bought the first house they had owned in their married life at 2518 Ocean Parkway in Brighton Beach. It was a small place, with no bedroom for me, so I moved into the basement of Doris's parents' house. They were so warm and loving that by then I already felt as though I were part of their family, and it became official on May 28, 1955, when Doris and I were married at the Empire Hotel on Broadway and Sixty-third Street in Manhattan.

It was a beautiful wedding, with wonderful food and music and plenty to drink. The dancing and celebrating continued into the wee small hours, and when it was over, Doris and I spent our first night together in the furnished basement apartment that we had rented on East Fifty-eighth Street, in the Flatbush section of Brooklyn, no more than ten blocks from where my in-laws lived.

Since it was approaching exam week in law school, I had to wake up early and hit the books, wedding night or not. When I opened my eyes and saw Doris looking so beautiful curled up next to me, I was tempted to delay memorizing some more case law, but at seven o'clock in the morning my study group was knocking impatiently on our apartment door.

Doris was a good sport about it: she cooked everyone breakfast. I wasn't surprised, not because these were the 1950s and wives were culturally bound to serve their husbands and to put their own wishes on hold. But rather it was because from the moment Doris and I were engaged, I knew that I had found my chief ally, that no matter what happened to me she would always be there, supporting me. She was just nineteen years old, and yet she was so capable and mature, both of which made me feel more loved and confident and safe than I had ever felt before.

This isn't to say that Doris and I didn't have to learn how to live as husband and wife or have our disagreements. On those occasions when we argued, usually over something I had forgotten to do, I developed a chant, thanks to our upstairs neighbors, that would come in handy throughout our married life. Our neighbors used to argue nearly every evening, the wife screaming at her husband without pausing to take a breath, letting out a stream of invective that would have embarrassed a longshoreman. Finally, when she ran out of air, her husband replied: "Ruby, Ruby, Ruby, what did I do, Ruby?"

Over the next five decades, whenever Doris became angry at me, she heard those words.

We had delayed our honeymoon for a few weeks until I could take my last exam. We were going to the Bahamas, a gift from Aunt Shirley and Uncle Harry, who owned the Fort Montague Hotel on Nassau. So when the day of our departure arrived, Doris packed our clothes, while I went into the city and completed the essay exam, promising to meet her when I was through at Idlewild Airport (renamed JFK after President Kennedy was assassinated.)

I blazed through the test, handed in my blue books, and was getting ready to hustle off to the airport when Professor Silverman said, "Shaw, how did you answer the last essay?"

I walked over to his desk, and he said, "You have a problem. You answered just two out of the three questions. That means the best you can do on the exam is a sixty-seven. That's failing in my class."

I explained about my honeymoon, how I had been in a rush and had never even seen the final question. Professor Silverman said we needed to discuss a solution with the dean. We went to his office, and I kept checking my watch, hoping I wouldn't miss my plane and not quite believing that I was on verge of not graduating law school.

Professor Silverman explained the situation to the dean. Then he said, "Shaw, what do you suggest we do?"

I admitted that I had no idea.

"You had better come up with some options," my professor said. "A good lawyer leaves himself options."

I said, "Well, if you want me to answer the question now, I'll stay here and finish it. Maybe that's too big a breach of policy. So you can give me a new question, and I'll answer that one."

The dean didn't appear particularly impressed with my ideas, and I was beginning to get nervous: I couldn't imagine explaining to my lovely new wife and in-laws how I wasn't going to be a lawyer any time in the foreseeable future.

Luckily, Professor Silverman pleaded my case: "Mr. Shaw has been an excellent student and a founding member and editor of the *Law Review*."

The dean thought that over, scratched his head, tugged at his jowls, and at last ruled that Professor Silverman should mark my two answers as if they were three. I thanked them both and bolted out the door, hailed a cab and just made it to the airport in time for my flight. Doris and I had our first taste of luxury on our honeymoon, and when we returned I got a piece of good news: I was going to graduate law school: I had scored the second highest grade on my last exam.

The most astonishing discovery I made after our honeymoon was on a Friday evening when Doris and I, as was our habit, ate dinner with her family. My mother-in-law was standing by the sink, smiling at me. Then she said: "Stanley, come over here a minute."

"What is it, Ma?" I asked.

She bent down, reached into her teapot, came up with a bank book, and gave it to me. I opened it. The numbers $18.40 ran down two pages. Every week, for six months, Betty had been cashing my paycheck from the law firm out of her own cash and then depositing the check in a savings account in my name.

"I know you'll be wonderful to Doris," she said.

I felt my eyes fill up with tears. Given my family situation, this was a new turn of events for me, parents who gave instead of received.

"Thank you, Ma," I said, and kissed her.

After our marriage Doris continued working as a switchboard operator at Carrilon Lingerie in the city. Meanwhile, I began to prepare for my law-school graduation and the bar review course that followed. One evening as we ate dinner, Doris said, "Stan, whenever I pass by a law office on my way to work I see that the lawyers' names always include a middle initial. But you don't have a middle name, so don't you think you ought to at least give yourself an initial?"

"It couldn't hurt," I said.

Doris and I pushed aside the dishes, grabbed pens and paper and began to try out every letter in the alphabet. We agreed that the letter J looked nice, and we started to experiment with it by sticking the J in front of Stanley instead of after it, and we liked the patrician sound of that even more, as though I would have to wind up a big shot with such a classy name.

It wasn't long before the J became a permanent addition to my identity, although I would have to wait more than twenty years before I achieved the success to go with it. I never did have my name legally changed to J. Stanley Shaw, so today, on my office wall, I have diplomas and certificates and awards that have been presented to me in both names, Over the years, people have often asked me what the J stands for, and up until now I didn't have a reasonable explanation.

Now I know: The J stands for all of the dreams Doris and I shared when we were very young.

The day that the results of the bar exam were published in the *New York Times*, Doris and I were just walking out the door to the corner newsstand when the phone rang. It was my friend and fellow law student Pete Fowler, whose father was the senior partner at Battle, Fowler, a major New York City law firm. Pete already had the results; both of us had passed the exam. I felt as though I was going to jump out of my skin. I couldn't actually believe that I'd made it, that I'd become a lawyer. I told Doris, and we kissed and hugged and stood looking at each other.

"What do you do now?" Doris asked.

"Fill out the forms to be admitted to the New York State Bar."

I went to work filling in the blanks, putting in my references, and mailed the papers. Then I was called to my interview before the Character Committee of the New York State Bar. I wasn't nervous. They were supposed to be evaluating my moral character. In the 1950s, bar associations took this phase of the process quite seriously. A bitter divorce could slow up the approval process, especially if adultery had been involved in the case. But I had never broken any laws, so I considered the interview pro forma. I was wrong.

"Mr. Shaw," the interviewer said. His name was Bernard Fergueson, and he was a former president of the Queens County Bar Association. "Our background check showed that you have an unresolved lawsuit with a Mr. Silverman."

I couldn't believe my ears. That SOB who forged a loan agreement was preventing me from becoming a lawyer. I explained what happened to the interviewer. He was sympathetic, but his hands were tied. I would have to get a judge to dismiss Silverman's lawsuit. I was enraged, but it was a good lesson, showing me that I needed to be on the lookout for the Silvermans of the world if I planned to be a decent lawyer and protect my clients.

It took almost a year for me to get the mess straightened out, talking to judges and filing papers, and getting Silverman's complaint dismissed because he had failed to prosecute the case within a three-year period. Then I had to wait for the Character Committee to run another background check on me. I continued working at Smith and Steibel, hoping that when I was admitted to the bar the firm would offer me a more permanent and higher paying situation as a full-fledged associate.

Meantime, my home life had become a lot busier, because my brother Sol and his wife, Evelyn, couldn't handle their eleven-year-old son, Seymour. Like his parents, who were in and out of psychiatric hospitals, Seymour was plagued by emotional problems, so Doris and I took Seymour in to live with us in our one-bedroom apartment. Doris was about to give birth to our son, Jeffrey, at the time. Caring for Seymour was a tremendous undertaking, but we did it, and Doris became a substitute mother to him. After several years, Seymour needed more care than we could provide, so we contacted the JCCA, and the agency found a place for Seymour to live.

A terrible sadness welled up in me when Seymour left us, and I wondered about this terrible burden my family was forced to carry.

At least my brother Eli only hated working in factories; he never went into a psychiatric hospital again. But Sol would continue his noble struggle against his demons and have to live as an outpatient for the rest of his life.

At last, I was officially admitted to the New York State Bar, but even that good news came with some melancholy. By that time, for reasons I never understood, Pete Fowler, who had a terrific career as a high-priced lawyer stretched out in front of him, had taken his own life.

I entered politics in 1958, the year Jeffrey was born, and I learned a number of unpleasant lessons I'd known since I was a kid and shouldn't have had to learn again, the most painful being that there are people you cannot always trust and people who will do anything to win—no matter how small the stakes, no matter what the cost to themselves and others.

However, I was also fortunate enough to learn that relative strangers can quickly become lifelong friends and, surprisingly, lead you to the sort of success you had only dreamed of.

By that year, Doris and I had moved out of our furnished apartment in Brooklyn and were living at 141-25 Northern Boulevard, in Queens. It was a nice brick apartment house, six floors with spacious rooms, high ceilings, and cranky elevators. Our rent was eighty dollars and forty cents a month, and the apartments were filled with many young people, all of them starting out in life. At first, money was tight for us. I remember one evening Doris and I had less than a dollar between us for dinner, so I suggested she buy a can of corned beef hash. When she returned from the store I put my experience from my coffee-shop days to work, showing her how to add eggs to the canned food so we could have a decent meal.

For fun, we could always go outside for a stroll. Back then, the heart of Flushing was a hectic, congenial neighborhood, an ethnic hodgepodge of Irish, Italians, and Jews, with plenty of stores and even a few shade trees. On Sunday mornings, when Doris and I had a few extra bucks, we would often walk next door to Horn & Hardhart, one of their classy automats with table service, and order French toast from a waitress with the loveliest Irish brogue I'd ever heard.

Despite the joy and excitement I felt with my new family, I was worried about our baby. At three months, Jeffrey was noticeably hyperactive, and we weren't sure why. He had been a forceps baby, and shortly after his birth, a staphylococcus infection had swept through the hospital nursery and he was sick with it for a week. (During her pregnancy Doris had been X-rayed, due to some minor illness, and although in the 1950s they were unaware of the effects of radiation on fetuses, years later we would wonder if the X-rays had contributed to, or caused, Jeffrey's condition.) In his ninth month, Jeffrey was stricken with roseola, and we thought we'd lose him. His fever hovered at a hundred and seven for forty-eight hours, and I'll never forget staying up with him through the night, along with Doris and the doctor, and wrapping him in cold sheets to lower his temperature and watching steam rise through the cloth. Fortunately, the fever subsided.

Doris was just twenty-two years old, but she stepped in and took over, making the rounds with Jeffrey to doctors, none of whom had any answers. Even with our troubles, we did manage every now and again to get away to the Catskills for a weekend. Once, we were seated at a table in the dining room with people we didn't know, and we played a game, trying to guess the occupations of the men. I picked out one guy and whispered to Doris that I was sure he was a salesman. She didn't agree, but had no alternative suggestions. The man's name, it turned out, was Murray Safrin, and he has been my doctor for the last forty years.

By the late autumn of 1960, Doris was pregnant again. With Jeffrey now an unusually active two-year-old, we had outgrown the apartment on Northern Boulevard, and my wife informed me that we ought to buy a house.

I wasn't sure that she was serious. I mean, how could she be. I was barely earning enough for us to get by; she had quit her job at Carrilon Lingerie to care for Jeffrey; and we didn't have any savings in the bank.

These were minor details, according to Doris. She had already discussed the idea with her parents, and they had agreed to lend us the down payment. Since we had come to enjoy living in Flushing, one Saturday afternoon we rode around that section of Queens looking at houses.

As I was driving down 143rd Street, Doris said, "Please pull over, Stan. You see that house? That's the house I want to buy."

The address was 29-43. It was a handsome, two-story Tudor with a rock garden in the front yard. The only problem with the place as far as I could see was that it wasn't for sale.

Because of Jeffrey's difficulties, Doris and I were nervous about the new baby on the way, and I didn't want to upset her, so gently, I said, "Honey, this isn't really how you go about buying a house."

She was incredulous. "No?" she said. "How do you do it?"

"You need a real estate broker," I explained.

"What for?"

"Oh," I said. "The broker takes you around and shows you houses that people really want to sell."

"Stan," Doris said, frustrated with my lack of know-how. "We don't need a broker for that. We have you. We'll go up there and if someone's home you ask if the house is for sale."

I accompanied her up to the front door and rang the bell. A middle-aged fellow answered the door. I introduced myself and Doris to him. His name was Mr. Dioguardi.

I said, "This may sound odd, but by any chance is your house for sale."

"As a matter of fact," he said. "It is. My wife and I are moving to Long Island, and Rabbi Applebaum—the new rabbi over at the Garden Jewish Center—has been over here already and says he's interested in buying this place. He's supposed to let me know by noon on Sunday."

I said, "How much did the rabbi offer you?"

"Thirty thousand," Mr. Dioguardi said.

As far as my financial status was concerned, he might as well have said thirty million. But Doris wanted the house; I'd work out the money later. I offered Mr. Dioguardi $31,000, and he said, "Nah, you can have it for thirty if the rabbi doesn't call me by noon. Try me on Sunday."

Before we left, Mr. Dioguardi and his wife gave us a tour. The interior was done up in a style I considered upper-middle-class Italian, and the Dioguardis appeared to be a couple who entertained frequently. There was a nice-size dining room and living room, and a paneled rec room with a wet bar in the basement. Mrs. Dioguardi, who looked like an ex-showgirl, was very friendly.

At 1 P.M. on Sunday, I called Mr. Dioguardi and asked him if he'd spoken to Rabbi Applebaum.

"Ain't heard from the guy," he said. "If you and your wife want the house, it's yours."

"We do," I said.

"Then stick out your right hand," he said.

"What?" I asked.

"Stick out your right hand."

Feeling foolish, I stuck out my hand.

Mr. Dioguardi said, "Is your hand out?"

"Yep."

"I'm shaking it," he said. "Ya unnerstan? We got a deal."

Doris was thrilled, and she told me that her parents had agreed to lend us the five-thousand-dollar down payment. Now I was thrilled, too, but while I was busy being thrilled Rabbi Applebaum phoned me at the apartment.

"Mr. Shaw," he said. "I want to buy the house you just bought. I spoke to Mr. Dioguardi and he gave me your number."

"I'm sorry, Rabbi," I said, figuring the worst he could do was give me a bad seat on the High Holidays. "We want the house, too. And I already made a deal with Mr. Dioguardi."

"That's what Mr. Dioguardi said," Rabbi Applebaum replied. "If you don't take it, let me know, will you?"

On Monday morning I went to the Williamsburg Bank and applied for a $25,000 mortgage. In order to qualify I had to get a letter from Smith stating that he was planning to raise my sixty-dollar-a-week salary. The mortgage was approved, and a few days prior to the closing I went over to the house so Mr. Dioguardi could walk me through a final inspection.

On the landing going upstairs to the bedrooms there was a shelf with a statue of the Madonna below a magnificent stained-glass window. Mr. Dioguardi showed me that behind the shelf was a hidden space where you could store valuables. Had Doris and I owned any valuables worth hiding we would have kept them in a safety deposit box in a bank, which was what I thought anybody would do. Thus, I wasn't exactly sure why Mr. Dioguardi was pointing out the hidden space, and not knowing what to say in response, I said that the stained-glass window was beautiful.

"And it comes in handy," he said.

"What for?" I asked, even more confused about the practical uses of the window than I was about the hiding space.

Mr. Dioguardi said, "Guy comes to the front door and you don't know who it is, you can open the window and look out and see who's there. You don't like the guy, you can shoot him, ya know what I mean?"

He laughed, presumably to demonstrate that he was joking. Then he led me downstairs to the kitchen, where he showed me another hiding spot, a private drawer built in behind the cabinets under the sink.

"Well, that about does it," Mr. Dioguardi said. He handed me a slip of paper with his new Long Island phone number on it. "Listen, you got any problems here you give me a ring, okay?"

I thanked him, and Doris and I moved in a couple of months later.

Rabbi Applebaum found a house two blocks away and our families became good friends. I was so happy with our new home that I forgot to tell Doris about my strange walk-through with Mr. Dioguardi or that at the closing he'd been represented by an assistant DA of Queens County. Back then, ADAs were permitted to have a private practice.

Anyway, a few years later, Doris and I were asked to buy a small interest in some trotting horses. To receive our racing license we had to be fingerprinted, and so we went down to our local police station. While Doris was pressing her thumb on the ink pad I ambled around the station and noticed a bulletin posted on the wall.

It said: "29-43 143rd Street should be kept under surveillance. New owner is related to old owner."

I headed straight for the duty sergeant, pointed at the bulletin, and said, "Why are you watching my house?"

"You live at 29-43?" he said.

"Sure do," I replied.

"Your name?" he asked, eyeing me suspiciously.

I told him, and he said, "You're not related to the Dioguardi who sold you the place?"

"No, I'm not. And who is he?

The sergeant said, "He's a relative of Johnny Dio."

I was stunned. Johnny Dio was a former protégée of the old-time gangsters Lepke Buchalter and Gurrah Shapiro. Around New York City, Dio was euphemistically known as a "labor relations expert," and according to Joe Valachi, the Mafia songbird, Dio had long put his expertise at the disposal of the Lucchese family.

His skills became big news in 1958, when Senator John McClellan's Senate Select Committee was investigating the link between organized crime and labor unions. The Senate committee had discovered that Dio was involved in, among other niceties, extortion, bribery, and shakedowns. He had supposedly helped Jimmy Hoffa gain control of the local Teamsters, and he had allegedly paid a man to blind Victor Riesel, a nationally syndicated columnist and commentator on labor affairs, by throwing sulfuric acid in Riesel's eyes.

Johnny Dio's relative was also alleged to be a member of the Lucchese family, which explained why I had been shown all of those hiding spots, and why men occasionally scared the hell out of Doris and me by knocking on our door after midnight and asking to see Mr. Dioguardi. Keeping a safe distance from my nighttime visitors by opening the stained-glass window above them, I yelled down that the previous occupant had relocated to Long Island.

At the police station, the duty sergeant didn't press me too hard for my identity, but for a minute or two I worried that the cops might drag me into the back room and question me about the origins of my birth with a rubber hose. When I saw that wasn't what the sergeant had in mind, I was content to let him think that I might be related in some fashion to Johnny Dio. Why not? Thanks to the Dio family, the Shaws now had their own private security force.

There were no complications while Doris was pregnant with our daughter, Lisa. Her birth went off without a hitch, and the doctor assured us that Lisa was in tip-top shape. On the heels of that happy news came a jolt of sadness. A few months later, the bell rang, and Doris answered the door, looked down, and saw a baby in a basket with a note that said: "I can no longer take care of this child. Please help." The note was signed by Evelyn, Sol's wife.

It was Sol and Evelyn's third child, Brenda. It turned out they were having problems again. Sol was back in the hospital. We called the police, and Brenda was handed over to the Social Services Department. Like her brother, Seymour, Brenda would also live in institutions. Brenda's older sister, Sheila, was still living at home and suffering terribly from her parents' instability. I decided to petition the court to put her in a foster home. That story, at least, had a happy ending. Sheila spent her whole childhood with her foster family and eventually became a geneticist, wife, and mother, and to this day not only remains part of her foster family, but has also created a close and loving relationship with Doris and me.

Although my Silverman snafu had been cleared up and I was now a member in good standing of the New York State Bar, I was sorely disappointed when Smith's partner, Leonard Steibel, informed me that the firm had no room for me as an associate.

Steibel was a fine transactional lawyer, meaning he could write an airtight agreement, but he had the personality of a frozen haddock, and I was aware that he considered me far too aggressive.

The next day, I mentioned to Bernard Smith that I would be leaving the firm because Steibel said they didn't have enough work to keep me on. Smith liked aggressive lawyers; they brought in business; and he told me to hang in there until he had a chance to talk with his partner.

Later that day, Smith told me he had convinced Steibel that I should stay with the firm, and they would pay me sixty dollars a week. I accepted, but I knew my days there were numbered. My dreams were far grander than thirty-one hundred a year could pay for, and so over the next nine or ten months I handled every case I could for the firm and developed a little law practice of my own on the side, working weekends at my house.

I realized that I had to leave, but before taking the giant step of going out on my own, I decided to see if I could get a job at a big, prestigious law firm. The father of a law-school friend, John Brosnan, Sr., who was vice chancellor of the New York State Board of Regents, had an excellent contact at the firm headed by the re-nowned Judge Joseph M. Proskauer.

The firm was predominately Jewish, an important detail in the early 1960s, when numerous New York City law firms continued to practice a quota system with respect to Jews. I met with the judge, but he couldn't offer me a spot, (even though one day I would be handling matters with his former colleagues). So after Judge Proskauer turned me down I decided one surefire way to get a job was to go into business for myself. I hired Ruth Koven, my secre-tary from Smith and Steibel, and started my own law firm in the city, renting space at 770 Lexington Avenue.

All at once it seemed I had a new house, new baby, and new law practice. Fortunately, stress wasn't as popular on TV and in the magazines back then, so nobody worried about it.

From day one I knocked myself out, working no less than twelve hours a day. I managed to do just a bit better than breaking even with my candy-store practice, taking every case that came across my desk in my little office on Lexington Avenue—wills, parking tickets, real estate closings, the occasional criminal matter—any type of legal problem that I could solve and get paid for.

One of my first cases came to me because of a family tragedy. At the age of eighty-four, my paternal grandmother, Sarah, was crossing the street near her apartment when she was hit and killed by a car. It was sad. Although I hadn't been as close to her as I had been to my maternal grandmother, Sarah had always been such a sweet woman, and even though she was old, she had been in ter-rific health. I got the family a decent settlement, but I didn't have the heart to take my rightful percentage.

My problem starting out was that while I knew I had to meet people who could become, or bring me, the sort of clients I needed to improve the quality of my practice, I wasn't exactly sure how to go about making these contacts.

Then one evening, Doris's cousin Stanley Rabin, who worked as an engineer for the borough president's office, asked me to join the Jefferson Democratic Club. The club was in Flushing, and the members would meet once or twice a month. So I went along with my wife's cousin and signed on, and for my trouble I was rewarded with a good, long look at politics at its best and its worst. The best part was the camaraderie, working and kibitzing with guys who would someday become judges and borough presidents. Later, this kind of socializing would be referred to as "networking." Yet even though we didn't know it by that term, the idea was the same and everyone there was aware of it.

The worst part?

None other than the club leader, Jim Roe.

Jim was a big, amiable guy, a classic hail-fellow-well-met, but he was a leader straight out of the darker traditions of Tammany Hall. And his cheerful, friendly veneer concealed a man who, to put it mildly, possessed a rather low tolerance for people who disagreed with him.

I joined the club and saw that they were in the middle of primary season—electing delegates to the County Committee Convention. It sounded exciting, but it took me about two minutes to realize that the primary process was a farce, all of it scripted by the bosses, in this case, Jim Roe.

Yet I'd long been curious about politics and wanted to see what this thing was about, so I became a sort of coffee guy, and I worked pretty hard, running errands with my mouth closed and my ears open.

On primary day, I was assigned to drive people to the polls, mostly elderly ladies. That morning I showed up at the club, and there was Jim Roe himself sitting behind a huge desk. One by one, all of us filed up to see him, and he said thank you for helping us, and then he handed everyone an envelope.

When it was my turn, I took the envelope and said, "What's this, Jim?"

"For expenses," he said. "You're gonna have expenses."

It was maybe twenty or thirty bucks. Today, I guess we call this soft money, but it made me nervous, and I moved away from the desk and said to my wife's cousin, "Stan, this doesn't smell right. I don't think I should take it."

"It's for gas," he said. "Keep it."

Being a neophyte, I pocketed the cash and went about my business, which must have been the right move, because the following year Jim Roe asked me to run for one of the hundred county committeemen.

There was a primary, and somebody in my tiny election district was going to challenge me. I did some campaigning, nothing fancy. It was a close election. Out of about fifty votes, I won by four. I don't know who I beat, but I'm sure I beat him because I had once lived in a bigger apartment house.

So now I was a county committeeman, and I can't recall precisely what I did, except for showing up and voting the way I was told to.

Call it feminine intuition—if you can still use that term without being stoned to death or sued, but Doris was less than enthralled with my entrance into politics, and she was quite vocal about her opinion.

"C'mon," I said, kidding around. "It isn't so bad. I won an election, didn't I? I'm going places."

Doris replied with a patient, loving smile. Good thing, too, because my wife would need that patience and love, since it would take me another fifteen years before I got to where I thought I was going.

When I met David Berg in the early 1960s, I was sure that I was finally en route to the kind of high-status clients I'd been trying to find.

David was in his late fifties then, a short, elegantly dressed man with impeccable taste, a first-rate reputation as an attorney, and an arrogance that would have impressed, and perhaps cowed, Napoleon.

Like the French general and emperor, David bore the unmistakable marks of a self-made man who had climbed far and fast. There wasn't a trace of sentimentality about him. He rarely smiled, and you could see that behind his eyes he never quit working, that he was constantly thinking about the next deal or client, or where you might fit, or not fit, into his plans. David was tough, shrewd, aggressive, always willing to take a chance, and by the time I met him, most of those chances had paid off in spades. He had earned a considerable fortune in real estate, and he was the majority stockholder and an influential board member of the Royal National Bank.

I had come to see him in connection with the bank. Along with a client of mine, I had invested in a small piece of property. I put up no cash for the deal, but I had personally signed for a construction loan from Royal National. I needed to restructure the loan and asked David if he would convince the bank to help me.

No problem, he said, and then we chatted about nothing in particular for a while. Since David operated his law office with just himself and one other attorney, I thought he might be looking to farm out work. I believe he did mention that he might have a matter I could handle, but then he casually added what may well have been the real purpose of the conversation.

"Stan," he said. "You know, I'm a vice chairman with the Liberal Party, and I'm soliciting money for them."

Being Jewish and raised during the Depression, my political leanings had long been left of center. Growing up, FDR had been a true American hero to the grownups around me. I had been a Stevenson supporter in 1952 and 1956, and voted for JFK four years later.

Yet truthfully, I felt there was more at stake here than my politics. David was letting me know that he had just done me a favor with the bank by restructuring my loan, and now it was my turn.

I didn't have to be asked to contribute twice. I didn't have two nickels to rub together, but I borrowed money from a friend and mailed in a check for five hundred dollars. I wanted to thank David Berg for his efforts on my behalf with the bank, but I also wanted to make an impression on him, hoping that he would prove to be a fruitful contact. Actually, over time, he was, helping to pull me back from the edge of financial disaster and introducing me to a man who would lead me far deeper into politics than I had ever expected, or wanted, to go.

The man's name was Alex Rose—the tall, broad-shouldered father of New York's Liberal Party. Alex was president of the United Hatter's, Cap and Millinery Workers International Union and a legendary figure in city politics, known not just for the impressive power he wielded on the local, state, and national level, but for his personal history—the almost mythical rise of the immigrant, which seemed to parallel so many New Yorkers of his generation.

Born Olesh Royz in Poland, his parents had sent him to America in 1913 at the age of fifteen because Jews weren't admitted to Polish universities, and they had hoped he would study medicine. World War I, however, forced his father to cut back on the funds he was sending his son, and so Alex went to work as a sewing-machine operator in a millinery shop for six dollars a week. He became active in the Labor Zionist movement, and in 1918 he joined the Jewish Legion of the British Expeditionary Forces and fought to throw Turkey out of Palestine.

After the war, Alex returned to New York , and began working his way up the ladder as a union official. He was instrumental in keeping Communists and racketeers out of his organization, and because of this, he developed a fanatically loyal following. Then, in 1936, Alex plunged into politics, helping to form the American Labor Party.

While the ALP was founded to head off civil war among the unionists, it also provided a political opportunity that wasn't lost on Alex Rose, with his preternatural political sense and flair for understanding the minutiae of elections and turning it to his advantage.

Since a substantial percentage of the membership of New York City's needle-trade unions were Socialists, the American Labor Party line on the presidential ballot allowed them to vote for Roosevelt's reelection without compromising their conviction that traditional American political parties were capitalist to the core and therefore unworthy of their support.

By 1944, though, the ALP had lurched too far to the left for Alex. So along with David Dubinsky, the powerful head of the Garment Workers, the largest labor union in New York, he founded the Liberal Party.

What Alex's experience with the ALP had taught him was that a new party line on a ballot could represent a swing force in elections. It was this discovery, and his peerless operative skills at putting it into practice, that served as the foundation of Alex's personal political power, a power that would reach all the way to the White House and last until his death in December of 1976.

Throughout his career, his genius was to characterize the Liberal Party as "the watchdog and the conscience" of the state, and then to use its line on the ballot to become the balance of power between the Democrats and Republicans. The Liberal Party line provided the margin of victory for Herbert Lehman's election to the Senate in 1950, for Averell Harriman's election as governor in 1954, and for John Kennedy's capturing New York's electoral votes in 1960.

And unquestionably, for a short while, Alex did see to it that the Liberal Party functioned as what the *Village Voice* referred to as an "independent and rebellious force in the city's political life." The party ran anticorruption candidates against Tammany Hall, and their occasional victories attracted thousands of young, well-meaning people to the party. Across the boroughs, neighborhood clubs were formed, and the members plunged headlong into grassroots reform politics.

Although I didn't know it when I met Alex Rose in the mid-1960s, all was not what it seemed to be in the Liberal Party. Their progressive reputation was wholly intact, but it was pure illusion. If the liberals had once represented a virtuous alternative to the patronage hustle and the assorted petty corruptions of the Democrats and Republicans, it was now afflicted with the disease it had promised to cure, and yet they still pretended to hold the moral high ground.

Alex was an old-fashioned political boss, pure and simple, as greedy for power and as dismissive of opposing points of view as Jim Roe had been, but a lot ruder about it because he was so much more powerful.

However, I didn't know that when we first met. He was an imposing presence. He spoke with an eastern European accent, pronouncing my name "Stand-ley," but he towered over me, and he gripped my elbow, hard, and walked me around, talking, hardly giving me a chance to get in a word. He had a booming voice as well as a talent possessed by every successful politician I've known—a way of making you feel like an insider and someone who is indispensable to their cause.

I thought, mistakenly, that Alex must have considered me the new rich kid on the block after I sent him the five-hundred-dollar check. Looking back, I wonder how I could have been so callow. With friends like David Berg, Alex didn't need me as a contributor.

Implying that there would be a reward waiting for me somewhere down the road, Alex suggested that I start a Liberal Party club in Queens. That seemed logical. It never hurt a politico to build distant power bases to help him spread the word and recruit sympathetic voters.

It wasn't until years later that I understood Alex was looking for young leaders who would be amenable to his—and only his—views on the prerogatives of power, mainly the uses and abuses of patronage. Eventually, I realized that his notion of a political club was a group of people who served as a mirror for Alex Rose, his wishes reflected without alteration.

Yet the rampant political activism of the 1960s, with its emphasis on good government, presented a dilemma for Alex. Sure, he had used the exciting climate of the era to attract scores of young people to the Liberal Party. But now they wanted to change things for the better, to elevate the moral plane of politics, and one of their primary goals was to curb the power of the bosses.

Not surprisingly, this was unappealing to Alex, a potentially fatal assault on his fiefdom. In effect, Alex needed me to help keep these activists—at least the ones in Queens—in line.

Maybe Alex figured that since he had met me through David Berg and I was trying desperately to build my law practice, that my drive to be successful would turn me into his unrepentant ally. That I would be his rubber stamp, meantime waiting patiently for his help—a list of well-heeled clients, or some legal work for the city, or a perhaps even one of the jewels of faithfully serving a boss, a judgeship.

It didn't work out that way. Not even close. I agreed to open a club and hold meetings at my house, but I suspect that Alex would have been a happier man if he'd never met me, for it wasn't long before I was battling him inside the Liberal Party and in the courts.

Nonetheless, as challenging as politics would prove to be it was really a welcome distraction from the central problem of my work life, because before I even had a chance to make my fortune, I had lost it, and I would spend nearly fifteen years teetering perilously close to the edge of bankruptcy and digging myself out of what seemed like a bottomless financial hole.

CHAPTER 6

SCHMUCK WITH A FOUNTAIN PEN: PART I

Like most Jewish immigrants of their generation, my in-laws Betty and Dave Meyerowitz believed deeply in the American dream. Their belief wasn't the least bit philosophical, but rooted firmly in their individual experience. They had come to the United States as impoverished youngsters from eastern Europe, and together they had, through hard work and their dedication to each other, carved out a far more comfortable existence than they could have imagined living as an oppressed minority in their European *shtetls*. Quite simply, Betty and Dave believed in the American dream because they personified it.

Part of that dream was to see their children achieve a measure of financial security and a secure spot in the upper reaches of the middle class. They knew Doris's older brother, Lenny, would have no trouble with the climb: Dave had taken his son into his thriving plumbing business. Doris was another story. She had married me, and I was a lawyer who had left a firm and was now out on my own, working seventy hours a week and barely making ends meet. I knew Betty and Dave were proud of my education, but they were also understandably anxious about the economic fate of their daughter, who had left her job at Carrilon Lingerie to raise Jeffrey and Lisa.

While Doris and I were dating, Betty had dealt with her anxiety by turning over the money she had saved for me during the years she had cashed my Friday paycheck from Smith and Steibel. Later, after we were married and the children were born, Betty supplemented our income by giving Doris substantial cash gifts on every occasion imaginable—birthdays, Chanukah, our anniversary, any excuse to assist us without injuring my pride. She also made certain that we had enough to eat by buying extra meat and chicken every time she went to her butcher and casually dropping it off at our house, explaining that she just wanted to save Doris a trip to the store.

Dave took a different and far more paternal approach. Shortly after Doris and I were engaged, he mentioned that a few of his neighbors were helping their daughters' husbands by setting them up in various businesses. After that rather leading observation, he asked me, "Is there something I can do for you?"

"Yes," I said. "There is something you can do for me," and Dave looked over at Betty with his eyebrows arched, as if to say, See, what did I tell you, I knew he wanted something from me.

Then I said: "All you can do for me is give me your love and your blessings."

I never saw Dave's expression of fatherly suspicion again. He would have been happy to place me in a business. Along with his brother and two brothers-in-law, Dave had invested in a paint factory in Boca Raton, Florida, and he offered me the job of helping to run it. I was grateful to have him in my corner, but I explained that I'd worked hard to be a lawyer, and I wanted to practice law.

Dave became my biggest booster, constantly filling the ears of his friends and associates with the latest news of his brilliant son-in-law, Stanley the attorney, meanwhile keeping his eye out for any legal work he could steer in my direction. And around 1958, he found me a paying customer, Martin Schulman.

Marty was in his midthirties, a pudgy, quick-thinking, fast-talking chain smoker who looked like he slept in his clothes. As soon as Dave introduced me to him, I remembered Marty from Brighton Beach. He had been one of the gamblers who hung around Chaim's Pool Room. I hadn't spoken to him then; he was five years older than I was, a big difference when you're kids, but I recalled that he was a fair-to-middling player, and he bet a lot of money on every game. I hadn't given it a second thought. My father and my mother's brothers were all heavy gamblers, and Marty wasn't in their league. Besides, betting was endemic to the atmosphere of the time, everybody out hustling to make an extra buck.

Marty was still betting when Dave got us together, mostly on sports, but he also appeared to have plenty of potential as a client. He was working with his father and brothers in the family business, Barrow Oil, which sold home and commercial heating fuel and installed furnaces. Even though Marty made a nice living at Barrow, he had grander dreams than his father's generation. He wanted to get rich. Not immigrant rich, with a bigger apartment and a month-long vacation at a Catskill resort, or a split-level in the suburbs and a new car every couple of years. Marty wanted to get WASPy American rich, chauffeur-driven-limousine rich, and he pursued his goal by packing away his tools and entering the real-estate business.

That was where I came in. Schulman needed a lawyer to handle his closings, and I was glad to do them for him because, after five minutes of listening to his plans, I was convinced that he was a genius.

This was my opinion of Marty Schulman before I had, thanks to him and my own dreams of grandeur, achieved the less-than-exalted status of "Schmuck with a Fountain Pen." Yet, even in retrospect, there is no doubt in my mind that Marty Schulman was brilliant and, had he been less greedy and more honest, he might have landed himself a spot on the Forbes 400.

During the Second World War, with building materials and able-bodied men in short supply on the home front, the stateside construction industry ground to a halt. However, with the return of millions of veterans in 1945 and 1946, there was an acute housing shortage around the country, especially in Manhattan, and the shortage grew worse as husbands and wives were reunited, or couples decided to marry, and the baby boom got underway.

Not only was there a lack of apartment houses in the city, but much of the existing housing stock, particularly in Greenwich Village, was unsuitable for families. First off, many of the apartment buildings were heated by coal furnaces, an inefficient and messy process. Secondly, the floors were chopped up into small living quarters with the bathrooms located at the end of the hallways.

Schulman was sharp enough to identify the problem and devise an incredibly profitable solution that was suited to his talents and his resources. He began buying up old, dilapidated apartment houses in and around Greenwich Village, paying between $150,000 and $450,000 per building. Using funds from Barrow Oil as his stake, he put down as little cash as possible, never more than 10 percent, and he financed the rest of the purchase price through an older friend in Manhattan, Irving Tropp, a senior loan officer at the Thirty-fourth Street branch of Manufacturers Hanover Trust Company.

The moment the deal closed, Schulman applied to the Federal Housing Authority for a loan to refurbish his building. As his plans called for making the apartments more hospitable to families, the FHA was delighted to lend him the funds, although not delighted enough that the government didn't require him to sign a personal guarantee that the loan would be repaid.

Enthralled with his own vision of the riches to come, Marty never gave a second thought to being personally on the hook for hundreds of thousands of dollars, and he signed loans as fast as the feds would lend him the money.

With the federal cash in hand, Schulman went into high gear. He put his crews from Barrow to work, converting the coal furnaces to oil and charging about $15,000 for the job, a considerable amount of money in the late 1950s. Naturally, once the furnaces required oil, the Barrow trucks would arrive and fill up the tanks, another source of profit for Schulman's family business.

As the crews were working away in the basement, carpenters were on the upper floors reshaping the small apartments into family-sized quarters, while plumbers—Dave and Lenny Meyerowitz among them—removed the bathrooms from the hallways and installed new ones in the apartments.

The moment the refurbishing was complete, Schulman applied to the New York City Rent Commission to raise his tenants' monthly rent. Since he had unquestionably improved the apartment house, the commission had no choice but to grant his request. Then Marty would turn around and sell some of the buildings at a handsome profit and go searching for more properties to buy and remodel.

Schulman knew a cash cow when he saw it, and he figured that he could increase his profits by buying and converting more than one building at a time. In theory, it was a marvelous idea, but as any experienced real estate investor knows, pouring your capital into multiple properties that you are also renovating can lead to a lethal cash squeeze, and if your money dries up, you can lose everything even though your accountant will swear up and down that you are worth a fortune on paper.

Yet Schulman, as is common with visionaries, was impatient. His dreams, and perhaps his greed, nagged at him, and he bought buildings with the reckless, gleeful abandon of a kid playing Monopoly.

He was impetuous, but not a total lunatic. He signed personally for loans when there was no other option for him to secure financing. Otherwise, Schulman hedged his responsibility for the borrowed funds by establishing a slew of corporations for his real estate ventures and—although I was unaware of it—by dipping liberally into the till of Barrow Oil.

I not only handled Schulman's closings, but I assembled his corporate structure. Nearly every Sunday evening between 1958 and 1960, I would skip dinner with my family and go to the offices of Barrow Oil and attend to Marty's mounting pile of legal paperwork.

During those two years, Schulman's legal bills were modest compared to the amount of capital he was investing. The work for setting up a corporation cost him about three hundred dollars, a closing four hundred. He always paid me, and having set up my own practice, I was relieved to have such a steady and reliable client.

Looking back I can see that I was also attracted to Marty's brand of wheeling and dealing and envious of the profit that he seemed to be earning. Beginning in childhood I'd always fantasized about becoming rich, and the reasons for my fantasy weren't fully clear to me until I was well into middle age.

Growing up, I'd seen the material comfort that my uncle Harry Miller and his family had enjoyed in the misty green paradise of Long Island, and the genteel manner in which my cousin Eddie and his brothers—and for a time, my brother Eli—were raised. That gilded life looked awfully good to a city boy whose parents fought so bitterly and were so broke that he was handed over to an orphanage and then bounced between foster homes. Money, I was sure, was the key that unlocked the door of happiness, and I had to have a bundle of it if I was going to be secure. My own childhood spelled out the proposition, and the Great Depression, with its sudden poverty, bread lines, and unemployed men huddling together on Brooklyn street corners, underscored its truth.

However, from the moment I began practicing law on my own I realized that a lawyer could never get rich in the way that I'd imagined as a child, the way Uncle Harry was rich. As a sole practitioner you had to do the heavy lifting yourself, and no matter what you charged your clients or how long you stayed in court or buried yourself at the office, there was only a finite number of billable hours in a day.

No, if I was going to do my Horatio Alger bit, I would have to use my legal skills as an entrée into the business world. I knew it was possible because when I'd been working for Bernard Smith, I'd struck up a friendship with Sam Buzzell. Sam was an older lawyer by then who had his own practice and was renting space from Smith. Sam was a copyright specialist, and years before, when he was starting out, Sam had occasionally accepted stock in a client's company in lieu of fees. In 1919, two brothers, Jack and Irving Mills, asked Sam to act as their in-house counsel for their new venture, Mills Music, a catalog company that purchased the rights to songs. Sam agreed and wound up with 10 percent of Mills Music, which would one day own, among other classics, "Take Me Out to the Ball Game," and "Stardust." Sam made himself millions of dollars with the Mills brothers, and he went on to develop a client list that included such celebrities as Duke Ellington, Cab Calloway, and Milton Berle.

Before I even had an opportunity to think through a plan, Marty Schulman told me that he was having cash flow problems. He couldn't get any additional funding out of Barrow Oil; they were tapped out. Then he suggested that since I was heavily involved in his affairs I might consider becoming his partner by swapping my legal fees for percentages of the buildings he was buying.

I was elated until he said: "I've had this operation going for a while, so you'll have to buy in."

That didn't strike me as an unfair request, except I hadn't even had the five thousand dollars for a down payment on my house. I knew I'd need more than five grand to become partners with a budding real estate magnate. I told Marty I'd be happy to swap my fees for a percentage, but that I didn't have any money to invest.

"We can fix that," he said.

"How?"

Schulman said, "I want you to meet Irving Tropp at Manufacturers Hanover. You'll sign a bunch of papers for him, he'll get you an FHA loan for thirty grand, you give me the check, and you'll be my partner. Once we convert the furnaces from coal to oil and remodel the apartments, the increase in rents we'll get will more than cover the loan."

I'd seen the sizable payoff that Schulman had made investing in these rundown apartment houses, and I was champing at the bit to get into the action. But I wondered why he didn't apply for an FHA loan himself, because he'd been doing that on a regular basis ever since I'd been involved in his affairs.

I asked him, and he replied, "I would, Stanley, believe me, I would. But the feds won't lend me any more money. I've capped out."

That sounded reasonable. Being new to this game, I didn't appreciate that business people were afflicted by two major varieties of cash illnesses. One was equivalent to the common cold, a fleeting discomfort that made you miserable but sooner or later went away. The second variety, however, resembled the more frightening types of cancer. It was insidious, and frequently terminal.

Thirty grand seemed like an astronomical figure to me. It is still a lot of money, but back then, prior to the inflation of the last five decades, it was equivalent to roughly $150,000 in today's numbers. Yet I learned that all you had to do to get your hands on that kind of money was to buy a subway token, ride the train downtown to Thirty-fourth Street and Eighth Avenue, shake hands with a personable, gray-haired fellow named Irving Tropp, and be escorted over to Carmine Messano, a young man in charge of FHA loans for the bank, and Carmine, who later became a dear friend, had me sign a stack of forms.

In this casual manner I received my thirty grand and became— for the first but not the last time—a Schmuck with a Fountain Pen, meaning that if the loan wasn't repaid by the profit from my investment with Schulman, I was liable for repaying it myself.

I gave Marty the check, officially transforming myself into a big-shot wheeler-dealer. I told Doris that I'd invested with Schulman, but knowing her nervousness about money in general and our financial condition in particular I was a tad evasive about the details, especially the part about me being personally on the hook for the government loan.

With the infusion of capital from my loan, Schulman immediately bought a couple more buildings in the Village, 10 Gay Street and 143 Waverly Place. In a matter of months, though, his supply of cash evaporated again, and he had to come up with another move to hang on to his—and now my—holdings.

His move was to introduce me to Emmanuel Kreisel, a savvy, successful, and honorable man who owned a company that managed rental properties. Manny had heard about a new legal instrument available for raising money—syndications. I read up on syndications in real estate newsletters, and they appeared to be a terrific idea. The primary investors—the general partners—would run the project. They would also seek money from other investors, the limited partners, who then shared in the profits while you owned your properties, and after you sold them they would reap additional benefits in tax savings.

Schulman was ecstatic about the syndication. More money, he said, meant more profits, and Manny said that he would invest with us but only if he became the managing agent of the buildings. I was glad to have Manny on board. He was experienced and less fanatical than Schulman.

I set up our first syndication, Laurence Associates, carefully writing out the term sheets, and listing all of the properties we owned, their appraised value, the current mortgage, every piece of financial information that I considered relevant to potential limited partners. Then we began hunting for investors. Since I didn't know anyone who dined regularly, or at all, with the Whitneys or Rockefellers, I turned to my family—my parents, Doris's parents, and their relatives—and any of my friends who had a buck to spare. I solicited dozens of people, as did Schulman and Manny Kreisel, a fact that wouldn't be relevant for a few years.

We ended up with just under twenty limited partners and $140,000 of capital. I was so grateful to all of the people coming through for me that I was about to elevate the art of being a Schmuck with a Fountain Pen to unheard of heights. Of my own accord, I signed a paper that personally guaranteed everyone's investment. If the money was lost, I would repay it out of my own pocket, plus 12 percent interest. Furthermore, I promised that if any limited partner chose to leave the syndication, I would refund their money within sixty days of their request.

I was feeling awfully noble about my guarantee, but I doubted that I'd ever have to make good on it, because Laurence Associates' opening investment—two apartment houses, one at 110 Thompson Street and the other at 40-42 MacDougal Street—was a smashing success. Schulman converted the coal heating system to oil, while the plumbers and carpenters did away with the hallway bathrooms and renovated the apartments. Manny Kreisel collected the rents, which were now higher due to the improvements, and he saw to the overall daily management of the buildings. We made money right away, paying 12 percent interest to our limited partners and plowing our personal profits into buying and improving more apartment buildings.

At that time we also started to invest in harness horses. The way it happened was that Marty called me one evening and said that tomorrow morning Irving Tropp wanted us to spend four grand to purchase a pair of trotting horses, one for $1,800, the other for $2,200.

"Marty, are you crazy? I don't know a goddamn thing about trotters."

Schulman said, "Irving's either at Roosevelt or Yonkers Raceway nearly every night, and he knows about trotters. Irving says he'll take care of everything if we give him 10-percent ownership. He's even got a first-rate trainer and driver, Charlie Fitzpatrick, to work with our horses."

"This is nuts," I said. "Besides, Marty. I've got a calendar tomorrow. I gotta be in court."

"Forget your calendar," said Marty. "Irving wants us to do it. I can't go so you have to, because we need Irving, don't we?"

We certainly did, and so I canceled my calendar for the next morning and attended the Old Glory sales at Yonkers Raceway with Irving and the new friend he introduced me to, the horseman Charlie Fitzpatrick. I stood under the crowded tent with them, while Irving told me when and how much to bid. A horse came up by the name of Action Hanover, and I called out, "Eighteen hundred dollars."

"Sold!" the auctioneer cried, making me part owner of a trotting horse.

He was a handsome animal, but I wasn't that excited about my new status and went out to call Marty.

"Congratulations," I said. "We're in the racing business."

"How much did you pay?" he asked.

I told him, and he said, "Remember, Stan. No more than twenty-two for the next one."

I hung up and ambled over to a stand for a sandwich and a cup of coffee. While I ate and looked around, I thought I had no business being at a trotting horse sale. Then I heard an announcement coming over some loudspeakers, saying, "Will Mr. Shaw please report to the auction tent immediately."

I double-timed it over to Irving and Charlie as the auctioneer said, "Do I hear nineteen for Mr. Childs?"

He heard nineteen and asked for twenty. In back, someone yelled out twenty, and someone else raised it to twenty-one. Irving nudged me, and when the auctioneer called for twenty-two, he got it from me. The tent fell silent, and the auctioneer exclaimed, "Sold! For twenty-two!" Suddenly I was surrounded by a crowd. Cameramen were snapping my picture, and reporters were hurling questions at me. Mr. Childs, it seems, was a splendid horse with an impressive lineage, and I was asked what it felt like to pay twenty-two thousand dollars for a trotter.

It felt like nausea, like I was about to lose my sandwich and coffee. Twenty-two thousand? I'd thought I was paying twenty-two hundred. Marty had said we were spending four grand total.

Frantic, I whispered harshly to Irving, "Give the goddamn horse back. I don't have that kind of money."

"Don't worry," Irving replied. "I'll get you the money. You can sign another note. And here it is."

He extended an official document toward me.

"The hell I will, Irving."

Irving said, "And I've got a blank check all ready for your signature."

He pulled the check out of his pocket. I stared at the two pieces of paper, and then at Irving. He smiled, and his message was loud and clear: Marty and I needed him or loans would be hard to come by.

"Okay, Irving," I said, scrawling my name across the note and the check. "We're in the horse business."

Beaming, Irving said, "Stan, Mr. Childs is gonna make us a fortune. You won't regret it."

At the moment, I regretted it plenty, and I went to call my partner.

"Marty," I said. "Are you sitting down?"

"Yeah."

"Good," I said. "Because we just paid twenty-two grand for a horse."

There was complete silence on the other end of the line. Then Marty said, "Twenty-two thousand?"

"Yep. Twenty-two thousand."

"Good luck," he said, and hung up the phone.

Mr. Childs would earn us over $200,000; we eventually sold Action Hanover for a handsome profit of about eight grand; and I never did regret owning trotters. Ultimately, I owned ten of them, renaming every one with the last name of Lindsay in honor of the New York City Mayor John V. Lindsay, whom, at the time, I considered a friend.

It wasn't the money that made racing so appealing to me. Truth is, after maybe a decade I only did a bit better than breaking even, but I had some adventures and encountered an amusing cast of characters that probably don't exist outside the world of racing. As a kicker I met Joe Licitra, a bright decent guy who would become my law partner and dear friend.

After succeeding with Mr. Childs we had the confidence, and the capital, to move up in class, and we got together $75,000 to buy a horse, the famed Meadow Grayson, from Del Miller, a vain, flamboyant man who was one of the most distinguished trainers and drivers in the world of harness racing and actually owned his own racetrack. But this icon proved to be less than candid with me. During one of the Old Glory sales at Yonkers Raceway, Del assured us that he had personally trained Meadow Grayson, and he was "sound of wind and limb." We gave him a check for the seventy-five, then put up a $2,500 stake payment to enter Meadow Grayson in a race the next evening.

On Saturday afternoon, Charlie Fitzpatrick called me at the house to tell me that our horse's knee had just blown up. He'd just spoken to Del Miller about it, and Del's response was, basically, tough luck.

Del must have been pretty impressed with himself to brush Charlie off, since Charlie was not exactly a shrinking violet. He was an artful handler of horses and as aggressive as any driver on the track.

Del Miller obviously needed some focused attention. Threatening him with a lawsuit might do the trick, but if I sued him he would get to hold onto our dough for quite a while, never a happy circumstance. He was, however, vulnerable in one area. He was unambivalently in love with his reputation, and I told Charlie to let Del know that unless he was at the track the next morning to refund our seventy-five thousand, plus our twenty-five hundred stake payment, and pick up his horse, I was holding a press conference to explain that the legendary Del Miller was not all he was cracked up to be.

Charlie passed along the information, and I imagine Del struggled over the decision, but he was an icon, after all, and in the war between his vanity and greed, his vanity won out. We got our $77,500 and Del got Meadow Grayson.

Charlie Fitzpatrick, it turned out, had not only spotted the trotter's injuries, he mentioned them to me at a significant, personal financial cost. Charlie claimed that he had been offered $20,000 to keep his mouth shut.

Except that wasn't Charlie's way. He may have been the Peck's bad boy of harness racing for his alleged involvement in a doping case, and he was tough as hell on the track, but he was a great friend to me. Given this set of circumstances, along with the fact that Charlie trained and drove my horses, it was probably just a matter of time before I got involved in a case on his behalf.

It started at Yonkers Raceway. Charlie won a big race, but he and the horse were disqualified due to a conflict of interest. Charlie not only trained the winning horse, but another horse in the race, and when the disqualification was announced, the fans began to riot.

The Harness Racing Commission suspended Charlie for thirty days. Not working for a month was a lot of money for Charlie to lose, and he needed a lawyer right away. I was glad to do it, not only because I liked him, but because the commission, an imperious group of misguided souls, was a royal pain in the ass.

I sued the commission in state court, claiming that in handing down their suspension they were acting as judge, prosecutor, and jury, thereby denying Charlie the due process that Americans have been entitled to, in theory, for a couple of hundred years. The commission wasn't overly intimidated by my argument, although while the brouhaha was playing out in the local press, I was denounced by George Morton Levy, the owner of Roosevelt Raceway, as a destroyer of standardbred racing, the man who was killing the handle and attendance, and generally ruining the integrity of the sport.

Meantime, one of the commissioners who had been in on Charlie's suspension made a terrible mistake. Prior to the hearing, he'd told the press that he had been present at the track and witnessed Charlie's contribution to the riot.

However, I knew that this fellow, a widely esteemed married man, was in the midst of a long-term affair with a woman, and they met frequently at a motel near the track on racing nights. I hired a private investigator to make sure that the night of the riot had been no exception, and sure enough the guy had been in bed with his mistress instead of at Yonkers Raceway.

I passed this information along to the commission's lawyer, explaining that before I ruined a man's reputation, I wanted to give him a chance to preserve his good name. On the other hand, if the commission lawyer wanted me to keep my mouth shut, all the commission had to do was reinstate Charlie and give him back his stall space so he could get on with his work.

The lawyer chewed on that information for a couple of minutes. Then I hit him with the closer. I said that I had called the court, and they were about to hand down their decision on the commission's abrogating my client's right to due process. From the secretary's voice, I assumed that I had won, but why should he (or I, for that matter) take any chances?

The lawyer went to speak to the commissioners, and it didn't take them long to reconsider. The commission cut Charlie's month-long suspension to five days, and the issue was settled.

Perhaps the most memorable character I encountered through racing was Vincent (the Chin) Gigante, who first achieved notoriety when he bungled the assassination of Mafia boss Frank Costello. Three decades after the assassination attempt, FBI agents identified Gigante as the brains of the Genovese crime family, and the tabloids had a habit of plastering him in their pages, showing him wandering aimlessly around Little Italy, unwashed and unshaven, decked out in a ragged bathrobe, pajamas, and slippers, muttering crazily to himself. The FBI asserted that Gigante was faking his psychosis to avoid prosecution on various racketeering charges. In his memoir, *Underboss*, Mafia informer Sammy (the Bull) Gravano seems to side with the FBI on the subject of Gigante's mental status.

I made Mr. Gigante's acquaintance when he was still bathing regularly, wearing normal clothes and making sense when he spoke. (I invariably called him Mr. Gigante, not only because this was the lawyerly thing to do, but because I suspected that only his really close pals could get away with referring to him as the Chin.) I met him through a chain of mutual acquaintances.

The first link in the chain was a casual friend of mine, a real estate broker in Greenwich Village, who introduced me to a big, heavy-set guy whom I will refer to here as Mr. Jimmy Salvatore, not his real name. At the time, Jimmy Salvatore, who was in the process of buying a dry-cleaning store, required the services of a lawyer for the closing, so I took care of it for him. Mr. Salvatore, I was told, wasn't a dry cleaner by trade, but he was attracted to the small retail cash business because it offered him a way to show a hard-to-trace source of income to the Internal Revenue Service, and he earned his true living as a bookmaker.

One day, shortly after I met Jimmy Salvatore, my Uncle Phil and I were spending a few idle moments reviewing the racing form. One of my horses, Dapper Lindsay, was running in the first race at Yonkers Raceway, but with my heavy schedule of client meetings I wasn't going to have the opportunity to get to the track. So Uncle Phil and I placed a bet on Dapper Lindsay with Jimmy Salvatore, and we also followed a wild hunch and bet two Daily Doubles.

As luck would have it, not only did Dapper Lindsay win, but our Daily Doubles came through. Our winnings totaled $3,800, and I called Jimmy Salvatore to check on his payment arrangements.

He said, "Go meet Ralphie in the clubhouse at Yonkers Raceway. He'll have your money for you."

"Ralphie?" I said. "I don't know any Ralphie."

"Oh Ralphie is a real nice guy," Salvatore said. "He works for the Chin. You know the Chin?"

"Vincent Gigante," I said, feeling a chill creep up my spine.

Jimmy Salvatore didn't help my chills when he added that Ralphie was one of Vincent Gigante's top assistants, a designation that I took to mean he was a Family capo, not the sort of guy you'd think would meet to pay off a small-time bettor like me.

I met Ralphie in the clubhouse. He was a quiet man dressed in a nondescript sports jacket and slacks, and after handing me an envelope stuffed with small bills, he politely requested that I serve as a tout for his boss.

He didn't mention his boss's name; I guess he figured he didn't have to. I answered that although I'd had been lucky once, I doubted that I could repeat my performance, and I would hate to be responsible for losing his boss's money.

I felt an enormous sense of relief when Ralphie replied that he understood my position, but it didn't hurt to ask.

I didn't meet Mr. Gigante in person for nearly another decade, until I got a call at my office from one of Jimmy Salvatore's sons. He said that his father had just died, but right before his death Jimmy had instructed him to invite me to his wake. I really wasn't very friendly with Jimmy Salvatore, nor had I bet with him again or done any more closings for him. Still, I was curious about why I had been invited to the wake, so I told Jimmy's son that I would go. His son gave me an address of a funeral home in Little Italy, and when I showed up there I felt as if I'd wandered into the pages of a Mario Puzo novel.

I offered my condolences to both of Jimmy Salvatore's sons. Ralphie was at the wake, and he brought me over to a chair in the corner of the parlor and introduced me to Mr. Gigante, who was sitting with his back to the wall. Although I'd never met Mr. Gigante, he greeted me effusively, as if I was his long lost brother. Ralphie mentioned in passing that Jimmy Salvatore hadn't left anything to his sons and that since he was their godfather, it was his responsibility to straighten it out. Ralphie had paid for the funeral, he said with a faint hint of pride in his voice, and there were other things he had to see to. Before I left he gave me a number where I could reach him.

A month later a $10,000 check from the Veteran's Administration arrived at my office. It was the payment from Jimmy Salvatore's life insurance policy, and it was made out to me because Salvatore had named me as his beneficiary.

I called Ralphie and told him about the check, adding that I was certain Jimmy Salvatore had intended it for his sons, and asked him where I might contact the boys.

Ralphie said, "Don't you give either one of them disrespectful bastards a dime till I give you the okay, you understand?"

"Absolutely," I replied.

"They was both disrespectful to their old man. That's why he made you his beneficiary. Listen, I'm gonna send them to you with instructions to apologize to you, as the representative of their father, for all the shit they pulled. When they're done, you give me a call, you understand?"

"Perfectly," I said.

I deposited the check in an escrow account, and within a week Jimmy Salvatore's sons stopped by and completed their mea culpa, telling me how sorry they were for disappointing their father while he was alive.

Immediately after the two boys left, I phoned Ralphie and gave him a recap of their apology.

"Good," he said. "I appreciate it. Send them each a check for five grand."

"First thing in the morning," I said.

"And what's your fee?" he asked. "We'll pay it."

"Free of charge," I said.

"Ah," he said. "C'mon, counselor. What'd you get?"

"In this case," I replied, "nothing. I didn't really do that much. I was glad to give Jimmy Salvatore a hand."

"That's nice of you, counselor," Ralphie said. "If you ever need me you can give me a call."

CHAPTER 7

SCHMUCK WITH A FOUNTAIN PEN: PART II

With the profits from Laurence Associates rolling in, I came to the conclusion that syndicating apartment buildings was the wave of the future, or at the least the future of J. Stanley Shaw, and I began setting up syndications as fast as Schulman and I could get our hands on buildings and investors. Carrol Associates and Arthur Associates were next, and within a couple of years we had four of these syndications.

As we expanded our holdings Schulman insisted that he, not Manny, should be managing the buildings. Manny didn't have access to enough capital to participate in our additional syndications, nor would he invest with us unless he was designated the managing agent of the apartment houses. Since our syndicates were hip deep in dollars, I didn't argue with Marty, but I did insist that he hire my Uncle Phil to help manage the buildings. Phil needed the job, and I figured he could be my eyes and ears, but I have to admit that I agreed to Schulman's demand without giving it a second thought.

I should have, though, because one morning, right after Marty took control of the buildings, I received a frantic call from him at the office.

"Stanley," he said. "Ya gotta help me."

"What's wrong, Marty?"

"I'm in jail," he said. "In Manhattan. On Center Street."

Schulman had been locked up by a magistrate of the Court of Special Sessions after pleading guilty to a violation of the Multiple Dwelling Law. When you stripped away the legalese, the simple truth was that Marty was in jail because he was a slumlord. Evidently, he wasn't the best apartment-house manager to come down the pike. Schulman was supposed to have made some badly needed repairs to one of his buildings, and he hadn't, and so the judge put him behind bars to encourage him to contemplate his failings as a landlord.

I knew this wasn't the first time that Marty had been in trouble for this type of violation. Previously, Schulman had pled guilty as charged. He had used a New York City attorney who was allegedly a proven hand with slumlord cases. This attorney had asked the judge to substitute the corporation for the defendant when he assessed the penalty, and one of those numerous corporate entities I'd set up for Marty had been ordered by the judge to pay a fine and make the repairs.

But on this morning, hundreds of Marty's justifiably angry tenants had stormed the courthouse, gathering on the steps and chanting "Slumlord! Slumlord!" Clearly, the judge sent Schulman to jail not only because he was angered by Schulman's despicable practices, but I suspect he was also intent on avoiding the unfavorable publicity that generally follows on the heels of a courthouse riot.

The reason for Schulman's neglect was unclear to me, but knowing him as well as I did, and that he was habitually short of cash, the cause should have been obvious and served as a warning to me. Yet now he was asking me to function as his lawyer, not as his real estate partner, and I didn't bother to reflect on the implications of his behavior.

I rushed to the courthouse next to City Hall, ordered an expedited transcript, hung around until I could pick it up, then ran back to my office to study it. Having identified a significant procedural error that the magistrate had made, I prepared my petition for a certificate of reasonable doubt, a document that claims there exists reasonable doubt as to whether a defendant received a legally proper hearing. Jamming the papers in my briefcase, I raced down to the supreme court on Center Street and presented my petition to Judge Owen McGiven, who, I later learned, was a close friend of my uncle, Harry Miller.

Judge McGiven saw me in chambers, where I made my argument. Schulman had been represented that morning by his New York City attorney, who, as a matter of course, had waived the public reading of his client's rights prior to the magistrate's accepting Schulman's guilty plea. Yet this was Schulman's second conviction for the same violation. His first conviction had been punished with a corporate fine. Now that he was pleading guilty again, the magistrate had a statutory duty to warn him that because he'd been previously convicted of this crime, he was risking a jail sentence. Schulman hadn't been warned, either by the magistrate or his attorney. I argued to Judge McGiven that this represented a grievous procedural error and that Schulman's jail sentence should be stayed pending my appeal.

I paced in the hall outside Judge McGiven's court for an hour or two while he read the transcript and my petition. At last, Judge McGiven gave me the certificate and ordered Schulman's release pending my bringing the case to the Appellate Division. I went down to the jail, where Marty was finally let out at 2 A.M., badly shaken and promising me that he'd take care of the repairs.

I won the case for Schulman on appeal, vindicating Judge McGiven's judgment. Yet over the next several years, I never connected the dots, never consciously perceived what I must have known at a deeper level: Schulman didn't make those repairs because he couldn't afford to, that he was collecting rents on our buildings and using the money elsewhere. I didn't discover what he was using it for until the day he came to see me at my office and said that the banks were starting to foreclose on an appreciable portion of our properties.

I was aware that we'd had various problems with a few of our investments, but I'd had no idea how serious they were or that we were in jeopardy of losing nearly everything we owned. Suddenly, my head was spinning, and my stomach was slowly and painfully contracting.

I said, "Marty, what do you mean, 'foreclose?' Why?"

He sighed and said, "My oil company is going under. I drained too much money out of it, and Irving's cut me off. I took a chance that we'd sell our buildings for enough so I could pay everyone back."

A decade later, it was the sort of answer that I would hear repeatedly from clients who had come to drop their legal troubles on my desk. I know now that while these explanations sound like greed and deceit to those who are listening to the explanation, particularly if they've lost money, they make perfect sense to the people doing the explaining. It took me years of experience to understand this all-too-human phenomenon, and Schulman was the one who gave me my first lesson. At the moment he told me I didn't hate him, and I have no recollection of feeling angry. I was devastated, though, and all I could think about was how could I ever tell Doris this terrifying news.

Schulman said, "Stanley, we may have a way out."

Screw it, I thought, how much more could it cost me?

"Tell me, Marty," I said.

His scheme for salvation involved a project on East Sixty-sixth Street in Manhattan, ten thousand square feet of prime real estate. The foundation was already in, and we stood to make a fortune, well over a million dollars. We had started building with the foolishly optimistic belief that we would have no trouble securing a construction loan to cover the cost of completing the project. My optimism was a product of my abject stupidity regarding these matters, because of course given our current financial status, getting any one to lend us money seemed impossible.

"If we can find the cash to finish," Marty said. "We're home free."

We called around and dug up some help, the real-estate investment firm of Punia and Marx, who were known for their extensive holdings in the New York City market.

They were represented by Dryer & Traub, an old, prestigious Brooklyn law firm (which has since been dissolved). I contacted the firm, and after some fast negotiations with the senior partner Abe Traub, Punia and Marx agreed to a sale-lease back. They would buy the building from our syndicate, and once it was completed, they would lease it to us so we could run it. The terms were exceedingly favorable, a mark of how valuable the building would be, and the cash injection would insure our survival. We would receive a nonrefundable $50,000 payment up front; another $250,000 three months down the road; and an additional $250,000 on closing.

Now, we had to get the building done, and yours truly, the inimitable Schmuck with a Fountain Pen, signed more notes to borrow the funds to pay the work crews. I wasn't worried. No way would Punia and Marx kiss fifty grand good-bye. Then we'd have another half a million and the banks would be off our backs.

I believed in Punia and Marx right up until Abe Traub phoned to inform me that his client was pulling out of the deal, letting us keep their $50,000 but not forking over the money that would have kept us alive.

At that moment, I knew I was ruined financially. As a lawyer I felt that it would be morally improper for me to declare bankruptcy, and since I was on the hook for every dime of our investors' money, I would have to repay it with interest, a burden that even then I saw would take me years to unload, if I was lucky.

I went home and told Doris what happened, skipping over the precise amount of my debt. Her reaction shocked me. The girl who had once been angry with me while we were dating because I owed her eight dollars didn't bat an eye. She simply listened and expressed her confidence that I would straighten everything out.

Decades would pass before Doris chose to tell me that her calm that day was due, in part, to the fact that she was terribly distracted at the time dealing with Jeffrey's ongoing difficulties and trying to look after Lisa. Instead of burdening me with her troubles, she talked to her friend, Lillie Marmelstein, whose son Lewis was in Jeffrey's class in school. Faced with a similar challenge, the two women became very close, and so Doris had a sympathetic ear to listen to her burdens.

Then, too, Doris reasoned, my business dealings weren't her responsibility: I was the one who was supposed to be earning the living, while she took care of the children and the house.

I understand that modern marriages are not organized along these definitive lines, that this marital bargain borders on the politically incorrect. Nevertheless, as a mechanism for survival during tough periods, it seemed to me the best route to follow. Doris and I each had our own responsibilities, and neither of us meddled in the other's business. Thus, we were able to protect each other from our respective, daily misfortunes, and considering what we faced—a hyperactive, learning disabled child and financial ruin—it made our burdens easier to bear.

Although Doris never said a word about it, I was aware that she knew we were in deep trouble. She managed our daily expenses skillfully and without complaint, an extraordinary feat of dollar juggling and emotional restraint given our vanishing finances. At one point, when my fiscal woes were at their worst, she brought her engagement ring to my Uncle Phil and gave it to him to sell at a pawn shop, adding the proceeds to the household kitty.

Doris was very attached to the ring and pawning it must have broken her heart. Yet she never reproached me for putting her in that situation. Actually, she never mentioned it at all, and I learned about it only when my Uncle Phil referred to the ring by accident. I was ashamed that I'd gotten my family into such a desperate situation, but I was proud of my wife and felt lucky to have someone like Doris in my corner. Many years later she told me that she wasn't worried for a minute. She always knew that I'd be a success. I wish I had been so confident. It might have saved me a few hundred sleepless nights.

My saving grace in this period of my life was my law practice. Every morning when I'd arrive at my office at 770 Lexington Avenue, I had a sense of relief. Throwing myself into other people's problems and using my head and legal skills to clear them up convinced me that I was at least competent at something—even if it wasn't wheeling and dealing in New York City real estate. My cases ran the emotional gamut from the hysterical to the dramatic, touching on the entire spectrum of the human comedy, though some were admittedly funnier than others.

One case that was not amusing arrived one afternoon when an older woman walked into the office, wrote me a five-thousand-dollar check for a retainer, and asked me to represent her daughter. According to the woman, her daughter was mired in a nasty divorce proceeding. The woman claimed that the son-in-law was harassing his estranged wife, refusing to negotiate, threatening her life, all the ugliness that divorces often bring and then some. I immediately went to court, got a restraining order, and tried to open negotiations with the husband's attorney. Nothing doing. And then, strangely enough, my client and her mother stopped returning my calls. The mother didn't ask me to refund the retainer, but I had the impression that she and her daughter had given up on the case. Then one morning I opened up the *Daily News* and saw a headline announcing that a woman had been arrested for hiring a hit man to murder her son-in-law. Below the headline was a picture of the woman who had retained me. I guess she thought she'd discovered a more efficient method for getting her son-in-law off her daughter's back. It didn't work out, though. I believe the woman was sentenced to prison.

Among the funniest matters that I got involved in came across my desk courtesy of Ken Levy, a pharmacist who was married to one of Doris's friends, Marcia. Ken had a brother, Stanley, who had been stationed in Germany during the war and decided to stay on and make his home there. Stanley changed his last name to Layton, married a German woman, and made some decent money by compiling and selling an international directory of Telex numbers, a useful book in those days before the fax machine, much like the Yellow Pages.

Stanley Layton had a friend, Peter Ackerman, an attorney who practiced in Munich. Ackerman needed some assistance with one of his clients, a German businessman who hoped to take his company public in the United States. Layton didn't know much about this type of law, so he suggested that Ackerman talk to me. We spoke, I told him I could give him a hand, and the next thing I knew I had a retainer and a plane ticket to Germany.

The tricky aspect of taking Ackerman's client public was that he was in the business of owning brothels. It was a highly organized and well-managed operation. The women were examined regularly by doctors and treated like valued workers by the management.

Shortly after I touched down in Munich and checked into my hotel, Ackerman took me for a ride past some of his client's holdings. A few of the pleasure palaces were right near the NATO military installations, an especially efficient location since the soldiers provided a steady stream of clientele to the working ladies, and a number of the married soldiers' wives, unbeknownst to their husbands, moonlighted as prostitutes. I don't know if any husband and wife were ever reunited in the brothel, but that would have been a marital spat for the record books. I do recall being amused by the signs over the houses: SEX WITHOUT LOVE. And years later I suddenly found myself thinking about that sign when President Clinton got into trouble with Monica Lewinsky.

I wasn't exactly sure how such an offering could be accomplished, but the idea had definite possibilities when it came to hyping the stock in America. Not only did the brothels appear to be turning a handsome profit, I could imagine a bunch of wealthy guys getting a real kick out of sitting around the bar at the country club with their friends and bragging that they owned a piece of a European brothel chain.

On my first night in Munich, Peter Ackerman and his partners showed me the sights, beginning with the beer hall where Hitler had made a name for himself as an up-and-coming political rabble-rouser and maniac, and ending with one of the city's biggest cabarets, three thousand square feet of glimmering lights, laughter, drinking, dancing, and flirting.

On every table at the cabaret was a telephone, and people were crowded around calling each other and introducing themselves, the German version of the Dewar's and double entendre. The cabaret also had a message-tube system, and people were sending messages all over the place. Peter Ackerman got a phone call, and with my pidgin Yiddish, I couldn't understand a word of his conversation in German. When he hung up, I asked him what was going on. He told me that a young woman seated across the cabaret had spotted me, and she was quite interested in dancing with me. I've never had reason not to be a faithful husband, but I was a visitor in a strange country and one dance couldn't hurt.

Suddenly, I saw that Peter Ackerman was looking over my shoulder, and he said, "Here she comes, Stanley."

Quite curious about the type of woman I had attracted, and a little nervous, I turned to see a blue-eyed blonde who must have weighed a minimum of three hundred pounds. I danced with her, much to the delight of Ackerman and his law partners.

Although I had a good time on my trip, I felt oddly out of place in Germany. I was uncomfortable with the way the harsh guttural sounds of the language echoed in my imagination. As I walked the streets or ate at the restaurants or hailed a cab, encountering men who were my age and older, I couldn't stop wondering what they had been doing from 1939 until 1945.

Were they fighting at the front, killing Americans or perhaps wounding my brother Sol? Or had they been assigned to the camps, standing at the train station when the boxcars of Jews were unloaded, choosing who should live and who should die? Maybe the older fellow who worked as a doorman at my hotel had helped introduce the Jews of Warsaw to the Final Solution. Or maybe he had fired at the lines of women and children who were murdered at Babi Yar. He might not have done anything at all, I realized, but this did nothing to mitigate my discomfort.

I felt particularly strange on the weekend that Doris flew to Munich to take a brief vacation with me. The Holocaust had devastated her father's family. Some forty-odd members had perished in German concentration camps, including his sister and her children. One cousin was at Dachau, managing to survive because she was a wonderful cook, and the commandant of the camp had her prepare his meals. After being liberated by the Allies, she made her way to Tel Aviv.

The day after Doris arrived we were invited to lunch at the family home of Stanley Layton's wife, the young German woman he had married following the war. We took the train from Munich out to the town, riding through the rolling countryside, passing streams and forests straight out of Hansel and Gretel.

At the station, Stanley was thrilled to see us—I always suspected that he was a bit homesick for America. His wife was an intelligent, gorgeous woman who spoke beautiful English. The town was quaint and backed by the lovely snow-topped peaks of the Alps. The first thing Doris and I noticed, though, when we walked into her family's home was an old, black-and-white picture of the woman's father. He was wearing a Nazi uniform with a swastika armband.

She saw us looking at the photo and commented that she could not be blamed for the sins of her father.

Naturally, we agreed with her, and we spent a rather pleasant afternoon at the house. Lunch was delicious, the conversation interesting, but I can't say that either Doris or I were terribly unhappy when it was time for us to say good-bye and go catch our train back to Munich.

I did finally figure out a way for the brothel owner to take his company public. He could characterize his holdings and business as hotels—with legal entertainment—which in Germany just happened to be the amusement provided by ladies of the evening. I had a prospectus drawn up, dotting every i, crossing every t. In the United States, the mid-1960s was an era of burgeoning social change. Rigid attitudes toward sex outside of marriage were loosening up, and the state in which they seemed to be loosening up

*Louis and Ida Shaw on
their wedding day, 1919.*

Me at age six months, 1930.

The Brooklyn Hebrew Orphan Asylum, known as Castle on the Hill, seemed to rise up on Ralph Avenue like a medieval stone fortress. This is probably how the BHOA looked on February 23, 1933, when my mother and her sister brought my brother and me there to stay.

To this day I can recite every address where I ever lived, a talent I suspect you will find in children whose first memories are of an orphanage.

261 New Jersey Avenue, Brooklyn, NY. My first foster home with the Greenberg family

1967 73rd Street, Bensonhurst, Brooklyn. My second foster home with the Winds.

238 Neptune Avenue, Brooklyn NY. The second apartment I lived in with Ida, Louie, and my brothers.

141-25 Northern Boulevard, Flushing, Queens. Doris and I lived here in the early years of our marriage.

29-43 143rd Street in Flushing, Queens. The first house I ever owned

The Bay Club, Bayside, NY. Where Doris and I live today.

Me and Sol outside the Greenbergs' house at 261 New Jersey Avenue in Brooklyn. It was my first experience of being treated like a special little boy.

Bugle Boy for the Jewish War Veterans.

My bar mitzvah picture, 1942.

Me and Sol outside the Winds' house, 1967 73rd Street in the Bensonhurst section of Brooklyn.

Living under the care of Mrs. Bella Wind was as close as I ever hoped to come to being a boy in a Charles Dickens novel.

Graduation class of 1943 from Public School 100. I am at bottom row, second from rig

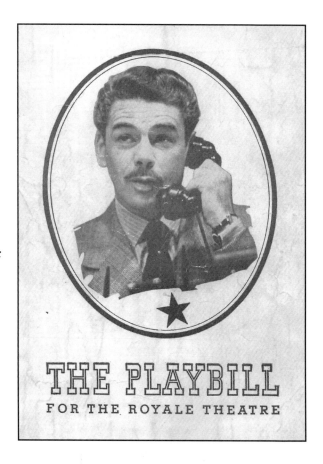

Playbill from Counsellor-at-Law, April 25, 1943. The show inspired me to become a lawyer.

Lincoln High School 1943 Championship Basketball team. Front row: Coach Lieb, Bob Cummin, Abe Becker, Murray Rost, Stanley Lampert, Max Cogan. Team seated on floor on right side.

That old gang of mine at the schoolyard: Left to right, kneeling: David "Duvie" Goldstein, —a "the German" Glassberg, Me, Herbert "Lavey" Hirschorn. Standing: Murray "Ace" Adler, —arvey Roth, Stanley Greif, Stanley Brahms, Stanley "Bucky" Kerner, Stanley "Shap" —apiro, Abe "the Walrus" Becker. Missing from the picture are Buddy "Max" Scher, Melvin —ones" Rothbart, Murray Gechtman, Irwin "Sonny" Spector, Herbie Lieber, Tommy —seph, Howard "Tatalu" Solomon, Bernie Schwartz, Murray Rost, and Sol "Schlomey" —andel.

Boy Scout Troop 361. My dear friend Bob Levine is the first Boy Scout in the second row from the top on the far left. I am in the top row, third from the left.

Me and Mother at Columbia University graduation day, 1951.

Left to right:
My dear friends
Christopher Jeffries
of Millennium
Partners, Joseph
Ferrara, Mike
Alexander, and me.

Me and Wilbur Breslin with
former United States Senator
Alfonse D'Amato.

With Governor George Pataki
holding the Bohack decision.

With Doris and former United States Senator Alfonse D'Amato.

Left to right: Alan Hevesi, comptroller of the City of New York, Parkhill Mays of Holland & Knight, Judge C. Albert Parente, Me, Preston Robert Tisch, Bill McBride managing partner of Holland & Knight.

Doris and my former partner and now Federal Bankruptcy Judge Dorothy Eisenberg.

My good friends Sam and Santa Albicocco. Santa is the treasurer of Nassau County.

Doris with William and Simone Levitt.

With Franklin Knobel and Wilbur Breslin.

With former Governor Mario Cuomo and his wife Matilda.

With New York State Comptroller H. Carl McCall and New York City Comptroller Alan Hevesi.

Me and Doris celebrating our fortieth wedding anniversary, May 28, 1995.

Our original maid of honor, Sandi Meyerowitz and our original best man, Eddie Miller, at our fortieth wedding-anniversary party.

Me with my partners at Shaw, Licitra. Back row, Left to right: Peter Marullo, Sarah Brenan, Roberta McManus, Jack Hall, Alan Marder, Stuart Gordon, Anton Borovina, Frank Livoti, Howard Kleinberg, Edward Flint. Seated, Left to Right: Robert Bohner, Myself, Jeff Schwartz, George Esernio.

With New York State Attorney General Eliot Spitzer.

Our son, Jeffrey Scott Shaw.

Lisa and Lon with our grandchildren Brittany-Lee and Ashley-Lynn.

the fastest was California. So I filed to take the brothels public there, and I was given permission to proceed.

However, just as the brothels were about to go out for public offering, Peter Ackerman contacted me and explained that the owner had suddenly become enmeshed in a serious financial scandal. The fellow had been privately selling shares in his company for a couple of years, and he had committed the con man's usual sin, selling each of his company's shares at least three times, behavior that I am told later got him thrown into jail. So I never got to take the brothels public, but I had a story I could tell at cocktail parties and dinners for the rest of my life, and I even managed to get another, far more serious case through Peter.

One day, I received a Telex at my office from Peter Ackerman, and he had a sad story to tell. Two young lovers, the man from West Berlin and the woman from behind the Iron Curtain in East Berlin, had traveled to New York City for a week-long holiday. Deciding that it would be interesting to observe the area from the air, they signed up for a tour with Heliair Helicopter. Tragically, the helicopter crashed, and the two lovers were killed. Peter was going to have pictures of the young man and woman airmailed to me, and he asked if I would please go down to the morgue and identify the bodies.

The photographs were delivered to my office, and I went to the morgue. Unfortunately, the police had recovered only the body of the young woman. I made the identification, and about two weeks later, when the young man washed ashore, I returned to the morgue and identified him. Shortly after the bodies were cremated and the ashes were flown to Germany for burial, I was asked by the parents of the couple to represent the families in a lawsuit against Heliair Helicopter.

The young man had been an architect with a promising career, and the young woman had been a nurse. I sued for $30 million, and the suit made headlines in Germany. I doubted that I would collect that sum, but given the age and the earning potential of the lovers and the pain and suffering of their parents, I was confident that I had a shot at a substantial award.

I had to travel to West Berlin and speak to the families. The young man's mother and father were easy to meet. I extended my condolences, gave them the necessary papers to sign, and told them that they would have to come to the United States for the trial, to explain to the jury about their son, his hopes and dreams and career, and their own anguish over his death. They agreed, and that was the end of that.

Now I had to meet with the young woman's parents. They had to travel across from East Berlin, and I had no idea how they were able to arrange it. (Incidently, I also never learned how their daughter had qualified to receive a visa from the East German government to visit New York.) The young woman's parents didn't speak or understand a word of English, and our discussion was passed back and forth by an interpreter. Their biggest concern was that even if I won the case against Heliair Helicopter, they would not be permitted to keep their portion of the settlement. The Communist government would take it from them.

That, I had to agree, was a problem, and I promised them that I would think about it and find a solution. After our meeting, I took a cab to Checkpoint Charlie, the border between East and West Berlin. A Russian soldier standing beyond the gate asked me what I wanted. I explained that I was an American lawyer, and I wanted to visit East Berlin for a few hours. He let me through, but I was back in forty-five minutes. I couldn't stand the place. There was a drab and sinister air about that section of the city, and I was glad to ride back to my hotel.

In the morning, I climbed into the shower, stood under the warm spray, and thought about how I was going to screw the East German Commies out of the money that they didn't deserve. By the time I was toweling off, I had cobbled together a plan. The method I devised required a round of phone calls to consulates, but it was a rather easy solution. I had the young woman's parents give the young man's parents power of attorney. Thus, any settlement check would be forwarded to them. They could cash it in West Germany and transfer the funds to the woman's family without the East German government knowing about it.

I drew up some papers and concluded the arrangements with the young man's parents. The next day I flew back to the States, but not before I made the taxi driver stop at a store so I could buy a Bavarian hat to celebrate my plan for outfoxing the greedy bastards in charge of East Berlin.

Back in New York I prepared for the trial. The case was going to be heard in federal court because the suit involved foreign citizens and an American company. I knew I had no chance of bringing the young woman's family out of East Berlin for the trial, but I contacted the young mans parents and suggested that it would be best for them to come to the States and testify.

Their response floored me. They absolutely refused, claiming that they would not come here because "the United States is our enemy."

When I'd met them in Berlin, I had no idea that I was dealing with folks stuck in pre-World War II history. Their refusal was devastating to the case. I was dead in the water without being able to put them up on the stand. First of all, they were the ones with power of attorney. Secondly, I wouldn't be able to suffuse my arguments with a living and breathing portrait of the real grief that the crash had caused, the part of my argument that went to pain and suffering. And finally, one of my major thrusts was going to be that had the son not been killed in the crash, he ultimately would have been around to help support his parents in their old age.

The matter was called to trial, and yours truly had no witnesses. I got a continuance for three days, insinuating that my witnesses were en route, and during those seventy-two hours I worked out a settlement. After my fees, Heliair Helicopter paid the families $150,000. I forwarded the money to West Berlin. Although I thought the young man's parents were a little odd, they turned out to be honest and shrewd because they maneuvered the proper share to the young woman's parents, who collected without any interference from their government. (One ironic footnote: Heliair Helicopter was later purchased by George Dempster, my client and friend, who renamed it Island Helicopter. In 1989, I successfully brought George's company out of bankruptcy.)

I have been described by many people as an eternal optimist, but one unfortunate fact I learned during my years of fiscal turmoil was that regardless of how grim your financial picture looks, it can always get worse.

With Punia and Marx dropping out of the equation, the bankers had no alternative, and they slated the East Sixty-sixth Street building for auction. This news was not greeted with joy by the unpaid contractors, who responded by slapping mechanic's liens on the building to the tune of $600,000.

Marty Schulman was in no position to come up with a plugged nickel. Plagued by severe cash deficits thanks to Marty's constant dipping into the company till to cover his cash shortages, Barrow Oil, the Schulman family business, would soon be sold for a song. At one point, Marty got so desperate that he broke into my office, ransacked it, stole my checkbook, and wrote checks on my account, signing my name. Then he filed for bankruptcy, but not before he stopped by the New York State Bar Association to lodge a complaint against me, claiming that our losses were caused solely by a combination of my legal incompetence and personal dishonesty. His complaint was summarily dismissed as being without merit. Then he attempted to complain to the state attorney general, saying that my prospectus didn't conform to state statutes. That complaint was also dismissed.

Arranging to settle your financial obligations and having the means to do it are two vastly different things, so I searched for creative ways to pay off my debts. I owed $50,000 in notes to Waller Construction, the general contractor in charge of the project. Waller was owned by Bill Crocker of the Crocker banking family. I called Bill and prevailed upon him to attend the auction of the foreclosure of the second mortgage on the East Sixty-sixth Street building. Quoting figures as fast as I could, I explained that there was a healthy profit to be made if he bought the property because the foreclosure sale would wipe out over half a million dollars of mechanic's liens.

The referee was already accepting bids when Bill Crocker walked in and sat next to me as casually as a guy who had dropped in at the neighborhood flea market. The bidding had reached $200,000 when Bill bid a quarter of a million. No one topped him, and the referee asked Bill for his cashier's check, the 10 percent that the winning bidder had to furnish to finalize the sale.

"I don't have it," Bill said. "But if you give me fifteen minutes I promise to get it for you."

The sole vested interest referees have in a foreclosure proceeding is to nail down the sale, and they shy away from taking chances. Better to sell to someone who can put cash on the barrelhead than to a higher bidder who promises to have the deposit fifteen minutes from now.

The ref informed Bill that he could have ten minutes, but that the price was high. He would have to return with a cashier's check for the full $250,000 if he wanted the building.

Bill nodded and said to me, "Let's go."

Outside, Bill said, "I thought I saw a bank around here," and I pointed toward a commercial bank on the far corner.

We crossed the street and went in, and Bill asked to speak to one of the vice presidents.

We were shown into a well-furnished office, obviously the home of a guy who had a little clout. After the introductions, Bill told the VP that he would like a cashier's check for a quarter of a million dollars.

Bill's tone was so matter-of-fact you might have thought he was asking for a drink of water, and the VP stared at him as though he were wondering if Bill had flipped his lid.

Finally, the VP asked him, "Do you have an account here?"

"No," Bill replied impatiently, as if he couldn't believe this guy would waste his time with stupid questions.

"Then I can't give you a check," the VP said.

Exasperated, Bill drummed his fingers on the VP's desk and replied, "Do you know the name of your bank's president?"

The VP told him, and Bill said, "Would you please call him?"

Keeping his eye on Bill, the VP dialed and asked to speak to the president. When he came on the line, Bill took the phone from the VP and had a fast, amiable chat with the president, telling him that he needed a check. Then Bill handed the phone back to the VP, who listened for a moment and hung up.

In two minutes, Bill had his cashier's check. I was totally flabbergasted, as was the VP, who ushered us out, smiling and assuring Bill that he was so glad that we had stopped by.

Bill bought the second mortgage on the building at East Sixty-sixth Street, and my reward for convincing him to attend the auction was that he forgave my $50,000 debt to Waller Construction.

Not a bad start, I thought, and like a gambler on a roll I instantly threw the dice again, hoping to cut a sizable wedge out of my debt.

Soon after, my Uncle Harry was trying to sell a parcel of land he owned on Central Avenue in Far Rockaway, Queens. Given the property's location and size, I believed it was a perfect spot to put up a garden apartment development, and a client of mine, Sam Gordon, agreed. Sam was a builder and, unlike Schulman, an extremely honorable man with a number of successful projects to his credit. Figuring I had a shot at substantially reducing my debt I secured a mortgage from the Royal National Bank and purchased the land from Uncle Harry.

We christened the garden apartment complex Lawrence Vista, because it was nearby the upscale community of Lawrence, Long Island, but the project was a disaster from the start. Looking back, I can see that I made two major mistakes that an experienced developer would never have made. First, I installed electric heat in the units. While this saved me money on my overall construction costs, it made the apartments terribly expensive to heat in the winter and discouraged would-be renters. Secondly, I never performed a thorough test of the market, a colossal error in judgment. The garden apartment complex was a spec job—we weren't developing for another company or partnership—and I should have at least canvassed the market to find out if anyone wanted to live there before taking out a huge construction loan.

Unfortunately, I had no idea what I was doing as a developer, and to make matters worse I repeated my Schmuck with a Fountain Pen act, and I personally guaranteed the construction loan.

By the time the garden apartments at Lawrence Vista were ready to rent that section of Far Rockaway had taken a precipitous dive. Rastafarian gangs had moved in and drugs were being dealt on the neighboring streets, and late at night it wasn't unusual to hear the bark and crack of gunfire mixing in with the beat of Reggae music and the whining of police sirens.

Understandably, a lot of the units went unoccupied. And my Uncle Phil, who had helped Schulman oversee our apartment houses and was now managing Lawrence Vista, was finding it difficult to collect the rents from a fair number of our less-than-upstanding tenants.

I had trouble meeting the payments on the construction loan, and David Berg, the majority stockholder at Royal National, helped me get some breathing room by asking the bank to restructure the payment schedule.

I limped along with my garden apartment complex for a while. The neighborhood continued its nosedive into mayhem, and all too soon I couldn't keep up with the restructured payments. By then, I had $200,000 of mechanic's liens on the property. Then Royal National was bought out by Franklin National Bank, and Franklin began foreclosure proceedings on Lawrence Vista.

I prepared the deed so I could turn it over to Franklin National and went to meet the bank president, whose last name, if I recall, was Gleason. When I walked in he said that he recognized me from some of the work that I'd done with the Liberal Party. I gave him a thumbnail sketch of my grim financial picture and told him that I had no hope of satisfying the liens, paying off the construction loan, or even reliably collecting rents from the occupied units. Gleason refused to accept the deed. Instead, he gave me $200,000 to pay off the liens, increasing my personal obligation to the bank to $585,000. I didn't even blink. What the hell, I thought. I couldn't pay them before, I could barely pay them now, even though Gleason reworked the figures so I could have a shot at making the payments. At least I could get out from under some debt and maybe, by some miracle, Lawrence Vista would pan out.

The miracle never came to pass. Believe it or not, things got worse, and not simply on the financial end. My Uncle Phil, the guy who was cursed at by tenants and had doors slammed in his face when he went to collect the rents, was arrested by U. S. Treasury agents. It seems that a bunch of wise guys operating a counterfeiting ring were using one of the garden apartments for a distribution center. Phil, as the managing agent of Lawrence Vista, was arrested along with them.

I got my uncle a lawyer, Bob Goldman, a first-rate litigator who had helped me navigate through my business reversals with Schulman. The trial lasted from Monday to Friday. I doubted that my uncle had been involved in any fashion with the counterfeiters, but despite Bob Goldman's best efforts, as I watched the jury file out to deliberate it didn't look good.

It was the first night of Passover, and by 7 P.M. the jury sent word to the judge that they were deadlocked. The judge ordered them to keep on deliberating until eight o'clock. I was supposed to be at my in-laws' for the Seder, but I wanted to know Uncle Phil's fate, so I waited around the courtroom, sitting on a bench behind one of the alternate jurors. The assistant U.S. attorney who had prosecuted the case wandered over to the alternate, whose presence was no longer required, and asked him what he'd thought of his performance during the trial.

"You did fine, man," the alternate replied.

The assistant U.S. attorney said that he'd wished that he could have introduced the defendants' background into evidence at the trial. They had all had their brushes with the law, including my Uncle Phil, who was a known gambler with a twenty-five-year-old arrest record for fighting. The prosecutor added that a lot of other convincing evidence against the counterfeiters had been excluded by the judge, and he proceeded to show these papers—whatever the hell they were—to the alternate.

Then, almost as if it were an afterthought, the prosecutor asked the alternate why he was still hanging around the courtroom after the judge had dismissed him. The alternate answered that there was a real foxy chick on the jury, and he'd made a date with her for that evening.

Immediately, I went over to Bob Goldman and told him the conversation I'd overheard.

"We have a mistrial here, don't we, Bob?" I said.

Bob said, "Let me talk to the judge."

The reason I thought we had an excellent shot at a mistrial was that the judge hadn't arranged to sequester the jury. Now let us suppose that the jury didn't reach a verdict on Friday, and the alternate got lucky that night with the pretty lady juror. They would be relaxing in bed afterward, and the alternate might mention what the assistant U.S. attorney had revealed about the defendants' past and the relevant excluded evidence that he'd showed the alternate during their post-trial chat. When the lady returned on Monday to continue deliberating, she would have information that would prejudice her against the defendants.

This was precisely the decision of the judge, and after scowling in the general direction of the loose-lipped assistant U.S. attorney, he declared a mistrial and sent everyone home.

The following week, Bob Goldman convinced the U.S. attorney's office that Uncle Phil had played no part in the counterfeiting ring and shouldn't have been on trial at all. So obviously, he shouldn't be tried again. The U.S. attorney cut my uncle loose, and that was the end of it.

I wish I'd been as fortunate at Lawrence Vista as my Uncle Phil had been in the courtroom. The neighborhood around Central Avenue in Far Rockaway slipped steadily downhill until it featured the noisy, depressing, and dangerous pathology that was sweeping the country's inner cities. Eventually, another bank, NatWest, that now owned my construction loan, foreclosed on the property and got a judgment against yours truly, the Schmuck with a Fountain Pen.

In the wake of that judgment, I sat down late one night with paper and pencil and recalculated each and every one of my liabilities, discovering that I was now over one million dollars in debt.

CHAPTER 8

POLITICAL MAN

T he Old Flushing Liberal Party Club was founded in my living room with a dozen of my friends. We sat around and discussed politics, did a little work in the community, raised a few bucks and, initially, I was unhappy with our role.

If I was going to do any job, I was going to do it well or not at all, and we needed more members to be effective. Now, it just so happened that one Saturday afternoon in 1967, when I was mulling over exactly how I was going to promote the club, a young man showed up at my door to drop off some Liberal Party literature. His name was Jerry Edelstein. He worked for Ben Davidson, executive director of the New York State Liberal Party. Davidson was the man who saw to it that Alex Rose's political strategy was carried out, and Jerry had been sent by the Liberal Party State Committee to help organize Queens County. Over the next couple of months, we became friendly. Jerry was a Brooklyn boy. His dad was a business agent of the International Ladies Garment Workers Union and also active in the Liberal Party. Jerry, however, was becoming increasingly dissatisfied with the direction of organized liberalism.

We both subscribed to the old adage, allegedly coined by a former political director of the ILGWU, that "it is the duty of the Liberal Party to keep Republicans liberal and Democrats honest," but Jerry felt that the party had rejected its trademark values. The scores of young people drawn to reform politics were registering Democratic, not Liberal, and this development unnerved Alex Rose, since his primary concern was to preserve the patronage that flowed to the party in exchange for its support.

According to Jerry, Alex's response was to undermine, as unobtrusively as possible, the reform Democrats. The party supported candidates, regardless of their philosophy, who could beat the reformers. (The height of this hypocrisy would come a few years later, when the Liberal Party supported Barry Farber, a reactionary radio-talk-show host, for Congress against Bella Abzug, the queen mother of New York liberalism.) In addition, Jerry said, the Liberal Party would gladly support some broken-down Tammany wheelhorse if he was sympathetic to tariff legislation that benefited the 400,000-member ILGWU. Hell, back in 1963, the Liberal Party quietly worked against raising the minimum wage because they were scared that an increase would chase the sweatshop owners out of the city and decimate their power base in the union.

I had noticed these trends, and the advantages for Alex were two-fold. First, he kept the reformers out of office, convincing the good-government types that their sole option was to register with the Liberal Party. Secondly, there were even more patronage jobs available for Alex when a more conservative candidate, backed by the Liberty Party, won an election. This was because when a Democrat won, Liberals got lost in the mad dash for the patronage jobs, since it is frequently difficult to tell the difference between a Democrat and a Liberal. On the other hand, Republicans or conservative Democrats do not attract the same job applicants, and so the patronage landed in Alex's lap.

Worst of all, as far as many reformers were concerned, was that Alex was so buddy-buddy with LBJ, refusing to challenge him on the escalation of the war in Vietnam. Considering Alex's extraordinary gift for judging the mood of the electorate, I was amazed that he didn't even publicly voice the mildest criticism of Johnson. From watching the news it was apparent that the war had created an enormous coalition of young men and women who were already organized and willing to become as active as necessary to advance their agenda, which ran well beyond forcing us to pull out of Southeast Asia, and included support for a host of classically liberal social programs. Literally thousands of these young people were living in New York, and while talking with Jerry I learned that he was plugged into that crowd. So I told him that I needed to attract members to my club, and in a matter of months, Jerry had introduced me to his colleagues and friends, and my membership problem was over.

They were "my potheads," or at least that's what I called the young people who signed on, although I'm not sure how many of them smoked grass. Like Jerry, the majority of them were in their midtwenties, bright, energetic, idealistic. And if they were addicted to anything, it was politics. I do know that they spent long nights in my living room and kitchen, talking and laughing with Doris and me, eating, drinking, and playing with Jeffrey and Lisa.

They had a spirit of fun that I'd never seen in people their age. I had always been too serious, too driven, always working, out to earn a buck—a result of my childhood and a mind-set that had not been improved by the financial troubles I'd gotten myself into with Schulman. My potheads were totally foreign to my experience. They were carefree, unfocused on the long-term mundane cares that had been at the center of my life for as long as I could remember. And they cheered me up to no end, providing a welcome relief from the law and my scrambling to get out from under the crushing debt I'd incurred.

Then, too, it turned out that it was a fortuitous time to have increased the membership of my club. At that moment, the Liberal Party was embroiled in a battle with the ILGWU. Back in 1965, the Garment Workers Union had strenuously objected to the Liberal Party's support of Mayor Lindsay, who was reputed to be anti-union. The rebellion had been put down by David Dubinsky, head of the garment workers and Alex's dear friend and staunch ally.

Now, however, Dubinsky had retired, and the ILGWU was at it again, fighting for control of the Liberal Party. They refused to go along with Alex and support Jacob Javits for reelection to the U.S. Senate, deciding instead to nominate Murray Baron, an outspoken hawk on Vietnam.

I admired Javits, his sensible liberalism and tireless support of Israel. Furthermore, I didn't want the Garment Workers Union, with its narrow concerns over tariffs and pay scales, to run the Liberal Party. A showdown was inevitable. You could feel it coming at our monthly meetings; tempers were exceedingly short during debates. Because I was a lawyer, I was asked to join the credentials committee, which I did, and then I sent my potheads door to door to draft new members and prevail upon them to sign proxies.

I don't remember where the final fight in Queens County occurred, but I do recall that it was at night. The hall was packed and hot and smoky and brightly lit, and there was so much yelling and screaming I felt like I was sitting ringside at a prize fight. The ILGWU was bringing their people in; we brought our people in;

and everyone was loaded down with armfuls of proxies, which they dumped on the card tables in front of me.

There were two of us and two of them on the credentials committee. I looked at the paper piled up and figured that we'd be there for a week of Sundays if we tried to determine the validity of each one of the proxies. Besides, in my own mind, I questioned whether some—no, make that most—of their proxies were legit. This isn't to say that the proxies on my side weren't suspect. My potheads could bend the rules with the best of them.

Meantime, the other three guys on the committee were frantically holding up all that paper on the palms of their hands, trying to determine the outcome of the vote by weight. It was one of the funniest things I ever saw, grown men trying to weigh proxies with their hands, while half of the forms floated off their palms like paper airplanes and the crowd shouted at us to watch what the hell we were doing. The trio wasn't making much headway, and finally I said to them, "Guys, forget the proxies. They really look even to me. Let's be democratic and have the vote on the floor."

That started an argument in the credentials committee. I listened, not saying a word. When they were done, I quietly explained that it was our only realistic option.

I guess all the noise from the peanut gallery convinced the two representatives from the Garment Workers Union that they'd win on the floor. I knew better. The ILGWU had elevated the collecting of proxies, both valid and invalid, to high art. My potheads were still learning that trick, but they knew the advantages of turnout, and they had been ferrying our people to the hall the entire evening.

The vote was close, but we won. The garment workers stormed out, and to this day I believe that if we'd counted the proxies we would have lost.

Of course, Alex Rose was pleased with the outcome. He was aware that if the ILGWU left the Liberal Party, he would lose their substantial financial backing, but doubtless to Alex that seemed like a small price to pay when faced with sharing his power. Shortly after our victory, I met with Alex in New York, and he took me on one of his elbow walks, gripping my arm, bending down, talking into my ear, congratulating me, giving me an update on his negotiations with the garment workers. Then he truly astonished me when he said, "Stand-ley, you interested in being chairman out there in Queens?"

"What about Izzy?" I said, referring to Isidore Levine, one of the party's founders and the current county committee chairman, who was in the middle of his third two-year term.

Alex replied, "Izzy, I think Lindsay might make him a judge."

That made sense. I'd heard that after Alex supported Mayor Robert Wagner for reelection in 1961, he was supposedly rewarded with a slew of judgeships. Something like one out of every four judicial appointees belonged to the Liberal Party. Lindsay was reported to be even more generous than Wagner, giving Alex a say-so over one out of three. And with court calendars lengthening every year, there were going to be fifteen new judgeships in Queens. Alex would get his share.

I agreed to run for chairman. It would certainly increase my visibility, which couldn't be bad for business, and it would also give my club the opportunity to do the things we had been talking about for the last couple of years. I returned to Queens and told my potheads that I'd been anointed by Alex. We had to keep it quiet because Izzy hadn't announced that he was resigning.

With Alex's blessing I doubted that anyone could take the chairmanship from me, but I wasn't taking any chances. On Monday evening, July 8, when the Queens County Committee of the Liberal Party met at the Jackson Heights Jewish Center, I made sure that my Old Flushing Club was in full attendance.

Izzy told the gathering that he was leaving, and we would have to vote for a new leader. I was nominated and ran against Ben Taruskin. According to the credentials committee, of which I was no longer a member, there were 201 accredited county committeemen at the meeting. I won the election 201 to 73. Go figure. Somebody later said that the vote was an example of the new math. Taruskin's people weren't buying it. When Izzy called for a vote on first vice chairman, they protested by walking out of the building.

Three weeks later I was sworn in as the head of the Queens County Liberal Party at a cocktail reception at Antun's restaurant. In passing on the chairmanship to me, Izzy Levine gave a little talk and made a big deal about turning over the reins of the party to somebody under forty. Ben Davidson, Alex's right-hand man, was there, and he echoed the same sentiments to reporters.

In my acceptance speech, I said I was proud of the young people we had attracted to our ranks, and I was going to devote every effort to keeping these resourceful, hard-working idealists with us and finding more of them.

I could see Ben nodding his approval. Looking back, I suspect that he had no idea I really meant what I was saying.

Before my group could begin working toward the social changes we envisioned in Queens County, we became involved in the national election. Vice President Hubert Humphrey was running against Richard Nixon for the presidency. Even with the ultraconservative third-party candidate Governor George Wallace of Alabama drawing support away from Nixon, the former vice president had held a commanding lead until the early fall when Humphrey publically broke with LBJ over Vietnam and started to catch Nixon in the polls.

The Queens County Liberal Party worked like mad for the Humphrey-Muskie ticket, and for Senator Jacob Javits as well. During the final two weeks of the campaign we mailed out nearly half a million pieces of literature. My potheads again went door to door, and they were exquisite. We organized and staged an antiwar march down Main Street in Flushing that drew a big crowd and several celebrities, including Tony Randall and Juliet Prowse. Ms. Prowse created the highest drama of the day. To protest the policies of our government in Southeast Asia, she tore up a ten-dollar bill, probably because she didn't have a draft card to burn, and Queens DA Tommy Mackel promptly told her that if she did it again he'd put her in jail. She refrained, and we managed to complete the march without any arrests.

Given that a large percentage of Americans had become thoroughly disgusted with the war and that one of the major planks in our platform called for an immediate halt to the bombing of North Vietnam so that meaningful negotiations could get under way, I knew we would do ourselves proud at the polls. But I was unprepared for how well we did.

Javits received 92,214 votes on the Liberal line in Queens, the most ever polled in the county for any Liberal Party office-seeker since the party's inception in 1944. The Humphrey-Muskie ticket got 61,900 votes, 28 percent of the total vote they received in all of New York City, and a new record for a presidential candidate on the Liberal line. The day after the election I told the *Long Island Press* that the turnout was proof that in Queens County the Liberal Party had at last established itself as a viable alternative to business-as-usual politics.

"We have demonstrated throughout the years the need for true individual independence in party politics," I told the columnist Robert Mindlin. "The day of the so-called controlled vote by organized leaders is the day of the past."

Not long after Mindlin's column appeared, I spoke to Alex. He complimented me and my organization on the fine job we had done and said that we would need another strong effort if Lindsay was going to get reelected next November. It was an upbeat conversation, and after I spoke to him, I wondered if he ever read the *Long Island Press*.

By the beginning of 1969, Mayor John Lindsay was in trouble. Rampant crime, shrinking budgets, rising taxes, racial unrest, and an overall perception that the quality of life in the city was rapidly deteriorating had eroded support for the young, charismatic mayor. Lindsay had appointed me to the Urban Coalition, a brainstorming group made up of successful businesspeople who were supposed to propose solutions to the city's problems. From my work with that coalition, it was easy to see that the social maladies plaguing New York were becoming a feature of city life across America. However, the previous fall, two strikes had given New Yorkers the impression that the city had lost control of its employees. That September, the teachers went on strike, keeping children out of the classrooms until late in the fall. Then the sanitation workers struck, illegally, and the leader of their union was tossed into jail. Trash piled up at the curbs until walking to my office on Lexington was like passing through a dump, definitely no way for a mayor to advertise to his citizens that he's in charge.

In an effort to spiff up the city and demonstrate that he wouldn't be intimidated by the unions, Lindsay asked Governor Nelson Rockefeller to send in the National Guard to collect the garbage and end the strike. Although both Lindsay and Rockefeller were liberal Republicans, there was bad blood between them, dating back to Lindsay's first run for mayor in 1965. Rockefeller had smoothed Lindsay's path from Congress to Gracie Mansion by having his family contribute $450,000 to his campaign. Yet when reporters asked Lindsay if the governor was his chief financial backer, Lindsay denied it, angering Rockefeller. Once Lindsay took office, he acted as though he were running the state Republican Party, behavior that was guaranteed to infuriate the imperious Rockefeller.

Consequently, I wasn't surprised that the governor's response to Lindsay's request for the National Guard was a blatant attempt to embarrass him: Rockefeller released the union leader from jail and promptly negotiated a settlement with the sanitation workers.

The governor's move had a steep political downside for both men. Rockefeller was portrayed in the press as having caved into the unions. And while some of the electorate appreciated the mayor's tough stance with organized labor, the ILGWU most assuredly did not. When the Liberals endorsed Lindsay for reelection, the executive committee of the Garment Workers Union voted unanimously to sever their quarter-century affiliation with the Liberal Party, specifically citing what they described as Lindsay's "catastrophic administration."

Understandably, New York Republicans, most of whom were beholden to Rockefeller, saw Lindsay as vulnerable, and they nominated State Senator John Marchi to run against him in a mayoral primary.

Despite Lindsay's faults I considered him a decent mayor. He was bright, articulate, creative, and willing to take a chance; and he had been fiscally responsible standing up to the demands of the unions. He was also a perfect candidate for the era, full of that brand of charm and ease with voters and the press that John Kennedy had used to get himself elected president.

And since the Liberal Party had endorsed Lindsay, I thought Alex would be eager to help him in the Republican primary against the far more conservative Marchi.

Alex, when I spoke to him, had a different idea.

"We're not gonna help Lindsay in the primary," he said.

"What do you mean, Alex?"

"In the election," he replied. "We'll help him in the election."

It took me a while to figure that one out, but it finally added up. Alex didn't want Lindsay running on the Republican line. He wanted him exclusively to himself. If Lindsay won, and Alex was betting that he would, then Lindsay would be particularly indebted to Alex, which meant even more patronage.

Of course, Alex wasn't the type to bet his last dime on a horse. At one point during the election season, he publicly stated that maybe it wouldn't be so bad if Senator Marchi beat Lindsay in the primary and became the mayor.

What Alex was doing didn't sit right with me. He had already placed an astounding number of Liberals in important posts—a deputy mayor, chairmen of the Youth Board and the City Commission on Human Rights, and a host of others in the Marine and Aviation Department, the Environmental Protection Administration, and the City Planning Commission. How much did he want?

All of it, I concluded, and let it go, not quite ready yet to buck the wishes of the boss.

Without the backing of the Liberal Party, the mayor lost the Republican primary. Hence, as Alex had hoped, in the general election Lindsay would have to run against Marchi and the Democratic candidate, Mario Procaccino, as a Liberal-Independent.

I met with Lindsay. He said that he felt if he could get a fifty-fifty split in the boroughs and win Manhattan's sizable liberal vote, he would be reelected. But, he added, he had to have Queens.

Winning Queens for Lindsay was a dicey proposition. The county was considered the biggest right-wing enclave in the city, encompassing a hefty number of Republicans and very conservative blue-collar families (a fact recognized by TV producers Norman Lear and Bud Yorkin, who less than two years later would make Queens the home of America's favorite bigot, Archie Bunker). Lindsay wanted their vote offset with an enormous turnout.

Alex turned us loose. We teamed up with Lindsay's man Al Unger and his organization (one of Al's assistants was Jeffrey

Katzenberg, the future Hollywood mogul), and right off the bat we began to make headway.

With the ILGWU gone, the Liberal Party had lost its major source of funding, so we had to raise money the old-fashioned way, dollar by dollar. We set up a phone bank at our headquarters on Parsons Boulevard, and we made thousands of calls, pleading with people to send us a donation and get out and vote.

We also mailed out campaign literature and seemingly knocked on every door in every neighborhood. In one single day, I chartered three new local Liberal Party clubs—Douglaston, Rockaway Beach, and Laurelton. I escorted Lindsay through the borough, and he stumped the streets hard and long, stretching his hundred-watt smile to the limit and dipping into his inexhaustible fund of charm.

Say what you will about John Lindsay, I am here to report that the man could definitely draw a crowd, friends and enemies alike. Once, on a swing through Astoria, I was standing with him on a flatbed truck when we got pelted with eggs.

That was the 1960s, though. Politics as Mischief Night.

Meanwhile, Alex wasn't taking any chances. He had another trick up his sleeve, which displayed his shrewdness, his determination to cover every base in pursuit of victory, his unwillingness to give up even the slightest edge.

In the 1969 New York City election, the first name you came to on the ballot was a candidate for an associate judge on the Court of Appeals. His name, if I recall, was James Gibson. Every party endorsed him—except the Liberal Party—because Alex calculated that by keeping Gibson off the Liberal line, the first mayoral candidate you would see in the voting booth would be John Lindsay.

It was an ingenious move. Topping the ballot for the Democrats, Republicans, and Conservatives would be a judicial candidate for the Court of Appeals, but Lindsay's name would be on top of the other mayoral hopefuls, sending a subliminal message to voters and making it easy for them to flip the lever.

And it may well have paid off. John Lindsay was reelected with 900,000 votes, and 800,000 of them came on the Liberal line, qualifying us as more than simply a third-party threat.

In New York City, at that instant, the Liberal Party had actually elevated itself to the same level as the Democrats and Republicans. In Queens, the Liberal Party pulled off a pair of small-time miracles: Lindsay won the county by approximately two thousand votes, *and* on Lindsay's coattails we elected Liberal enrollee Alvin Frankenberg as a councilman-at-large, unseating a Republican incumbent.

I spent election night at our Parsons Boulevard HQ, monitoring our phone bank, which was calling around to election districts checking the returns. In the days before TV's sophisticated computer tracking, it was the best method for keeping a running score on an election. We were pretty sure Lindsay was going to win, and then a call came in from one of his assistants, who said that the mayor wanted me to visit him at his hotel.

Thinking we were off to a victory party, Jerry Edelstein and I got into his Karmann Ghia and drove toward Manhattan. As we entered the Midtown Tunnel, we suddenly got an unhappy surprise. WINS radio announced that Lindsay was losing by 50,000 votes. I couldn't believe it. I asked Jerry what the hell went wrong. He shrugged and lit a cigarette. Had Lindsay called me so we could cry together in our beer?

That was the longest ten minutes I ever spent in a tunnel. We came out the other side just as WINS admitted that they had made a mistake. The mayor was actually winning by 50,000 votes.

I can't say for sure, but I think Lindsay was at the Roosevelt Hotel that night. However, I vividly recall that when Jerry and I walked in, the downstairs ballroom was packed with revelers, laughing and drinking and plenty of them smoking victory cigars. I spotted Lindsay chatting with a couple of people, and the next thing I knew he was hugging me and kissing my cheek, and we were both crying, and he kept saying, "We carried Queens. We carried Queens. Stanley, I can't thank you enough."

I stood there, savoring an accomplishment that has remained, twenty-five years later, as one of my proudest moments in politics. Then I wished the mayor good luck and went home.

A few weeks later, I was at the Drake Hotel meeting with a client, when the phone rang. My client picked up and said it was for me. John Lindsay was calling from his car phone, an awfully high-tech instrument in those days.

"Stanley," he said. "Listen, I'm in a bind. I need to appoint somebody fast for the City Planning Commission. You got a name for me?"

"Not off the top of my head," I replied. "I'll call around and get back to you."

"*Right* back to me, Stanley. I'm in a hurry."

Perhaps I should've reflected on the implications of my actions. But the Mayor of New York phones from his car and requests a name, you get him one. I called around, and everyone I spoke to came up with the same guy, Marty Gallant. I called back Lindsay in his car and told him.

"Good," he said. "Marty Gallant was on my short list. Thanks, Stanley."

Making that recommendation seemed like a harmless thing for me to do. But then nothing is viewed that way when you are dealing with a boss who is convinced that every patronage job belongs to him. Word about my emotional exchange with Lindsay at the hotel had already filtered back to Liberal Party headquarters, and now I had helped somebody get on the city payroll.

My war with Alex Rose had begun. Only I didn't know it yet, because Alex was a pragmatic man, a careful man, and he would never fire a shot until he was sure he could hit you.

CHAPTER 9

MUSCLING THE BOSS

Once the dust cleared from the campaign, the Queens County Liberal Party had 25 percent of the city's 60,000 registered Liberal voters, making us a major power base of the statewide Liberal organization. We had attracted the new legions of young people by pledging to get involved in social issues. Hence, I was soon busy supporting the creation of methadone clinics, going after the Queens County Bar Association because they excluded women from their leadership, and engaging in a series of debates with Serphin Maltese, the conservative leader of Queens (and now a state senator from the county's Fifteenth District). The debates were held at churches, synagogues, anywhere we could attract an audience. We generally got a sizable turnout, and mainly what I recall is that Serph and I would do our shtick, then he would attack me as a radical, and I'd reply, "If it's radical to be against the war in Vietnam, if it's radical to want to get drug addicts off the streets, and if it's radical to be pro-women, then you're right, Serph, I am a radical."

Serph may well have recruited as many members for his party as I did for mine—hey, this was Queens. But the debates provided something valuable that appears to be missing in today's civic life, an open forum where people can gather as a community and express their most profound feelings on the issues of the hour. No matter how deeply Serph and I and the audience disagreed, there was the sense that our fates were intertwined and our voices mattered. Regardless of where we stood, each of us held the conviction that a community which remains uninvolved will one day cease to be a community.

The speaking was heady stuff, and it made the workaday drudgery of dealing with bosses and raising money feel far away. However, it proved to be only a momentary respite from the grimmer aspects of politics, for after the new Lindsay administration took office, I began receiving phone calls from some of my people, all of whom had a similar complaint: The New York State Liberal Party had promised them jobs with the city, and nothing had come through for them.

Currently, I know it is fashionable to denigrate government workers as pampered, overpaid whiners whose salaries and perks bleed taxpayers dry. This belief wasn't as widespread in the winter of 1970—actually, quite the opposite. Twenty-five years ago, millions of young people felt that government possessed the power to alter the lives of its citizens—especially its poorest and most powerless citizens—for the better. That was unequivocally the case with the group who were waiting to be contacted about their city employment. They were industrious men and women brimming with ideas and ideals, and they had worked like dray horses for the Liberal Party and Lindsay's election. Now they were eager to dive in and try to make a difference for a salary that was barely above a liveable wage.

Having no answers for them, I promised to look into it and contacted Jerry Edelstein, who was still with the Liberal Party State Committee. Jerry isn't the kind of guy to mince words, and he said, "It's bullshit. There are jobs galore, but Alex keeps saying there aren't. He's screwing you, Shaw."

Figuring that Jerry was overreacting and that I'd straighten the whole thing out with a quick meeting, I called Dick Aurelio (who today is a force in the cable TV industry.) Dick had served as Lindsay's campaign chairman and had become his chief deputy. I got an appointment, but I was put off for a month. I was annoyed; here I am the chairman of the Liberal Party in Queens and I get the runaround when I try to get in to talk to the deputy of the man who had hugged and kissed me in a hotel ballroom on election night. Yet I didn't draw any conclusions about the delay in my meeting with Dick until I finally met with him and saw the slightly embarrassed expression on his face. Then I knew I was in for some less-than-happy news.

"Dick," I said. "Four weeks to see you?"

"Sorry, Stan," he replied. "But I gotta be honest. Alex told us not to deal with you directly."

"Listen, " I said. "The mayor asked me for a name for the City Planning Commission. I didn't go running to him for favors."

Dick said, "Possibly the mayor didn't understand the protocol."

I was incensed. These people waiting for their jobs were being jerked around by some worn-out boss who had a serious case of champagne-of-the-mind. Who the hell did he think he was? Eventually, I wangled a meeting with Lindsay, thinking that he would be brave enough to tell Alex that *he* was the goddamn mayor and he'd deal with anyone he wanted to.

As I entered Lindsay's office, he was on the phone with Jacqueline Kennedy Onassis. Glancing up at me, he asked her to hold on, covered the mouthpiece with his hand, and said, "Jackie's being harassed by the local paparazzi and wants me to do something about it. What do I do?"

I felt like replying he should get Alex Rose to help her, but I said, "Tell her you'll send the cops, then say something nice and hang up."

That's what he did, but when I mentioned the situation with Alex he shrugged, letting me know that his hands were tied.

I suppose this is the gratitude that politicians are famous for. I should've known better, and yet, to this day, I am dismayed when somebody you help win an office turns his back on you. A few years later, for instance, Frank Padavan was running for the New York State Senate from the Eleventh District in Queens. It was an awfully tight race, and Al Unger called, saying that the Liberal vote would put Frank over the top, and then he asked me if my organization would get behind him. I didn't agree with several of Padavan's positions on the issues, but a friend was asking me a favor, so I met with Frank and got my organization to pitch in. Lo and behold, Frank won. Now, maybe ten years later, I was at some political dinner, and Frank was seated nearby and I went to say hello.

"Who're you?" Frank asked.

I told him my name, and he said, "I don't know you."

For an instant, I was worried that the poor fellow was suffering from Alzheimer's. Except he looked too young and fit. I reminded him that I'd been the leader of the Liberal Party of Queens County, and we had provided his margin of victory in 1972.

"No you didn't," he said.

"Yeah," I said. "We did."

"You couldn't have," he replied. "I never heard of you."

This could've gone on indefinitely, but my soup was getting cold.

"Don't worry," I said. "I'm not looking for a job."

He stared at me, probably debating whether he should summon a trooper to cart this nut off to jail, but I left on my own, wondering how I could, after all those years in the game, be so naive.

I blame it on my lifelong devotion to wishful thinking, my tendency toward cockeyed optimism. When I was a kid I remember lying in bed at night, knowing, without question, that my folks would suddenly appear and reclaim me from foster care. It didn't fall out that way; it took time and a furious negotiation on my part. Yet I never stopped wishing for it and believing it would happen.

My chronic hopefulness aside, I'm evidently expecting too much from your average politician, and as of late I've concluded that short memories are a qualification for office.

As I write this in the spring of 1997, Frank Padavan is still a state senator.

By the time I walked out of City Hall I had calmed down, and as I rode the train home to Flushing, I tried reasoning it out. Maybe Alex didn't have a bone to pick with me personally. Perhaps Lindsay had made a slip in protocol, and Alex was reminding him of who's who in the Liberal Party pecking order. Fine. That must be it. Then all I'd have to do is straighten it out with Alex.

Before I could arrange a meeting with Alex, he blindsided me by recommending Allen Moss as a criminal court judge in Queens. That wasn't right. There were lots of lawyers waiting for that slot, people who had been active in the Liberal Party for decades. At best, Moss was a newcomer. In addition, I'd heard that he didn't have the experience for a judgeship, nor did he have a kosher Queens address, but one had been gussied up for him to satisfy the residency requirement. Moss's most notable qualification was that he was a law partner of Alex's son, Herbert.

I went to Liberal Party headquarters in Manhattan, at 165 West Forty-sixth, right off Broadway, and politely told Alex that Moss was a major problem. My people with seniority were hurt that they'd paid their dues and now they were being stepped over. If he had consulted me, I could've prepared them for the news and gotten Moss through with a minimum of fuss by reassuring them that Alex had to sit Moss on the bench, but they were next in line. How could I function as the county leader if my people couldn't depend on me to go to bat for them and get them the jobs they're qualified for and deserve?

Alex gazed absent-mindedly at me with his big, droopy eyes, like a bored owl perched on the beam of a *shtetl* barn. When I finished, he said with his heavy accent, "Stand-ley, this is de vay things are done."

That was it. He wasn't in the mood for an elbow walk. He knew I was beyond persuasion. Then again, so was he, and he sat there, looking as though he was wondering, Where did this guy get the nerve to question me?

I came away from that encounter believing that under Alex Rose's leadership the Liberal Party was neither liberal nor a party, but a half-assed politburo run by a man with a visceral love of power. He would support anyone who would trade him jobs for votes and couldn't have cared less about the thousands of well-meaning people who did the party's work for him. Who knows what happened to the Alex of the 1930s and 40s. Maybe he wearied of the good fight or found collecting perquisites a bigger kick than idealism. For all I know, Alex could have polished off a fifth of vodka one night and woke up in the morning with the unshakeable conviction that he was Joseph Stalin. The reasons didn't matter anymore. We were weeks away from open warfare.

In 1970, Nelson Rockefeller was seeking a fourth term as governor. His polls were down, with two-thirds of the electorate in favor of replacing him. A friend of mine, State Senator Seymour Thaler, a Democrat from the predominately Jewish, vociferously liberal, Forest Hills section of Queens, told me that his party's leaders were optimistic that they had a real shot at ending twelve years of Rockefeller's dictatorial rule. Sy had discussed possible candidates with two of his top staffers, Dick Brown (now the district attorney of Queens County) and Alan Hevesi, (the current comptroller of the City of New York), and they had determined that for the Democrats to win the governorship they had to nominate someone who could match Rockefeller's national presence and recapture the strong support he received from organized labor. A seven-term senator with a high profile among voters as a crusader against the deplorable conditions in many of New York City's hospitals, Sy had a good deal of clout inside his party, and he successfully pushed for the nomination of one of the most distinguished men in America, the Honorable Arthur Goldberg.

A former justice of the Supreme Court, secretary of labor under Kennedy, U.S. ambassador to the United Nations, and general counsel to the AFL-CIO, Goldberg was also a natural to run on the Liberal Party line. And at the state Policy Committee meeting in New York City, we tried to put him there. Trouble was, Alex Rose wanted to wait until the last minute to finalize the nomination, giving himself the maximum amount of time to sniff the political winds and pick a winner.

Needing a warm body to fill the spot temporarily at the top of our ticket, Rose's minions nominated Reverend Donald Harrington, the titular head of the party. It was understood that Harrington would step down and be replaced by Alex's choice once Alex had decided on a candidate.

Granted, Goldberg as a campaigner was so soporific he could have cured a hospital full of insomniacs. Joseph Persico, a Rockefeller speechwriter who later wrote a biography of his ex-boss, recalled that although the Democratic nominee unsettled the governor's staff, Persico himself was "unperturbed" because "I had heard Goldberg make a speech."

However, Goldberg was the true essence of a liberal, and Alex was hurting his candidacy by not immediately putting the full weight of the party behind him. Facing the Policy Committee, I spoke for a half-hour straight, saying more or less that delaying the nomination of Arthur Goldberg was cowardly and destructive. I had enough experience arguing in front of judges and juries to know when my words were beginning to sway opinions. There were five hundred people there, and I could see the changing expressions on many of their faces, hear their murmurings of approval whenever I paused.

Sensing someone standing beside me, I turned and saw David Dubinsky, retired leader of the Garment Workers Union and co-founder of the Liberal Party. Dubinsky was revered by liberals as the grand old man of the cause, the living embodiment of its past, when labor held the moral high ground. He tugged on the sleeve of my suit jacket and called out, "Can we break for ten minutes? I'd like to talk to this young man."

We sat in the back, and Dubinsky said, "Son, I guarantee you that Goldberg will be the candidate of the Liberal Party. Give me a few weeks, and stop your speech. Your speech is going to hurt us. You do this, you have my word, Goldberg will be our candidate. Alex, he needs to demonstrate he has control of the party. You understand?"

I said, "Mr. Dubinsky, I'm a loyal person. I'm not here to make waves, but Goldberg should be our candidate. You give me your word on Goldberg and ask me to stop, I'll stop."

"Son," he said. "After Goldberg addresses us, he'll be our man. You have my word."

I agreed and lived to regret it, since I firmly believe that had we taken the vote Goldberg would have been our candidate right then and there.

Today, approaching my seventieth birthday, I can say with relative certainty that I have had more troubles than most to be angry about in my life: the breakup of my family when I was kid; the Dickensian circumstances of my second foster home; Louie's appropriating my savings to pay his gambling debts while I was off in the Army; Jeffrey's painful struggle against his handicaps; and Schulman's dishonesty, which ruined me financially for a decade and a half. My childhood anger was tempered by my feeling that you owed your parents love and respect, and by my recognizing, even as a youngster, that my mother and father were deeply flawed but doing the best they could. As an adult, the burdens I faced were made manageable by my marriage. Without Doris's love and support and her watching over my physical well-being, I would have a different tale to tell. My point is that despite my troubles, anger wasn't an overwhelming day-to-day presence for me. That is, not until the spring of 1970, in the aftermath of the Policy Committee meeting, when Alex Rose announced that in order for Arthur Goldberg to win the Liberal Party nomination he would have to write a long, public letter proving that his beliefs were in accord with the tenets of liberalism.

My reaction to that announcement was literally to shake with rage till I became sick to my stomach. What a hideous goddamn joke. The demand for a letter was nothing more than an aging, increasingly insecure boss making a candidate kowtow. Alex was humiliating not only one of the authentic giants of the public arena, but perhaps the most esteemed man in American Jewish life. The pathetic irony of it was painful. Arthur Goldberg, like Alex Rose himself, came out of a generation of American Jews who were sadly too well acquainted with closed doors—in industry, politics, universities, housing. By sheer force of will, hard work, and intellect, this generation had managed to swim into the mainstream. They had seen the Holocaust and responded by playing a central role in the creation of Israel and the American civil rights movement. As a community, of which Arthur Goldberg was a prime example, their unflinching dedication to the principles of liberalism was a matter of record. But Alex Rose needed a seven-page letter. Goldberg was enough of a gentleman to supply him with one.

I'm proud to say that I hadn't waited for this perversity to run its course: I had already informed the press that Goldberg would be the Liberal Party candidate. By then, I had annoyed Alex sufficiently that he decided it was time for me to explore another avocation. He began shoving me out of the party leadership. At the end of June, I was dropped from the Executive Committee of the Liberal Party, making me the sole county chairman who was not a member. My war with Alex was heating up, and I had no illusions about his goal. As I told reporters, "Queens has the strongest Liberal organization in the city, and Alex wants to control it."

Two weeks later, he made his move.

With my first term as county chairman ending, I was up for reelection. On July 1, the Queens Liberal County Committee convened at our headquarters, the third floor of an office building on Parsons Boulevard.

We had twelve hundred people on our committee, but luckily just over two hundred showed up, because there was no air conditioning, and it was an unbearably hot and humid evening. In the jungle weather New York City summers are famous for, crowding into that room was like being jammed into a *shvitz* bath.

Eric Barr was heading a slate to challenge me. Eric and his allies, young people interested in issues not patronage, had formed a splinter group within our Queens organization known as Liberals for New Politics. The meeting was called to order. I remember seeing Morton Greenspan, deputy traffic commissioner for the city and a Liberal Party vice chairman, standing off to the side, fanning himself with a rolled-up newspaper and puffing on his pipe. Morty was a friendly acquaintance of mine, and he was supposed to nominate me. However, minutes before the call for nominees, Morty said that he would be running against me. Alex wanted it that way.

I was taken aback by Morty's betrayal, but I had been prepared for that sort of maneuver. Wiping the sweat from my eyes, I calmly stated that I would be presenting proxy votes on my behalf. The place went nuts. Like a bar fight without the flying chairs, or a borscht-belt hotel on free steak night. Greenspan's backers, a number of whom worked city jobs courtesy of Alex Rose, demanded that we do it over.

I replied that you do it over in punch ball, not politics.

They promised to take me to court over the use of my proxies. So what, I thought. I'm a lawyer, I been to court plenty.

After an hour of *Sturm und Drang*, it became obvious to me that Alex was using economic blackmail to win supporters, threatening to take away their municipal livelihoods if they didn't deliver for him. I knew I was going to have to adjourn the meeting without a vote, but I told the group that we would have to reconvene in less than three weeks because I suspected that Alex, a master of election arcana, was aware that under the rules the county committee must elect officers no later than twenty days following the primary or the Liberal state committee would take over the delinquent organization. Chances are Alex was hoping the whole thing would blow up, we would miss the deadline, and then he could run Queens from state headquarters in Manhattan.

Round Two of the vote was rescheduled for the evening of July 13, at the Jackson Heights Jewish Center. That afternoon, I held a press conference at the Overseas Press Club in Manhattan. My fight with Alex had generated a healthy amount of media coverage, and the place was packed. I began by informing the reporters that I would be running with Eric Barr as my vice chairman. My supporters had put together the Queens Coalition for an Independent Liberal Party, and I was sanguine that we would prevail against the Greenspan slate. Then I said that the Liberal Party should—and would—be a "massive party," except that the present "autocratic leadership opposes this concept as it depends on ultimate control in the hands of a few. The present leadership would rather have 'dummy county organizations' and 'paper political clubs,' whose only function is to elect state committeemen who would do its bidding at any convention which designates statewide and citywide elected officials." In conclusion, I stated that the era for this type of exclusivity had come and gone, although certain leaders continued to live in the past.

At the press conference I had more in mind than thumbing my nose at Alex. I can't say for sure that he understood my message, but his gifts for deciphering political nuance were large. His efforts to dislodge me over the next four years were unrelenting. Therefore, I assume he had figured out what I was driving at. Besides, if he didn't catch my drift that day, my message was interpreted for him in a lengthy piece about our battle that soon appeared in the Sunday *New York Times*. After recapping our dispute the reporter wrote that the splinter group in Queens was "remarkably similar to the original Democratic Party reformers who chipped away at Carmine G. DeSapio, once the most powerful political leader in the state."

DeSapio was one of the last great Tammany Hall bosses, running the Democratic Party in Manhattan with an iron fist. From the late 1940s onward, he controlled patronage and brokered deals for the great and small. He was Alex Rose with bigger muscles and a far longer reach. The 1960s, though, proved to be a perilous era for political bosses. A reform movement inside the Democratic Party, led by Senator Herbert Lehman and Eleanor Roosevelt, attacked DeSapio as a corrupt holdover from a moribund system. As a result, DeSapio lost his district leadership position to a reformer, and by the time the second Lindsay administration rolled around, DeSapio was being tried for conspiring to bribe a former water commissioner and to extort contracts from Con Ed in exchange for kickbacks. He hadn't been convicted by the afternoon of my press conference, but the smart money around the city said DeSapio was going to jail. (He would eventually serve two years.)

At the very least I wanted Alex to be aware of the stakes we were playing for and that I was serious about winning. I wanted him to know that bosses did indeed dissolve into history and, as DeSapio proved, sometimes they didn't fade comfortably into oblivion, but were drummed out tainted with scandal. Hell, I even had fantasies about going over to Alex's apartment in Washington Heights and telling him that I was a big fan of Eleanor Roosevelt, that I had, in fact, brought her to Lincoln High School my senior year as a speaker. Maybe that would have done the trick, made him back off.

Probably not. Say what you will about Alex Rose, he wasn't a quitter. Me either. That was the problem, the unacknowledged cause of our war.

The air conditioning was blowing full blast at the Jackson Heights Jewish Center when the Queens Liberal County Committee convened for a second try at a vote. The count was 120 for Greenspan and 93 for Shaw. Then I presented the 118 proxy votes I had collected and declared myself the winner, 211 to 120.

With everyone shouting at each other, and at me, I adjourned the meeting.

Doris had been present that night, her face frozen somewhere between fury and grief. She couldn't stand the abuse aimed in my direction, and as we walked to our car, she pronounced politics a disgusting racket, a verdict I was beginning to share, especially when I discovered that the battle over the chairmanship wasn't over.

Funded by Alex and represented by Herb Rubin, a member of the Liberal Party and a high-profile New York City attorney, Greenspan took his grievance about my use of proxies to the Queens County Supreme Court. His complaint was absurd; the Liberal Party had permitted the use of proxies for decades. I never did think their case was anything but Alex acting on the shibboleth that the best defense is a good offense.

Bob Goldman was representing me, and in response to Alex's harassment I had Bob subpoena the Reverend Donald Harrington, chairman of the statewide Liberal Party; Ben Davidson, the party's executive secretary; and Alex. Sometime later I heard that

Harrington and Davidson accepted service of the subpoenas, but Alex became incensed and slammed the door in the process server's face, refusing to open it again. My potheads and I got a big kick out of imagining that scene.

As I waited for my legal battle to begin, I continued as the county leader and suddenly found myself locking horns with Alex again. He was attempting to fill a vacancy on the Queens Supreme Court with former city councilman-at-large Joseph Modugno. Alex pushing Modugno was an obvious payoff to Rockefeller. What marked Alex's choice as a blatant effort to help the governor settle some political debt was that Modugno wasn't just a Republican, he was a die-hard conservative who belonged on the Liberal Party line about as much as I belonged on the mound at Shea.

The man who deserved the Liberal endorsement was civil court Judge Louis Wallach. Sy Thaler had introduced me to him years before while we were both attending a Chinese wedding in Chinatown, sampling one of those hundred-year-old eggs. At the time, I didn't attach any mystical significance to meeting Judge Wallach, although given what would happen I probably should have.

So, at our County Judicial Convention, held at the Queens Bar Association Building in Jamaica, I nominated Louis Wallach. Maybe it was my disgust about the fight over the chairmanship, but when Alex's supporters nominated Modugno, I felt like my head was going to explode.

Standing up, I launched into one of the longest, most impassioned speeches of my life. I said that I had nothing personal against Joe Modugno, but surrendering the Liberal line to him would make us a party to fraud, condemning us to the same cynical circle of hell inhabited by Alex and every boss who claimed that prudent compromise was the name of the game, and then proceeded to sell his soul in a smoke-filled room for two cents on the dollar.

I wound up my speech around midnight. The convention called for a vote. Alex's supporters didn't like the look of Modugno's chances, and they requested a five-minute adjournment. If I recall, it was Morty Greenspan who went out to phone Alex. I was confident that Modugno wouldn't make it, though not due to my persuasiveness on Louis Wallach's behalf.

From the moment I popped up to speak, I'd been betting that at this early stage in the struggle for control of the Queens County

Liberal Party, Alex would conclude that he couldn't afford a public defeat.

After all, a boss doesn't endure purely because of his real power—the patronage he dishes out, the nominations and elections he can swing. A boss survives based on the power that others perceive he has. Once a group successfully slips out from under his control, as we were doing in Queens, the perception of his power changes. Seeing that the boss is vulnerable, other groups, voicing their own resentments, decide they no longer owe him their absolute allegiance, and slowly but surely the boss loses both his perceived, and real, power.

With a quarter-century of experience under his belt, Alex knew the mathematics of bossism down to its last decimal point. He wouldn't risk damaging the public perception of his power over a judicial appointment, not while he had a shot at taking the chairmanship away from me in court. He was too good a gambler, and too in love with his exalted position on New York's political food chain.

Morty Greenspan returned, and Alex's verdict was relayed quietly around the floor: We lost this one to Shaw; forget about Modugno.

Louis Wallach was given the Liberal line on the ballot. Wallach had listened to my speech while sitting in an anteroom off the main meeting hall, and after the vote he came flying toward me, teary-eyed and puffed up with gratitude. A few months later, he won a seat on the bench in the general election. Shortly thereafter, I appeared before him in court and came away thinking that had I known about Judge Louis Wallach's dearth of wisdom and compassion, I would have nominated Joe Modugno myself.

CHAPTER 10

MAYBE A DIVINE HAND

N
ow that my potheads and I were a full-fledged dissident faction of the Liberal Party, we chose to support our own slate of candidates in the upcoming November election. Initially, over at the statewide Liberal Party headquarters in Manhattan, they weren't taking us seriously. Then we held our annual Queens dinner at Terrace on the Park, and the candidates, at our invitation, showed up to woo us.

Arthur Goldberg came, as did Senator Charles Goodell, Attorney General Louis Lefkowitz, and their respective Democratic opponents, Representative Richard Ottinger and Adam Walinsky. With nearly a thousand people there, Goldberg in particular made some flattering remarks about me, and I am told that when Alex found out about it, he went off the wall, complaining that we were splitting the Liberal vote, when what we were essentially doing was undermining his authority.

I was glad that Doris, who loathed politics more with each passing day, enjoyed herself at the event. She spent a pleasant hour or so talking to Mrs. Goldberg about their recipes for chicken soup. And though the evening was immensely enjoyable for me and proved that I could hold my own against Alex, it did have a bittersweet moment.

During the cocktail hour, I was outside one of the dining rooms having my picture taken with the candidates, when I noticed a sign announcing that the Brooklyn Hebrew Orphan Asylum was holding their annual fund-raising dinner next door. I hadn't thought about that place in years, and I walked in and spoke to the woman who appeared to be in charge of the event.

I said, "Everyone here was taken care of by the orphanage?"

Yes, she replied.

"Me too," I said, gazing at the crowd around us, sad and a little stunned that so many children back in the 1930s had grown up as I had, with the same lonely feeling in the pit of their stomachs. The trick is to keep your loneliness from turning into a progressive disease, to stop yourself from believing that it's your fault, that you deserve it. You wrestle with that challenge every day as a child and into adulthood. If you're lucky and marry someone as loving as Doris, you get to put it behind you.

I said, "Why don't you mail me a letter. I'll send you a contribution."

She promised to take care of it, and I was thinking that maybe I'd go back and look in on the place, but I never heard from the orphanage again.

Along with the New York State Liberal Party, out in Queens we endorsed Goldberg and his running mate, Basil Paterson, the first African-American to run for lieutenant governor in New York. I was proud of the Paterson nomination, the way I'd been proud in 1947 that it was my beloved Brooklyn Dodgers who first crossed baseball's color line with Jackie Robinson. We had a strong, vocal black contingent in the Queens County Liberal Party; in fact, it had been their outspoken disapproval of Modugno that convinced Greenspan it was time to call Alex.

Along with this contingent, my potheads and I had drummed up support for the Paterson nomination in the county and the press. Congressman Ben Rosenthal of Queens worked with us. In the early 1960s, Ben had given me my only paying job in politics, a forty-dollar-a-week stint as a fact-finder, which required me to attend local functions in his place, hear out his constituents, and then report my findings to Ben.

I can't say that I was of enormous help to Ben, but he was enormously helpful to my family, because with Jeffrey's skyrocketing medical costs, my ongoing financial woes, and working as a solo practitioner, I wouldn't have been able to purchase medical insurance at an affordable rate without that job.

Anyway, together Ben and I brought in a pair of well-known conservative congressmen, the Republican Seymour Halpern and the Democrat Joseph Addabbo, to stump for Basil Paterson, and pictures of them smiling and standing beside Paterson appeared in newspapers and on TV around New York.

However, while the Queens County Liberal Party was in accord with the statewide Liberal Party on the top of the ticket, we differed with them by voting to endorse Adam Walinsky for attorney general, who was more of a traditional liberal than Louis Lefkowitz, and Richard Ottinger for the Senate.

Personally, I was fond of Ottinger's opponent, the incumbent Charlie Goodell. He was a left-of-center Republican, as Lindsay had been before Alex talked him into switching to the Democrats. Also, like Lindsay, Goodell was handsome and charming.

Yet Goodell hadn't won his Senate seat in an election: Governor Rockefeller had appointed him to complete Senator Robert Kennedy's term following Bobby's assassination in June 1968. And the polling data on Goodell indicated that while he wouldn't beat his arch-conservative rival, James Buckley, he would sap substantial support from Ottinger, thereby handing the election to Buckley, an outcome my group was intent on avoiding.

In the waning days of the campaign, Senator Birch Bayh flew up from Washington to endorse Ottinger during a meeting at the Grand Hyatt. I spoke after Bayh, saying that "my change in support should not be construed as a repudiation of Senator Goodell, but rather must be construed as sanctioning the greatest good for the greatest number. I urge all other leaders of my party to determine their position on the basis of their personal convictions, which must lead to their backing [Ottinger], the only possible Liberal candidate in the race who can win the Senate seat. The Buckley threat must be stopped."

My speech was enthusiastically received, but I left the hotel feeling that Ottinger wasn't going to make it. Goodell had become quite popular with liberals for his outspoken criticism of the war, which had drawn fire from Vice President Spiro Agnew, the quickest shortcut to induction in the Liberal Hall of Fame.

For Ottinger to win, Alex needed to get involved, but he was sticking by Goodell because he was reluctant to cross the governor, who had pushed the Republicans hard for Goodell's nomination.

One of the fascinating, unwritten stories of this slice of New York politics is the collusion between Alex and Rockefeller. Both were so imperious by nature that they may have felt a spiritual kinship the less arrogant were unable to share. They were also pragmatists when it came to the nuts and bolts of politics, and I suspect they recognized that there was no use butting heads because their interests were widely divergent. Alex coveted the power that accrued to him in New York City by waving his magic patronage wand, while Rockefeller ran the state with one eye trained south on his life's ambition, the White House.

During the spring of 1970, the two men saw their dreams slipping from their grasp. Despite the surge in antiwar protests following the U.S. incursion into Laos and Cambodia and the tragedy at Kent State, Nixon was solidly ensconced in the Oval Office, sentencing Rockefeller to at least another term and a half in the Executive Mansion in Albany. The governor responded with a frenetic expansion of state government, establishing programs, appointing commissions. Unlike Rockefeller, Alex was unrestrained by law and legislators, so upon discovering that the fiefdom he had built over the last twenty-six years was under siege, he reacted in the predictable, yet grander, tradition of a tyrant: He threatened to conduct a purge.

First, he came after me. With my matter pending, he set his sights on the Manhattan Liberal leader, Edward Brook, whose crime had been to urge the Liberal Party State Committee to support Adam Walinsky's nomination for attorney general and to reject Alex's candidate, Louis Lefkowitz.

Brook lost his position to Ed Morrison, Mayor Lindsay's liaison between the City Council and the Board of Estimate who was frequently characterized in the press as the heir to Alex Rose. On the surface, it looked like nothing more than a county leader losing a race. However, as Brook and I ascertained after the election, Alex had let it be known that any municipal employee who didn't support Morrison would soon be collecting unemployment checks. Considering that 150 of New York's leading Liberals were either city or judicial employees who owed their jobs to Alex, his threat was effective.

Brook and I hammered Alex in the press, stating that he controlled the Liberal Party because the majority of county leaders held municipal jobs. We pointed out that fifteen of the eighteen newly elected Liberal county officers worked for either the city or the judiciary.

Alex told reporters: "There is no basis for such charges. No one in our party is denied the full Democratic right of his opinion. The charges were pure fabrication. No one cited any examples."

Of course, Brook and I didn't cite examples of the people coerced by Alex since they would have been fired.

The one man who might have talked sense to Alex was John Lindsay, if he had chosen to use his power. Upon taking office in 1965, Lindsay had said that people should be prohibited from holding political-party office while employed by the city. Now, though, seven months into his second term, the mayor had developed a highly evolved fantasy that had him one day sitting in the Oval Office. Accomplishing such a dream would require the muscle of bosses like Alex Rose, and Lindsay refused to comment on our charges.

No surprise there. The mayor owed his job to Alex as well.

In the middle of my fight to take my rightful place as the county chairman, I had to dive into a legal case because our son Jeffrey's bar mitzvah was coming up, and I was flat broke.

I never subscribed to the theory that a bar mitzvah had to include a fancy enough party so all of your relatives and friends would ooh and aah about it until your son got married, but Jeffrey was in a special situation. By his fourth birthday, Doris and I realized that our son was learning disabled and in all likelihood would require some type of managed care for his entire life.

According to Doris, who was and has remained very active in nonprofit agencies for the learning disabled, when Jeffrey was young the special ed classes offered in the New York City schools were perhaps the finest of their kind in the country, public or private. Today, all of that has changed, but back then Jeffrey was making noticeable headway in school.

He was also studying for his bar mitzvah with a tutor and by listening to tapes for hours on end. My son may well have put more energy into learning his Hebrew prayers than I did preparing for the bar exam.

Watching Jeffrey try to read and memorize the words was both thrilling and heartbreaking. I hurt for him seeing his struggle, and yet I was awestruck by the fierceness of his efforts, his ability to cope with the inevitable frustrations. More than anything, I wanted to make him a party to celebrate his accomplishment and to show him, in a way that he could readily comprehend, how proud Doris and I were of him, how glad we were that he was our son.

All I needed was the money.

One morning, a Dr. George Ginandes showed up at my office with a sad story to tell. Along with two other men, Dr. Ginandes had been involved in a limited partnership, and the general partner, David Shusett, proved to be an opportunist who had raked the three men over the coals, running a rather sophisticated Ponzi scheme on them. Dr. Ginandes asked me if I could recoup some of his and his other partners' losses.

I explained that as limited partners, per se, they didn't have the right to sue on behalf of the limited partnership unless they were granted that express right in the agreement. Since Dr. Ginandes and his partners didn't have that option, I suggested that we sue Shusett, Inc., the corporation owned by the general partner, David Shusett.

As it worked out, Shusett, Inc., was in the middle of its own legal squabble on the West Coast. Luckily for my clients, Shusett was suing a fellow with deep pockets, H. F. Ahmanson, one of the wealthiest men in California, whose company was the parent of Home Savings of America. The suit involved one of Ahmanson's pet undertakings, the construction of a magnificent high-rise at the corner of Fifth Street and Pershing Square in the commercial heart of downtown Los Angeles.

I sued Shusett, Inc., in civil court and won judgments against the company for three of its creditors. With these judgments in hand, I was then able to file an involuntary petition of bankruptcy against Shusett, Inc. Once I put the corporation into bankruptcy, I had myself designated as the attorney for the trustee, which gave me the right to pursue assets, and the asset I pursued was Shusett's potential judgment against H. F. Ahmanson. In effect, I won the right for my clients to step in and take Shusett, Inc.'s place in the company's suit against Ahmanson.

I can't recall the value of the building Ahmanson was putting up in L.A., but I do remember that the price tag seemed about the size of Israel's defense budget. I figured stopping work on the building would give me a terrific negotiating position against H. F. Ahmanson, since I assumed that he was hoping the building would stand as an eternal reminder to future citizens of Los Angeles that his magnificent presence had once graced the city.

Thus, I commenced an action against Ahmanson and at least one of his companies, the one that owned the building.

To sue Ahmanson in his home state, I needed an attorney who was a member of the California bar, and I contacted Frank Desser, my erstwhile mentor at Smith and Steibel, who had relocated to Los Angeles. At our old firm, Frank and I had been friendly with Sam Buzzell, the lawyer who wound up making a fortune in the music business. Sam had introduced Frank to his oldest daughter, and they fell in love, got married, and eventually moved to L.A.

After Frank and I talked over old times for a while, I quickly explained the case to him. Then I said: "I'm flying out to Los Angeles with the papers, but I need you to file the *Lis Pendens* against Ahmanson."

A *Lis Pendens*—Latin for "a pending lawsuit"—is a hell of a weapon. It means that pending the suit, nothing should be changed, and in this instance it would prevent the title to the building site from being legally vested in Ahmanson's company unless he disposed of the lawsuit.

I got to L.A. just in the nick of time for Frank to file the papers that day. Then I turned around and returned to New York. Within twenty-four hours, Ahmanson's attorney, Richard Coleman, called my office and asked me what sort of settlement I was looking for.

Why not, I thought, and replied, "A quarter of a million dollars." These were 1970-dollars, and if I got any amount near $250,000, I would be doing a bang-up job for my clients and me.

Ahmanson's lawyer said, "You're not kidding?"

I felt like telling him that I was too broke to kid around about money, but that wouldn't have been the smartest card to play. So I tried an unusual tactic for me and most lawyers: I said nothing.

To which he replied, "Your figure's way out of the ballpark.

"Then we'll litigate," I said.

I took out one of my much-abused credit cards and purchased an airline ticket for Los Angeles. Frank met my plane at LAX, and together we served the summonses and complaints.

Almost as soon I was back at my desk in New York City, I heard from Ahmanson's attorney.

"Why don't you come out here," he said. "We'd like to explore whether we can resolve this."

Off I went to California again, going straight from LAX to haggle with Richard Coleman. In less than an hour, I was holding a check for $150,000, and the building (which turned out to be gorgeous and is still standing today) was free to go up and immortalize Ahmanson.

I flew to New York. Jeffrey's bar mitzvah was five months away, and my financial status hadn't yet officially improved, but it was comforting having Ahmanson's check in my briefcase.

As the attorney for the bankruptcy trustee, it was my responsibility to advise the trustee how to distribute the money, so a couple of days later I made my first trip to the Bankruptcy Court of the Southern District of New York and appeared before Judge Roy Babitt.

My purpose was to prove that the $150,000 was reasonable, and I submitted the papers that would demonstrate the fairness of the settlement. I also had to submit an application to Judge Babbitt to receive payment for my services. Since I hadn't been in bankruptcy court before, I had no idea how to calculate my fee and simply wrote up everything I'd done in the case, my disbursements and my time, and multiplied my hours times my rate. I knew that lawyers usually didn't receive the entire amount they requested in such cases, but I thought my figure was fair, since it accurately reflected my investment of time and effort.

Judge Babitt read over my papers. Then he said: "Settlement approved. Please step up, counselor."

I approached the bench, and Judge Babitt said, "You're entitled to get paid here, Mr. Shaw."

"I know, your Honor." I replied.

"So?" Judge Babitt said. "How much will it be?"

I shrugged. I didn't want to seem like a pig, but I didn't want to cheat myself either.

"Your Honor," I said. "The truth is I have no experience with this type of procedure and don't know what I'm entitled to. I gave you an accounting of what I thought was fair. That's the best I can do."

He said, "You've got time invested, right?"

"The majority of it was traveling between here and California," I said. "I mainly negotiated over the phone."

The judge said, "Okay, Mr. Shaw. You think about it and come see me at two o'clock this afternoon and tell me what fee you'll accept."

After lunch, I returned to Judge Babitt's court and stood before him. He said, "You look like a nice guy, Mr. Shaw. How much?"

I said, "You're Honor, let me be frank. I'm really looking for the money to pay for a bar mitzvah."

"Ah, *mazel tov*," he said. "You've got a son."

"Yes," I said. "And I'm not seeking sympathy from the Court, but Jeffrey is a disabled child, and his having a reception to celebrate his bar mitzvah is special to us and to him."

The judge said, "Well, how much is the bar mitzvah?"

"I don't even know yet," I answered. "My wife and I didn't plan it because we didn't have the money."

"I'll tell you what, Mr. Shaw," said Judge Babitt. "Here's what you do. Go talk to your wife, find out the price of the bar mitzvah, and come back and we'll see what we can do about your fee."

It was a kindness from a judge that I had never seen before, nor since.

That evening, I walked in the door of our house, hugged Jeffrey and Lisa, and kissed Doris.

Having grown accustomed to my string of financial setbacks and my ongoing face-off with Alex, my ever-vigilant wife said something to the effect: "You look happy, Stan. What's wrong?"

"Jeffrey's going to have a bar mitzvah," I announced.

A smile lit up her face like sunrise. "Where?" she asked.

"Wherever you say," I replied.

"Terrace on the Park," she said.

My wife has good taste. The Terrace had great food, a lovely view of Flushing Meadows and the former site of the 1964 World's Fair.

"How many people?" I asked.

"A hundred and fifty," said Doris.

I did some fast figuring in my head. We had to hire a band and photographer; and then there were invitations, floral arrangements, the bar and bartenders, hors d'oeuvres, and dinner.

In the morning, Doris started planning Jeffrey's bar mitzvah, and I went to talk to Judge Babitt.

He said, "What's it going to be, Mr. Shaw?"

"About twenty thousand, your Honor. Without buying a new suit for me or a dress for my wife."

Judge Babitt said, "Then let's set your fee at twenty-two thousand. That ought to cover the whole *schmeer*."

Jeffrey had his bar mitzvah service on a Thursday morning in a private ceremony at the Garden Jewish Center and the reception a few days later. Like a lot of learning-disabled children, Jeffrey had a tendency to rise to the occasion. In Hebrew, he recited the small portion of the service that he had been practicing for close to a year. He performed beautifully, and his joy at doing so well was evident on his face.

Standing there, full of pride for my son, I thanked God that I'd been able to come up with the money to make a party that Jeffrey wouldn't forget.

I don't count myself as a formally religious man. As an adult, the synagogue was where I went on Rosh Hashana, Yom Kippur, or if somebody was born, got married, or died.

When I was a child bouncing between foster homes I did wonder about God, and why He, with all of his power and wisdom, didn't see to it that I, like my school friends, lived in a house with my parents and brothers.

After pondering long and hard, I concluded that my dilemma had a lot more to do with my mother and Louie than with the Almighty, and my theosophical inquiry fizzled out.

Nonetheless, standing in the Garden Jewish Center with my wife, son, and daughter on that Thursday morning, I had this wonderful, peaceful feeling that God had been watching over my family.

Later on, I would refer to it as an example of Divine Intervention, but naturally nobody knows such things for sure, and I feel faintly embarrassed suggesting that God, busy as He must be, would have either the chance or the impetus to meddle in my pedestrian worries.

However, I paid for Jeffrey's bar-mitzvah reception by handling my first bankruptcy case, and while of course I was unaware of it at the time, by doing so I not only provided my wife and children with the joy they deserved, but I also uncovered the focus of my life's work.

CHAPTER 11

THE ART OF THE IMPOSSIBLE

Morty Greenspan's complaint about my proxies in the county election was heard in Queens County Supreme Court by Justice Moses Weinstein, a former Democratic chairman of Queens County and a friend of mine.

Greenspan's attorney, Herb Rubin, argued that my election should be nullified on the basis of three issues: that I had used proxies to win the election; that there should have been another vote on an appeal to my ruling to allow the use of proxies; and that I refused to allow weighted voting, a mathematical formula in which the vote of each member of the county committee represents the number of votes that the Liberal candidate for governor had received in the committee person's election district.

Because of my mistakes, Rubin concluded, the court should order a new election.

My attorney, Bob Goldman, countered by asking the court how Greenspan could complain about proxies when he had tried to solicit them for himself, further evidence that proxies were utilized by the Liberal Party and had been since its inception.

Furthermore, my ruling on his appeal for another vote and my disallowing weighted voting wouldn't have changed the outcome of the election.

This sounds like legalistic nonsense because it is. But that didn't stop both sides from arguing it point by excruciating point for hours, while Justice Weinstein sat behind his polished mahogany bench listening respectfully, doing a fair impersonation of a man trying to be impartial.

The last week of August, Judge Weinstein issued an eight-page decision. I'm not the greatest lawyer in the world, but I can read a decision and there was more horseshit in those eight pages than I saw in a year at Roosevelt Raceway.

"There is a strongly-felt tradition today that the public interest can best be served by removing any cloud of doubt surrounding an election of public or party officials," Justice Weinstein ruled. "The process of selecting political leaders requires the highest possible standards. . . . In view of the indicated irregularities, [the election is at best in doubt]. Under the circumstances, the court directs that a new organizational meeting be held."

I wasn't shocked by the ruling. Sources had already indicated to me that the rumor from the start was that the judge wasn't going to write the decision and that it was being written for him by a political guru in Brooklyn, who happened to be a dear friend of Alex Rose. I never learned if the rumor was true.

Confident that Weinstein would be overturned, I immediately appealed, and within a month the Appellate Division, in a 5-0 decision, overturned Weinstein's ruling, opining that the use of proxies was proper and left "no doubt as to the officers chosen by the members of the County Committee. The results of the election are not impugned by any of the alleged irregularities."

Again backed by Alex and now represented by Herb Rubin's wife, Rose, Greenspan took his case to the Court of Appeals in Albany. I don't recall her arguments, but they didn't do Greenspan any good. The court unanimously affirmed the decision of the Appellate Division.

The story has a pair of footnotes, one amusing, one less so.

Several months later, I was at a formal dinner function, and I met Judge Scileppi, one of the seven judges who sat on the Court of Appeals and had heard my case. Since the court hadn't offered an opinion along with its affirmation, I asked Judge Scileppi his view of my legal arguments.

"Stanley," he answered. "You don't understand. You won, but don't you know why you won?"

"Why?" I asked.

Judge Scileppi said, "Who argued in the Appellate Division?"

"Herb Rubin."

"Correct," he said. "And who argued in the Court of Appeals?"

"His wife, Rose Rubin."

"Exactly," Judge Scileppi replied. "Stanley, do you think the Court of Appeals, in all of its majesty, would allow a wife to beat a husband so for the rest of his life he'd have to know that his wife was a better lawyer than he was."

Judge Scileppi was laughing now, and he patted my shoulder, wished me luck, and walked away.

Rose Rubin's name came up again a couple of years later, but it was not in the context of a joke.

After Governor Rockefeller introduced his harsh New York State Drug Law, the courts required more judges to hear the flood of cases created by the stricter standards. At Alex's behest, Rockefeller appointed Rose Rubin to the Court of Claims. It was a terrible appointment. Even the governor's own screening board didn't fully approve of her. That didn't bother Alex, nor did it bother the New York State Senate Judiciary Committee who held a hearing on her appointment on the twenty-fourth floor of the State Office Building at 270 Broadway.

I testified against her at the hearing, telling them that Rose Rubin was "unqualified to sit on a bench, presiding over trials in which people's lives may hang in the balance of judicial decision." I pointed out that she had already been rejected for lower court posts because she was found not qualified by the City Bar Association and her appointment to the Court of Claims was nothing more than a political payoff to Alex Rose. But Alex had friends everywhere from Manhattan to Albany, and he wanted Rose Rubin on the bench. She got the judgeship anyway.

Following my victory in the Court of Appeals, I received an interesting phone call from Judge Moe Weinstein. He wasn't calling to apologize for his decision, but rather to explore if I would be interested in joining him on the bench. He offered to broker a deal with Alex and John Lindsay that would make me a judge. I guess this was Alex's version of "If you can't beat him, join him."

I told Moe that I wasn't interested in a judgeship.

"You sure, Stanley?" he said. "I could try to do this for you."

"I'm sure, Moe," I replied, knowing full well that Moe couldn't do a damn thing without Alex's say-so.

Although I was now legally the chairman of the Queens County Committee, the New York State Liberal Party was only recognizing Morty Greenspan as the committee head, a turn of events that worked out nicely for my young supporters and me. Alex more or less left us alone to pursue our passions and dismissed us in the press as an island of raging nuttiness in the placid Liberal kingdom he had made.

In the election of 1970, my group went all out supporting Goldberg for governor, though it was quickly clear that he was a lost cause. Stumping across the state, he was the opposite of compelling, and Rockefeller was outspending him on radio, television, and print ads by a ratio of four-to-one. (According to Persico's biography, *The Imperial Rockefeller*, the governor spent $7.2 million on the campaign, "a new American record for any election except for the Presidency.") Rockefeller also didn't miss an opportunity to drive home the message that he was the governor and would continue as the governor for as long as he chose to favor New Yorkers with his presence.

Just prior to Election Day, I was asked to host a dinner in honor of Murray Bergtraum, a legendary New York City educator who was dying of cancer. (He was such a good fellow that they named a high school after Murray. You can see it when you drive over the Brooklyn Bridge.) The dinner was a politically ecumenical affair. I invited the Democratic, Republican, and Conservative leaders of Queens—Matthew Troy, Sydney Hein, and Serph Maltese—to join me as cohosts, and all of us agreed that no candidates should be permitted on the guest list.

Then one morning the governor's office called, informing me that Rockefeller would like to attend.

"I'm sorry," I said. "It's not a political dinner. I'm the designated host *and* the guy backing Justice Goldberg, and he's not going to be there either."

"The governor won't be a candidate at the dinner," I was told.

"What will he be?" I asked, not quite believing my ears.

"He'll be the governor," came the reply, and then the phone went dead.

Rockefeller showed up with a great deal of fanfare, and an aide bearing his personal bottle of sherry. The governor sat on the dais between Doris and me, and we chatted. The photographers tried to

168 : *I Rest My Case*

get our picture, but I turned my back to the cameras because I doubted that my mug plastered across the papers with Rockefeller would be the best advertisement for my candidate.

I was obliged to introduce the governor before he spoke, and standing on the podium, not wanting to use his name, I said to the three or four hundred guests, "I'd like to introduce you tonight to the highest elected official in the state of New York. I give you, the governor."

Rockefeller was laughing. What did he care? Given his separate peace with Alex, he owned the Liberal Party. Then he shook my hand, and with tongue in cheek, whispered, "You bastard, I'll get you yet."

During that political season I also managed to do some legal work and retire some of the crushing debt I had incurred during my adventures with Martin Schulman. The most profitable case I worked on actually came to me through a fellow I met in the Schulman days. His name was Bill Barrett, and he had helped Schulman secure construction loans. Bill phoned one afternoon to say that he knew of a land development company that was trying to put together a deal to build retirement homes in the Ozarks, right outside Branson, Missouri. The company was already selling the building lots and had collected $3 million in home contracts from the future retirees.

"Stan," Bill said. "Maybe you know a bank that could get them financing based on the signed contracts?"

I told Bill I'd see what I could do. The only banker I knew well enough to pitch on this kind of thing was David Berg, the man who brought me into the Liberal Party. David Berg was an incredibly successful real estate investor, as well as a majority stockholder and board member of the Royal National Bank. I always suspected that my networking in politics would help my career as a lawyer, and I sensed this might be my chance. I called David, and he told me to come right over. When I walked in, David greeted me decked out in one of his impeccably tailored suits. As I said earlier, David was a tough, shrewd, and aggressive investor, and nearly always willing to take a chance. He listened as I told him about the plans in the Ozarks.

When I finished, David thought about it for a moment, and then he said, "Stan, do you think these guys can afford to pay ten percent interest?"

"I believe they can," I said, and David sent me over to one of the major loan officers at the Royal National Bank.

I spoke to the loan officer, whose name was Sidney. Sid said the deal sounded pretty good, but he wanted to take a look at the property with me. By then, there were other investors, two oil men, Clyde Mumma and Tim Dunne, and another guy from Missouri, who turned out to be a real Shylock.

Sid and I flew to Springfield, Missouri. The land development company, in reality a group of five or six partners, sent a car that drove us from the airport to Branson. The development site included a thousand acres of virgin forest with a magnificent lake in the middle of it. The developers told us that they were ferrying potential buyers in by seaplane, which landed on the lake, and they were giving tours of this pristine wilderness that, according to them, enabled their company to sell building lots like hotcakes. The deal they were offering to buyers was 20 percent down and the rest over the course of their lifetimes. When the company had collected enough down payments and financing they planned to put in roads and water and sewers. It was dream deal, they said. A fortune waiting to happen.

Sid fell in love with the land, and Royal National approved an $800,000 loan for the land development company. This was especially good news for me because I received a substantial commission for brokering the arrangement. Right before the bank cut the check I again went to discuss the deal with David Berg.

"David," I said. "I don't know much about these guys and their land development company. So I want you to take out title insurance on their collateral."

"I hadn't thought about that," David said. "But just to be safe why don't you take care of it."

On behalf of David Berg I made another trip to Branson, this time taking Doris along. It was enjoyable watching this nice Jewish girl from Brooklyn mixing with the ladies of Branson, who put on a special breakfast in her honor.

However, my joy with the deal didn't last very long. It seemed that one of the developers had conned the other two by collecting money from potential home buyers and financing from investors and not putting a dime of it into the land. Furthermore, he didn't have all that many contracts on building lots. He'd had his sales-people submit phony contracts, and he even paid sales commission to his people to make it seem that the deal was legitimate and probably to keep the salespeople quiet. The whole shebang wound up in district court, where the judge did his best to straighten out the mess. Even though the deal fell apart, I felt that once again Divine Intervention had come to my rescue. Given the debt I was carrying, the commission I collected for putting the deal together was a financial lifesaver, and I was pleased that David Berg and Royal National Bank didn't get hurt. The title insurance paid off, thus preserving my credibility with Berg, and even the land development guy escaped from the scam without too many cuts and bruises.

It was also at about this time that I found myself involved in another deal that turned out to be far less profitable than the bustout in the Ozarks, but far more amusing. As luck would have it, I became the part owner of a dude ranch in the Catskills. It wasn't my idea of a solid investment, but a client of mine who had picked up the place in foreclosure owed me money for work I had done for him, and he couldn't pay me. In lieu of my fees I accepted some paper on the ranch. I doubted that I'd wind up with any cash in my pocket, and I didn't. But I did get a story out of it that I've been able to entertain my friends and colleagues with for years.

It was in the summer. I had to go to work in the city every day and couldn't look after the ranch during the week. So while I lived in Queens, Doris stayed up in the mountains full time with Jeffrey and Lisa and ran the place along with the owner's wife, seeing to the needs of the guests, making sure everything ran properly, and managing the help. Some married couples would come up to relax and swim in the Olympic-size pool and enjoy the cool summer air and take horseback riding lessons. Most of the clientele, however, were young, single Jewish women from New York City who had a hankering to meet cowboys, the wranglers we employed to look after the horses and give the lessons.

One afternoon I was at my office and phoned Doris to see how she was doing. I always knew she was quite handy at juggling responsibilities and managing details, but I was about to learn that Doris also had a unique and creative management style that would make our friends laugh for the next twenty-five years.

"How is it going?" I asked her.

"Well, we had a problem last night," she said.

"What kind of problem?"

Doris said, "The busboys and waiters are showing up late to work in the dining room because they're so tired."

"Why are they so tired?" I asked.

"Because we have a nymphomaniac here," Doris said. "It's one of the married ladies who's up here for the summer, and her husband is in the city during the week. The boys line up outside her room in the evening or wait their turn in the lobby. It goes on all night."

"Honey, you can't let that go on."

"I know, Stan," my wife said, perhaps a bit exasperated with my apparent lack of faith in her abilities.

"What did you do?" I asked.

Doris said, "I went over to one of the boys who was waiting his turn in the lobby. I said hello and sort of mentioned to him that I'd heard the generous lady upstairs had come down with gonorrhea."

I laughed. "Did he believe you?"

Doris said, "He must have, because he told all his friends, and the lady has run out of suitors and the dining room has a wide-awake staff."

Despite my wife's efforts, fiscal woes forced the dude ranch to close it doors after the summer season, but it was worth that little tale.

With gubernatorial candidate Arthur Goldberg trailing badly in the polls, I tried to come up with a strategy that would narrow the gap in Queens, which was how I wound up in court again, this time with Francis Smith.

Francis, whom everyone called Frank, and who was running for the New York State Senate from the Twelfth District of Queens, stopped by one day and asked if we would support his candidacy on the Queens County Liberal Party line. Frank was a moderately conservative Democrat, but he was also a very affable and popular guy, and I figured that if he were on the line it would be an excellent draw for the Goldberg-Paterson ticket. I told Frank that he would need to meet with my group, we'd take a vote, and maybe he'd get the line.

Frank presented his views, after which my group gave him their standard third degree. They saw that his candidacy would attract voters to the polls, and it would be a boost for Goldberg to be on the same line with him.

At these exploratory meetings, I usually asked potential candidates what they would do if they were faced with a close decision: Would they vote as their constituency wished or would they vote their conscience? The question is the political version of how-many-angels-can-dance-on-the-head-of-a-pin? While I leaned more toward voting your conscience, I wasn't completely inflexible about it, and I was truly more interested in the candidate's answer as a method for gauging if he had the ability to articulate a position on his feet.

But I already knew Frank Smith was a good talker, and I recall at this meeting that I dispensed with philosophy and asked him a single question: If you are offered a judgeship after the judicial nominating convention, will you quit the race for the senate? I explained that we couldn't afford to get stuck without a candidate on the line. Frank replied that he was after a senate seat, not the bench. We voted, and Frank got the line.

Then a funny thing happened. Frank was offered a judgeship, and he took it.

Normally, this petty variety of double-dealing would have rolled off me. During my fight with Alex Rose and Morty Greenspan I had maintained a semblance of composure. Yet reflecting on it, I have to admit that the nastiness and duplicity and crude displays of power, all of them briefly legitimized by Judge Weinstein's faulty decision, had been eating away at me.

I seethed at Frank Smith's betrayal and sued him for fraud, claiming that he had to stay on the Liberal line for state senator. After I lost in Queens County Supreme Court and the Appellate Division, I flew up to Albany to present my case to the Court of Appeals. The judges will grant you an informal audience in the morning to determine whether they will hear your argument on its merits in the afternoon. When I arrived a secretary ushered me into a beautifully appointed tea room with leather couches and chairs and lazy spring sunlight pouring through the high windows. The seven judges were seated around a polished oak table that seemed as long and wide as an ocean.

After I outlined my case for them, the chief judge, Stanley Fuld, said, "Mr. Shaw, what is your real complaint?"

I replied, "Frank Smith lied to me and the Queens County Liberal Party."

Judge Fuld said, "What would you rather be, Mr. Shaw? A senator or a judge?"

"That's not the issue. The issue is fraud. We relied on Frank Smith's promise to run."

The chief judge sighed. "Does Frank Smith want to be a judge or a senator?"

"Obviously a judge."

"Then I suggest you go home, Mr. Shaw," Fuld said. "And leave Mr. Smith alone to become a judge."

Indeed, Frank Smith became a judge, but this little tale has an ending worthy of Aesop.

Three years later, while Frank Smith was sitting on the bench, he was indicted and then sentenced to jail for criminal conduct.

Arthur Goldberg lost in 1970, and as I feared, Senate hopeful Richard Ottinger lost to the conservative James Buckley by approximately 125,000 votes. A quarter of a million voters cast their ballots for incumbent Senator Charles Goodell, and to this day I believe if Alex had backed off his support for Goodell, Ottinger would have gone to the Senate.

Over the next two and half years, until the mayoral primary of 1973, my war with Alex Rose degenerated into a smattering of predictable skirmishes with a full-blown battle here and there to remind us that one day, in the not too distant future, we would have our final showdown.

One of our biggest confrontations during this period was in 1971. New Yorkers were being asked to approve a $3.5 billion transportation bond issue in November. With his uncontrollable urge to build anything he could fund with public money, Rockefeller desperately wanted the bond issue, and not surprisingly, Alex was in favor of it, too. Besides pleasing the governor, my guess is that Alex ordered the state Liberal Party to support the measure because he never saw a piece of pork he didn't like.

The bond issue had been slapped together after the Transit Authority claimed that an infusion of $150 million was needed to maintain the subway fare. How that translated into $3.5 billion in bonds was a mystery to me, but Rockefeller threatened to raise subway fares if the issue didn't pass.

As I told the press, the whole deal was "a case of smog." Rockefeller really wanted the money for highway construction, which explained why the bond issue lacked a detailed mass transportation proposal.

From my perspective, the young people moving into Queens and buying houses and starting families were being asked to mortgage their future without a promise that they would have anything to show for it other than the knowledge that they had jumpstarted the bond market and a bunch of politically connected companies had made a killing on sweetheart deals.

"That seems to me," I told Frank Ross of the *Daily News*, "to be a very expensive way for the people to keep friends in the banks."

My wing of the Queens County Liberal Party formed a committee to combat the issue's passage, focusing our efforts on dissecting the plan in the media. Bond issues are full of hidden costs. The reason the issues are frequently approved by voters is that the arguments made in favor of the issues are generally emotional, and this obscures economic reality. Then, too, it requires a fair amount of financial sophistication to calculate the true cost of a bond issue, and the majority of voters don't have degrees in high finance. In my opinion that was why Rockefeller threatened to hike subway fares; it's easier to comprehend a daily fifty-cent increase in your ride to work than it is to ferret out the thousands of dollars you will pay over decades in increased taxes.

Fortunately for the future fiscal health of the state, my feelings panned out to be in synch with a substantial majority of New York voters, who soundly defeated the bond issue at the polls.

It was with Alex in mind that I told reporters, "The people of this city and state will not be hoodwinked by autocratic politicians concerned with special interests rather than the welfare of the majority."

For the most part, though, the political memories I have of the years up until the spring of 1973 are steeped in nostalgia, a series of anecdotes that blend together in a mix of humor and sadness. I recall the odd moments of politics, the mistakes, the silliness, the blatant vanities.

For instance, not long before the primary season of 1972 I received a call from Senator Henry Jackson, a Democrat from Washington State. Scoop, as he was known, was considering a run for the presidency. He told me that he was unsure how he would do in New York, especially with black voters, a must-have bloc for any Democrat to win the White House. He asked if it would be possible for me to get him a speaking engagement in front of a good-sized black audience?

I said that I'd do my best, and I contacted a number of black leaders, including, I believe, New York Congresswoman Shirley Chisholm, the first black woman to serve in the U.S. House of Representatives.

I recapped Jackson's request to the leaders and asked them if they could give me a hand, which they generously agreed to do. A chamber of commerce dinner was coming up, and I prevailed upon the members to invite Jackson as the featured speaker.

The black leaders delivered. Half the seats were filled with black men and women. I was sitting on the dais, and as the senator approached the rostrum, he paused to shake my hand and thank me for my assistance.

The audience gave him a polite round of applause. He graciously thanked us for inviting him. Then he adjusted the microphone, leaned forward, and said, "My name is Scoop Jackson, ladies and gentlemen, and the main reason for my being here tonight is to call a spade a spade."

The rest of his speech is a blank to me now, but I do recall glancing over at Shirley Chisholm and that, like me, she seemed to be experiencing an overwhelming desire to crawl under her chair.

I'm told that Scoop was a decent man, but in view of his attack of foot-in-mouth disease, he may well have saved himself and America an indignity or two by choosing not to run.

The other faux pas I won't forget illuminated the phonier side of politics.

Donald Manes was the Queens Borough President who tragically took his own life when he got caught up in a scandal. Donny and I were relatively friendly, and as the leader of the Democratic Party in Queens he would invite me to his political dinners. Now, one year, Senator Ted Kennedy was scheduled to speak. The dinner was at Antun's, a terrific restaurant in Queens. Donny called me and bragged a little about how tight he was with Kennedy, how they'd been friendly going back fifteen years. He said I could come early and get into the VIP room and meet Ted.

So I went and shook hands with Kennedy and got a kick out of seeing Donny standing right by his side, both of them acting as chummy as old roommates at a college reunion.

Now, while Donny spelled his last name M-a-n-e-s, it was pronounced *Man-iss*, a fact that Ted Kennedy proved to be unaware of after dessert when he stood before the crowd and announced, "Ladies and Gentlemen, I'm here to congratulate my dear friend, Donald M-a-i-n-s."

You know the cliché about a room being quiet enough to hear a pin drop? I never believed it until I attended Donny's dinner. Yet it would be one of those painful moments you would laugh about with the passing of time, if only Donny's life hadn't ended so sadly.

Donny had that illness endemic to lifers in the political racket, a near obsession with people's opinion of him, and the humiliation of the scandal must have been too heavy a burden for poor Donny to bear. I prefer to remember him in the VIP room, shaking everyone's hand and glad that he could call Ted Kennedy his friend.

Let me end these fast recollections on a happier note.

In 1972, Senator George McGovern was running for president, and the statewide Liberal Party invited him to be the guest of honor at their annual dinner, a huge, ritzy affair at a big hotel in Manhattan. It goes without saying that my gang of young activists and I weren't exactly welcome at Alex's shindig. So we held our own, the Undinner Dinner, at Pete's Tavern, a historic bar and grill in Gramercy Park, where the writer O. Henry used to hang out— before or after he went to prison, I'm not sure.

We invited McGovern to our less-than-formal gala, though we doubted that he'd come. After all, there was nothing in it for him as a presidential candidate. We were a small splinter group, not an apparent force in the outcome of a national race. Then, too, we didn't do any advance work with McGovern's aides, and with the assassination of Bobby Kennedy in 1968, and the attempted assassination of George Wallace in 1972, the Secret Service was a bit touchy about presidential candidates making unplanned whistle-stops.

We ate and drank and made merry, and most of our attendees had hoisted three sheets to the wind when George McGovern ambled into the bar. At first, I couldn't believe my eyes, but I walked over to him and introduced myself and ordered him a drink. McGovern talked to us for a while and then he apologized for not being able to stay, saying he had another dinner uptown.

I didn't always agree with George McGovern, but I always thought he was a hell of a guy, and a framed picture of us sitting side by side and drinking at Pete's Tavern still hangs on my office wall.

CHAPTER 12

THE STRANGE CASE OF JUDGE LOUIS WALLACH

One of the reasons I entered politics was to help build my law practice, but I soon discovered that I had a passion for the political action and a deep distaste for the kingly machinations of bosses and what I considered their lack of pragmatic idealism.

While I didn't immediately sign up the well-heeled clients I had originally been seeking, my increased visibility as chairman did attract plenty of cases. However, my war with Alex had evolved into a career unto itself, leaving me no time to handle the additional load, and I took on Jesse Levine as my law partner. Jesse was active in the Queens County Liberal Party. He had a fine mind and "golden hands," meaning his legal briefs were immaculately researched and written.

I kept Jesse busy enough for two lawyers, and yet I couldn't climb out of my financial hole. Still, the cases poured in. In New York City, there is a continual convergence of politics and the practice of law. Before joining the Liberal Party, I'd thought that this connection would prove profitable, but by the early 1970s it hadn't paid off for me. Often, when these two segments of my life touched, it was terribly disappointing, and in no case was this more true than when I bumped into Judge Louis Wallach, a year after he ascended to the Queens County Supreme Court, thanks in no small part to my efforts.

The story begins when my friend Jerry Edelstein introduced me to an elderly married couple who were members of the Queens County Liberal Party Committee. The husband and wife, both in their eighties, were in frail health and mired in a lawsuit that had drained them physically and financially. They owned a cracker-box house in Queens and were squeaking by on their meager savings and small Social Security checks. They had retained a lawyer, but as their legal troubles dragged on, they had run out of money to pay him, and Jerry asked me if I would take their case pro bono.

I agreed. It was a sad situation, and the legal aspect of it seemed like a simple matter. The elderly couple had been entangled in a feud with one of their neighbors. Ordinarily, the old man and his neighbor, a much younger fellow, yelled mild obscenities at each other from the safety of their respective yards. Then, one afternoon, their shouting match escalated until they charged across their demilitarized zone, and the old man hit his young neighbor across the back with a piece of metal pipe. The neighbor filed criminal charges, which were dismissed, but the elderly couples' lawyer was either incompetent, moronic, or an ill-starred combination of the two, because he didn't secure a signed release from the neighbor, who then turned around and sued the elderly couple for monetary damages.

I received the case file in September, the first day of the new trial term, and I walked into court with the elderly couple in tow to ask for time to study the file. I went before the assigning judge, who basically serves as a traffic cop, directing cases to the other judges for disposition.

I figured I'd have no trouble getting an adjournment since the assigning judge happened to be James Crisona. I'd known Jimmy for a while and considered him a friend, and when a judge respects your work, he will generally give you the benefit of the doubt. Jimmy was the former borough president of Queens County, and my faction of the Queens Liberal Party had vigorously supported his election to that post.

I approached the bench and said, "Your Honor, please, the file only showed up on my desk this morning. I'm representing two elderly people, and I'll require a week's adjournment to read the file and explore the possibility of a settlement." The fact is with such sympathetic clients I would have preferred a jury trail, but the couple's prior attorney had convinced them to waive that right.

Jimmy surprised me. "Nobody gets any adjournments here!" he barked, like you would've thought I'd asked him if I could take his wife to Vegas for the weekend. "You're going to try the case today."

I couldn't believe this arrogant nonsense from my pal Jimmy Crisona. Before I could say another word, Jimmy banged down his gavel, announced a fifteen-minute recess, and disappeared into his chambers. His clerk was in the court, and we knew each other quite well. I caught his eye, and he came over to me.

"What's wrong with Jimmy?" I asked.

He said, "Stanley, I've got to apologize to you. Jimmy didn't have his glasses on. He's half-blind without them, and he didn't know it was you."

"I haven't even had a chance to read the goddamn file," I said. "Can't you cut me a break here?"

The clerk said there was nothing he could do, and I was really pissed off until I discovered that Judge Louis Wallach had been assigned to hear the case. Now I'm thinking, hey, maybe the gods are watching. I'll go to Louie, tell him my story and get my adjournment, no sweat.

It was about 11:30 A.M. when we made it to Wallach's courtroom, and the elderly couple were fading fast. They were walking even slower, if that was possible, and their eyes were glazed and sleepy as they sat waiting around for their case to be called.

Louis Wallach had the stern craggy face and sonorous voice of a judge straight out of central casting, and right off the bat he said that the case should be settled. So bip-bop-bip I read the file and then Wallach had me and the plaintiff's lawyer brought to his chambers.

I said, "Judge, these people have no money. The only asset they have is a small equity in their house. They're sick and elderly, and they shouldn't be examined or cross-examined on the stand. Furthermore, there was a screw up: They should have gotten their release after the criminal matter was disposed of, but their lawyer didn't take care of it. Here's what I propose. I will personally arrange a two-thousand dollar loan for them, they'll give it to the plaintiff, and we can get rid of this thing, because I'm afraid taking the stand will cause irreversible harm to their health. These are eighty-five-year-old people, your Honor."

Glaring at me, Judge Wallach said, "I am not accepting your two thousand dollars. Where do you get off making such a chintzy offer? You've got a lot of nerve. I don't give a damn who you think you are. This case is easily worth fifteen thousand if it's worth a dime."

Wallach was literally screaming, excoriating me and my offer. I stood there wondering if this could be a charade for the benefit of the plaintiff's lawyer, to show him that I wouldn't be granted any favors due to my past relationship with the judge.

I mean nearly everybody in the Queens County legal community was aware of my role in getting Judge Wallach his spot on the supreme court, but in my humble opinion he was laying it on a bit thick in the interest of displaying impartiality.

The fact is I helped numerous judges get on the ballot and win elections, and I didn't expect any favors from them other than to be treated at least as politely as I treated the waitresses at the Seville Diner. Evidently, I was expecting too much from Judge Wallach.

I left his chambers convinced that there were worse options than having a conservative like Joe Modugno sitting on the supreme court in Queens.

Now, it was almost noon, and there was nobody in the courtroom except the elderly couple, the plaintiff, and the plaintiff's attorney. I told my clients that we would have to go to trial and they would have to take the stand and testify. They looked frightened, but I assured them that I'd get them through it okay.

I just wished that I felt as confident as I'd tried to appear to them. Ambling over toward the counsel table, I asked the plaintiff's attorney if could speak with him in private.

He got up and came over, and I said, "Listen, you don't know me, and I don't know you, but do me a favor. You've got to have a little *rachmanes* with these people. You know what *rachmanes* is?"

The guy either didn't understand Yiddish or was running a serious empathy deficit, because he said, "What do you mean, '*rachmanes*'?"

I said, "You're going to cross-examine these people, so do it easy. Don't go through the lawyerly histrionics. They're old, and I'm fearful for their health."

He said, "I can't promise you that. I represent a client, and I'll be as tough as I have to be to win this for him."

At that moment it was entirely fitting for me to recall Shakespeare's suggestion that the first thing we ought to do is kill all the lawyers.

Judge Wallach had returned to the bench by then. Peering down at me, he said, "You will be back here in one hour, and we will begin the trial right after lunch, and there will be no more nonsense from Mr. Shaw."

What a jerk, I thought, and then I approached the bench and said, "Your Honor, please. I would like to now move that you recuse yourself because you have prejudged this case."

For the record, I recapped the entire conversation that had occurred in chambers, adding, "I think your behavior lacks the fair-mindedness required of a judge in any case, but particularly with respect to the tenuous medical condition of these elderly people sitting here. I made an offer in good faith, and while it may not have been sufficient in your mind, excoriating me in front of the other side was not a fitting response and falls far short of what every lawyer expects from the judiciary."

I went on in this vein for ten minutes, with Wallach gazing off as though he were out on a fairway trying to decide which iron to use for his approach shot to the green.

When I ran out of steam, Wallach said, "Your motion is denied, Mr. Shaw. You'll be ready here in one hour."

Over lunch, I briefed the elderly couple, taking them through some of the broader twists and turns of trial procedure. Then we went back to court. The plaintiff's lawyer put the elderly gentleman on the stand for two full hours. His strategy was to wear the old man out with the rat-a-tat rhythm of his questions. I did the best I could to protect my client, objecting at regular intervals to give him a chance to catch his breath and organize his thoughts between answers.

Meantime, Wallach was making a big show of it, sustaining my objections with a real flourish, as if he was auditioning for the producers of *Perry Mason*.

The old fellow didn't hobble off the witness stand until after three o'clock. His wife was called and sworn, and the plaintiff's lawyer beat up on her for an hour. Again, I objected as much as possible to protect her, but like her husband before her, she was clearly out of gas.

The plaintiff was called, and his lawyer questioned him with that smugness you notice in second-raters who are certain they've proved their case even before the other side has mounted its defense.

At four-thirty, I cross-examined the plaintiff. Out of frustration and rage that the matter had gone this far, I teed off on the young man. Having not thoroughly read the case file, I had to fire from the hip, but I threw everything I could think of at the plaintiff, making sure to be as venomous as I could, using every grand and puny courtroom trick I'd picked up in my two decades of practicing law.

It was close to six o'clock when I got done with my act, and the other lawyer said to Judge Wallach, "Plaintiff rests."

I responded, "Your Honor, I move to dismiss on the grounds that plaintiff hasn't proved a prima facie case."

Judge Wallach did his King-Solomon-the-Wise schtick, glancing heavenward with a contemplative frown, like he was receiving instructions from God on solving the conundrums of dispensing justice. Then Wallach said, "Decision reserved," which meant that he was going to have to hear my case before determining whether to dismiss.

I had no choice but to put on my case tomorrow, and the elderly couple would have to go through the same crap all over again. That night, I prepped them, and then went home and boned up on the file.

In the morning, I put the couple on the stand. They were exhausted. I frequently had to restate my questions for them, and their answers were halting and occasionally missing crucial details, but overall they performed valiantly. Then I called one of their neighbors to testify on their behalf. He said that the young man had repeatedly threatened the couple with physical harm and that the elderly gentleman had possessed good reason to fear for his safety when his next-door neighbor came charging at him. Thus, the use of the pipe to protect himself was justified.

The plaintiff's lawyer cross-examined my three witnesses until lunchtime. After the break, I renewed my motion for Judge Wallach to dismiss the complaint on the grounds that the plaintiff hadn't proved his case by a preponderance of evidence.

Wallach looked at me and said, "Granted."

The sanctimonious blowhard had known all along that I'd been right as a matter of law, and had push come to shove and I'd lost, he knew on appeal I'd get him recused for his semipsychotic pretrial tantrum in chambers. I remember standing there, staring up at Wallach and saying to myself, You son-of-a-bitch. You dismiss the complaint now like you're some big deal, and meanwhile you allowed these old people to go through what was probably one of the most traumatic experiences of their lives.

I would like to report that the story ends here, with a lawyer ticked off at an insensitive judge. That would be a fairy-tale ending compared to what happened.

Two weeks after the trial, the old man died of a heart attack. A week after he died, his wife passed away in her sleep. My worst fears had been realized, and I blamed Louis Wallach.

Several months later, Judge Wallach sent me a reference, appointing me as a referee in a foreclosure case. It was supposed to be a plum for a lawyer; you earned about three hundred bucks. He attached a note to the reference which gave the impression that he felt by sending me this prize he was doing me the biggest favor in the world.

I wish I had the letter that I wrote him in reply. I could reread it whenever I doubted my aptitude for translating my outrage into the written word. I recall firing off five pages of pure invective, which, in sum and substance, suggested that Wallach take his reference, roll up the document into a pointy cone, and forthwith shove it northward into any orifice of his choosing until his eyes popped out of his head. Then I told him what I thought of him, how the trial had been responsible for the death of the elderly couple—a trial, I stated, that would not have been necessary if his Honor hadn't been such an ignorant, pompous, self-righteous, and inexorable piece of human garbage.

A month or two passed, and I had to attend a political function in my capacity as chairman of the county Liberal Party. I was lining up with some other people to walk onto the dais when who did I find myself standing behind? None other than Judge Louis Wallach.

Pivoting toward me and putting his hand on my shoulder, he said, "Stanley, how have you been, dear friend?"

Either the guy didn't read his mail or he was brain dead. Loud enough for everyone around us to hear, I said to him, "Take your dirty hands off me. I want no part of you. I will not sit next to you. You're a disgrace as far as I'm concerned. You caused the death of two old people."

With an expression of horror on his haughty face, Judge Wallach made himself scarce, and after that evening I never saw him again.

He died within the year. I recount this story because the presumption among the majority of citizens is that all politicians are prostitutes. Although that is a presumption that is rebuttable with many stellar exceptions—notably the ones I've mentioned in this book— the truth is that generally to win a judgeship you have to be as political as any elected official, and I wouldn't choose to face a jury using the late Judge Louis Wallach as my sole evidence to rebut the popular and unflattering view of those who lead and judge us.

CHAPTER 13

THE PRIMARY

T he beginning of my end as a front-line player in politics came
in 1973, when Governor Nelson Rockefeller, for reasons
known solely to himself and his Heavenly Father, decided
that after John Lindsay left office Robert Wagner should once again
be Mayor of New York. Wagner had served as mayor from 1954 to
1965, so he was unquestionably familiar with the job, and he told
Rockefeller that he would be happy to leave his law practice for
Gracie Mansion.

The governor's dilemma was that he was a Republican and
Wagner was a Democrat. Nevertheless, as Joseph Persico wrote of
his erstwhile boss, for Rockefeller "party loyalty was a sometime
thing. . . . If he liked the Democratic better than the Republican
candidate, he expected his party to go along with him."

Rockefeller met with Republican chieftains and cheerfully
shoved Wagner down their throats. One detail the governor didn't
have to worry about was Wagner securing the Liberal Party endorsement. Alex Rose would do his bidding, and on this occasion,
do it gladly. Alex relished the idea of having Wagner in charge of
the city again, a mayor accustomed to the realities of bossism, who
had made his peace with the bent rules of the game.

Liberal leaders rubber-stamped Alex's selection of Wagner, but
then they crashed into a roadblock. They couldn't get the required
number of signatures (something like four thousand and change)
on the nominating petitions. The Liberal rank and file were no
keener to see Wagner on the ballot than their Republican counter-
parts, both preferring a candidate of their own ilk.

The situation was shaping up into an immense embarrassment
for Alex and Wagner, so they went to Plan B. Wagner declined the
GOP nomination and publically attacked "peanut [Republican] politicians who don't know anything about good government." As Tim
Wicker observed in the *New York Times*, this tack gave Wagner an

"inside lane to campaign as an independent liberal." It also loosened up Liberals, who gradually and somewhat reluctantly began signing Wagner petitions and prevented Alex from looking like a feckless sellout.

Out in Queens, my potheads were—to borrow one of their stock phrases—freaking out. The idea of Robert Wagner back in city hall was anathema to them. The young people who joined me in the Liberal Party were issue oriented—against the war in Vietnam, pro-choice on abortion, in favor of treating drug addicts in lieu of incarcerating them. Nonetheless, the energizing factor for these men and women wasn't a specific issue. It was their desire to alter the system itself, to bring an openness and honesty to governance that would have doomed Alex and his kind to the boneyard of history. Watergate was in the air then, trials were starting, the word impeachment was being bandied about, and Americans in general, and young people in particular, had seen enough corruption to last them a lifetime. To be sure, my potheads suffered from periodic bouts of naiveté, but they weren't cynical, which was why I loved them. To them, and to me as well, Wagner was a throwback, a business-as-usual candidate, and he would have offset any gains we had made against Alex.

We realized that it was imperative to stop him. The question everyone was asking was how we could do it. The newspapers were reporting that allegedly Wagner's deal with Rockefeller and Alex didn't include suffering through the indignities of a primary.

That was the answer, of course, to stopping him, but I was hesitant to suggest it because I recognized that it would herald my showdown with Alex and present the possibility of sinking me into politics more deeply than I'd planned.

Maybe it was ego that made me take the step, or my anger at Alex, my ambition to beat him. Whatever it was, by then I didn't care what it would cost me.

Finally, I told my group: "You get me the signatures on the petitions, I'll run myself and challenge Wagner in the Liberal Party primary in June. You watch: He won't risk the humiliation of losing. He'll try to drop off the ballot and we'll do what we can to keep him there. If I beat him in the primary, Alex will have to find himself another party to be the boss of."

God bless my potheads. They went at it hammer and tongs, canvassing neighborhoods, working the phones, collecting signatures. Added to the reality that your average member of the Liberal Party rejected Wagner, signed petitions were soon piling up at our headquarters.

When it became obvious to Alex that I was going to qualify for the primary, he came after me with a vindictiveness that was breathtaking.

He told the *New York Times* I was a "liar," a "manipulator," and a man with "a shady record." Then he circulated a two-page letter around political circles in New York. It was signed by State Chairman Donald Harrington and Morton Greenspan, who was now billing himself as Queens chairman of the Committee to Preserve the Liberal Party. The letter rehashed some of Martin Schulman's false charges against me and concluded with the observation that "the character of Mr. Shaw is best shown by his defaming the Liberal Party and its leaders by charging them with helping Nixon, Rockefeller and Buckley."

The letter was infuriating, but worse yet from my perspective was that Alex blatantly lied to the press. As Michael Kramer wrote in *New York* magazine, "Rose now denies prior knowledge of Shaw's business difficulties. In his typically disarming, self-deprecatory way, Rose told [me], 'I'd have been crazy to have supported Shaw if I knew about his problems in [1968].' "

That was nonsense. I had thoroughly explained to Alex about Schulman's charges when he recruited me for the Queens County chairmanship. And I am eternally grateful to Michael Kramer for not taking Alex's word on it, for digging until he found the truth.

Kramer wrote: "State Liberal Party assistant secretary Josephine Gambino, a Rose ally, and Rose Rubin, the attorney representing the regular Liberal faction in its legal attempts to purge Shaw, both confirm the existence of 1968 correspondence relating to the matter and the fact that Liberal higher-ups, including Rose, were apprised of Shaw's activities at the time. Rose's present outrage at Shaw's 'less than exemplary character' would, of course, appear ridiculous if he admitted prior knowledge. Apparently, however, Rose knew all about Stanley Shaw five years ago and is only now making waves because it happens to suit his 1973 politics."

If I was going to enter the primary, I needed a war chest. Senator Sy Thaler had recommended that I use his public-relations man, Al Lawrence, as a campaign manager, and Al would cost me five thousand dollars. I figured another twenty thousand for advertising, since that was all the debt I could afford to pay back.

I called my friend Carmine Messano at Franklin National Bank. "Guess what, Carmine?" I said. "I'm running for mayor."

"That's what I hear," he replied.

"Carmine, I need a loan. Could the bank lend me twenty-five grand?"

He laughed. "Stanley, have you paid off your old debt yet?"

"I'm working on it," I said.

"The bank won't lend you a dime more, Stanley. But I know you're good for the twenty-five, and I got a guy for you to meet."

The guy was Joseph Ferrara, a general contractor who, over the next decade, would become the largest supplier of concrete in New York City. I had a cup of coffee with Joe and arranged the loan. I was grateful for the money. I was also grateful because next to Doris and Frank Knobel, Joe Ferrara would one day be among my closest friends.

By the spring of 1973, the scuttlebutt was that Robert Wagner couldn't garner enough signatures to get on the ballot in the Liberal Party primary, and he was going to reject the nomination. He hadn't won the nomination, just Alex's blessing, which in the past had been one and the same. Since my potheads had gotten me the requisite signatures to qualify for the June race, Alex and Wagner sensed that whether they got the petitions or not, Wagner would lose to me in the primary.

The state Liberal Party had a Committee on Vacancies, which provided a route for a candidate in Wagner's situation to withdraw with his dignity. Alex had previously used this process to hedge his bets until determining which direction the wind was blowing. To dethrone Alex, we had to have Wagner on the ballot. So we took him to court to keep him as a candidate for mayor, arguing that he couldn't turn down a nomination he hadn't received.

Had we won our case Alex Rose's days as a boss were over (and mine might have been beginning). After all, if you can't deliver your own party, then what good are you? However, the court held that the law can't compel a man to run in a primary. The best we did was to embarrass Alex and Wagner, insinuating that the former mayor couldn't dig up four-thousand-plus registered Liberals to support him, and by extension, Alex.

Even today, I have no idea if Robert Wagner had, or could have had, the petitions he needed. I do remember thinking back then that Alex was too clever to let this happen to his mayoral choice again. He recognized that for his career as a boss to continue, his man had to prevail in the primary even if he had no shot at winning the general election. Alex would have to come up with a candidate that Liberals, and the liberal press, loved.

Give Alex Rose his due. There were kinder leaders than Alex in politics, but you would be hard pressed to find one who was smarter.

His next candidate was Assemblyman Al Blumenthal of Manhattan, a reform Democrat with excellent name recognition who had been the principal and most effective spokesman for New York City's interests in the state legislature.

In May, what the newspapers referred to as a "a dissident faction of the Liberal Party" held a convention in Manhattan and approved a slate of candidates for the primary. I was officially put up for mayor; Mel Feit, my friend and accountant, who had authored some innovative articles on taxation, was nominated for comptroller; and Joan Slous, a student at Brooklyn Law School, got the nod for City Council president.

Although my name had been mentioned with increasing frequency in the press due to my differences with Alex and the state Liberal Party, I was a relative unknown to the general public and a newcomer to big-time, New York City electoral politics. So at first, my campaign manager, Al Lawrence, had trouble booking me into venues to speak.

Al called around, cajoling, wheedling, and finally got me and my campaign off to a less than auspicious start when he scheduled me for a speech at a Jewish nursing home in the Bronx. I arrived and found one elderly woman wandering around a hallway.

"What're you doing here?" she asked.

"My name is J. Stanley Shaw and I'm running for mayor. I'm here to talk."

"Sonny," she said, "you wanna talk? So talk."

Before I could give her my pitch, she said I looked like a nice young man and walked away.

Al Lawrence had mixed up the dates. It was the wrong evening, and I drove home to Flushing hoping that the trip had been worth at least one vote.

I fared better as June approached. At the Civic Affairs Forum Plan Association, I held my own in a debate with Blumenthal and the three other Democratic candidates, Representative Herman Badillo, City Comptroller Abe Beame, and Representative Mario Biaggi.

I spoke in the Turtle Bay section of Manhattan with Congressman Ed Koch and other politicians, and stirred up the audience enough for Koch to trip me, inadvertently or otherwise, as I walked back to my seat. I knew Ed from some real estate closings we'd been involved in as lawyers, and as I recovered my balance he laughed and said, "You upstaged me. Don't do it again."

During a debate at Queensborough Community College sponsored by the Queens League of Women Voters, my exchange with Blumenthal was moderately interesting and exceedingly nasty. He said that until the election I'd been "a great guy," but I had suddenly developed "hoof-and-mouth disease."

I replied that my verbal affliction, while apparently strange to professional politicos like Mr. Blumenthal, was nothing more than my obsessive tendency to tell the truth: Indeed, Alex Rose had been "the tyrannical leader" of the Liberal Party since the 1940s, and Alex, along with Governor Rockefeller, was backing Blumenthal to perpetuate this tyranny.

Blumenthal laughed, answering that he had made no deal with Alex or the governor.

A word to the wise: Beware when some politicians laugh. A load of horseshit will surely follow.

Al Lawrence redeemed himself handsomely for his scheduling faux pas at the Bronx nursing home by getting me a free half-hour in prime time on Channel 5. Al's argument to the network had been that they were allotting air time to the other four candidates, and by his interpretation of FCC rules I deserved the same treatment.

I was also invited on the Sunday New York talk shows and repeated the same message I'd been carrying throughout my campaign: The era of bossism was over.

I'll never forget doing Gabe Pressman's Sunday morning show, on which I again debated Badillo, Beame, Biaggi, and Blumenthal. Doris's niece, Sheri, was getting married the Saturday night before I had to go on the show. I'd been rehearsing my position in my mind during the ceremony, and I was as nervous as a high-school kid on his way to his first prom. When the waiters served the main course, I couldn't stand it any longer, and I said to Doris, "Can we leave?"

"Stanley, my niece gets married only once. I will not leave early."

I pleaded with her until I made her crazy. Just after we had the coffee, but before the Viennese table came out, I said we're leaving. Doris said all right, we're leaving.

For all of these years, Sheri rarely misses an opportunity to remind me that I left her wedding before the Viennese table.

Everything went fine with Gabe Pressman, and as soon as we were off the air, Gabe leaned over and gave me a compliment I've treasured ever since: "Stanley," he said, "you won the debate."

That was generous of him, though I must've done pretty well on his show because on Monday morning my office received calls from people who said they'd never heard my name before and now they were eager to vote for me. It was explained to them that they had to be registered Liberals, and unfortunately none of them were, but at least I felt that New Yorkers were hearing my message.

My appearances on TV had an unforeseen dividend. One morning at my office I received a phone call from a Mrs. Smolkin. I didn't recognize the name, but the voice was unmistakable when I called her back. It was Rita Greenberg, the daughter of the foster mother I'd so deeply loved. My throat closed up when Rita told me her mother, Jenny, whom I hadn't seen since my wedding, had passed away, but it was wonderful talking to Rita after almost forty years, and we never lost touch again.

High points aside, I couldn't outpoll Al Blumenthal. On the other hand, he couldn't win against the Democratic front-runner, Abe Beame. Alex had known that from the jump. He chose Al to beat me, to protect his own turf, not to make a mayor. Yet there was a way for both Al and me to get what we sought. With a week to go until the Liberal Party primary, I invited Al to lunch at Longchamps.

We chatted about the campaign for a few minutes. Then I said, "I ran to stop Wagner. I've done that."

Blumenthal said, "Alex wants to beat you awfully bad."

"The feeling's mutual," I said. "I'll give you my people if you'll come out against business-as-usual. We'll work for you, whatever you need. Maybe you'll win."

He seemed to consider it for a moment. Then he shook his head no.

Al Blumenthal beat me two-to-one in the primary. The outcome had never been in doubt. On June 4, few of my potheads hung around to witness the results. Jerry Edelstein, in fact, went to the movies. Abe Beame won the Democratic primary, and within days of his victory I got a call from him inviting me out to his home in the Rockaways. I drove out to see him. He lived in a charming old house with a screened porch off the master bedroom, and we sat out there enjoying the warm spring air and talking about everything but politics.

Abe was a kind man without a deceitful bone in his body, and I thought he might be having trouble steering the conversation around to what was obviously the purpose of his invitation. So I said, "Abe, I'll be glad to work for you in the election. And I don't want anything from you if you win. Just the opportunity once in a while to share my ideas on things.

Abe smiled, and we shook hands. My potheads and I formed Liberals for Beame, and we worked in Abe's campaign. He defeated Blumenthal, and the Republican candidate, John Marchi, in the general election, and in January 1974, Abe appointed me to an unsalaried post on his Urban Design Council.

I had six months to go before I had to run again for the chairmanship of the Queens County Liberal Party. I knew Alex and the New York State Liberal Party were logging a lot of overtime in an effort to replace me with someone less antagonistic to their agenda. They were out making deals, registering new members, collecting signed proxies, lining up support wherever they could. I was fully committed to fighting them, but I must admit that after the primary something went out of the game for me. I had the feeling that unless I was willing to enter politics as a full-time player, a constant candidate for serious office, keeping Wagner off the ballot was the best I could do to counter bossism.

I had no desire to live in that arena. As Doris had observed long ago, it was an ugly place to spend your life, and I already regretted the time my chairmanship and primary campaign had stolen from my family. Besides, I loved being a lawyer; I wanted to make money without being on the take; and last but certainly not least, ever since the spring of 1972 I'd been busy trying to keep my friend Sy Thaler from going to prison, an experience that would leave a bitter taste of politics in my mouth forever.

CHAPTER 14

MY FRIEND SY THALER

Seymour Thaler, his wife, and two children lived in a beautiful home on Groton Street in Forest Hills, a short drive from my house in Flushing. I met Sy around 1960, a couple of years after he was elected to the New York State Senate.

He had grown up poor and smart in the Bronx, and graduated from Brooklyn Law as the valedictorian of his class. Beginning as an assistant district attorney and then as a deputy commissioner in the city's Department of Investigation, Sy made a name for himself as a crusader by leading inquiries into the illegal use of inferior lumber in construction, the rent gouging of welfare recipients, and the improper behavior of city marshals. It was as the ranking Democrat on the Joint Legislative Committee on Public Health and Medicare that Sy became famous for his dogged investigation of New York City hospitals. He exposed a raft of payroll-padding, waste, patient neglect and abuse, and an astonishing shortage of essential medical equipment. When his fellow senators expressed skepticism about his findings, Sy took them along with him on one of his impromptu inspections, and it wasn't out of the ordinary for a handful of previously skeptical senators to become physically ill upon witnessing the substandard conditions and callous patient care.

Sy was tall, dark, and intense, a liberal Democrat with a deliciously independent streak, a finely honed intelligence, boundless compassion, and a penchant for hollering at anyone whom he considered cruel or dishonest, an inclination that earned him the sobriquet "Instant Indignation" from his legislative colleagues. Despite his successful thirteen-year tenure in the New York State Senate, Sy dreamt of being a judge, a dream he'd been harboring since childhood. In November of 1971, endorsed by both the Democrats and Republicans, Sy was elected to a judgeship on the state supreme court. He was perfect for the job, a fair-minded man with

endless patience for listening to people and appreciating their perspective.

Then, four days before Christmas, Sy was indicted by United
States Attorney Whitney North Seymour, Jr., for crimes I still believe Sy didn't commit. But his distinguished, unblemished career
in public service, so unremittingly and skillfully pursued, was reduced to the tragically banal, a soon-forgotten footnote to New York's
political history.

Sy's troubles began in September of 1970 when a lawyer who
rented space in Sy's suite of offices on West Forty-fourth Street
told him that he represented a client from Long Island, who, for
tax reasons, needed to sell $800,000 of United States Treasury bills
at a substantial discount. T-bills are short-term securities sold by
the government in large denominations and are about as close to
cash as you can get. Under oath, Sy declared that he didn't know
why any person would sell them at a discount, but one of Sy's clients, a real estate investor, offered to buy the T-bills if they weren't
stolen.

Sy brought the Treasury bills to a Manhattan branch of Chemical Bank and informed a bank vice president that the buyer planned
to cash the T-bills at Chemical and asked the VP to verify that they
were legitimate, which the bank officer promised would be easy to
do within forty-eight hours. According to Sy, Chemical never notified him that the T-bills were stolen, but the deal fell through.

At this juncture, events grow murkier, depending on whose
version you trust. Sy later testified that since the lawyer he knew
vouched for the seller of the T-bills, saying that he was a reputable
businessman from a well-to-do family and the owner of the securities, he arranged to sell $250,000 of the T-bills at the Second Na-
tional Bank of New Haven for 25 percent of their full worth. This
was a whopping discount, given that the securities don't generally
sell for less than 96 percent of their face value. Sy pocketed his fee
and handed over the remainder to the other lawyer and his client.

The lawyer, who would be a key prosecution witness at the
trial, testified that Thaler knew his client was merely a commis-
sion-earning broker of the securities, which turned out to have been
pilfered from the private Wall Street bank of Brown Brothers,
Harriman & Co., and when an insurance company started making
inquiries into the theft, Sy cooperated with them and offered to

return his profit from the sale. During the fall of 1971, a grand jury looked into the situation and indicted everyone involved for conspiracy, fraud, and interstate transportation of stolen securities. Sy was also charged with perjury for allegedly lying to the grand jury about his role in the sale.

Sy was tried in the federal district court at Foley Square. The trial ran for three weeks in March of 1972, and Sy was defended by Milton Gould of Shea, Gould, one of the preeminent firms in New York City. Milton Gould was an ego wrapped in an expensively tailored, pinstriped suit, but he was a bear in the courtroom defending Sy.

Sy's acquittal hinged on his convincing the jurors that he had no idea the Treasury bills were stolen. It may have been a long shot for the jury to believe that a fifty-two-year-old former state senator and judge didn't smell something fishy about T-bills being peddled for twenty-five cents on the dollar, but the jury didn't know Sy as well as I did.

The bottom line on Sy and money was that he was about as sophisticated in financial affairs as a college freshman with a generous allowance. As ridiculous as that sounds, it made absolutely perfect sense, because as a practical matter Sy didn't need to know even the basics of personal finance. Since his career in government had never earned him a large salary, the elegant lifestyle that he and his wife, Mildred, enjoyed was largely made possible by her extremely wealthy family.

Actually, I believe that Sy's ill-fated foray into wheeling and dealing was an attempt to prove to his wife and her family that he, too, could cut a big money deal. Sy realized that once he became a judge, his investment opportunities would be severely limited by conflicts of interest, and so he made his move before running for the supreme court.

At his trial, Sy took the stand in his own defense. His testimony was heart-wrenching. Sometimes he seemed on the verge of tears; at other times, he yelled out his answers. For instance, after pointing out to the jury that he had conducted the entire transaction with checks, letters, and bank documents, he shouted, "Even an idiot wouldn't do it that way if he thought [the Treasury bills] were stolen." Then Sy was suddenly calm, his voice trailing off as he said that he truly thought the securities were legitimate. "I would have staked my life [on it], and I did stake my life, unfortunately."

Assistant U.S. Attorney Edward Shaw (no relation to me) hammered at Sy, and yet he couldn't shake his testimony. And Sy may well have persuaded the jury of his innocence except for a highly questionable piece of evidence which appeared to indicate that Sy was a liar.

Now remember, Sy had asserted that a lawyer he knew had assured him that his client was completely reputable and the owner of the securities. On the other hand, the lawyer had testified that Sy had known from the start that his client was purely a broker in the deal, not the owner of the T-bills. The lawyer referred to a signed agreement regarding commissions on the sale of the securities that would back up his claim, but he couldn't physically locate the agreement.

But his client could, or at least a wrinkled photostat of it, and he pulled the paper out of his pocket while he was testifying on the stand. It was the most dramatic moment in the trial. The agreement, allegedly bearing Sy's signature, seemed to prove that he knew this guy wasn't the owner.

On the stand, Sy almost broke into tears when he inspected the signed photostat. He claimed that it was a forgery, and an expert testified that it was entirely possible Sy was correct. The agreement was really a photostat of a photostat, and for my money Judge Murray Gurfein shouldn't have allowed it into evidence. Yet he did, rejecting Milton Gould's argument that the photostat couldn't be substituted for the original, and the document impeached Sy's previous testimony.

I didn't accept the photostat as genuine and still don't. During the trial, a rumor circulated that the U.S. attorney had to have his findings reviewed by the Nixon White House before bringing the case against Sy. The Republican president would be up for reelection in November. In a traditionally, left-wing Democratic stronghold like New York, in a trial involving one of the state's foremost liberals—and a Jewish liberal, to boot—the Nixon administration would have wanted to make doubly sure that the U.S. attorney would win and do maximum damage to Nixon's political enemies.

The rumor was passed on to me from a handful of sources, and Sy had heard it from friends in Washington. I sincerely believe that when it appeared Sy might persuade the jury of his innocence, the photostat was manufactured by someone for political reasons and used to turn the tide of the trial. If that has a ring of paranoia to it, it should be remembered that 1972 was the year of the Watergate burglary and a host of dirty political tricks born in the White House. Most everything I've read in the transcripts of the recently released Nixon tapes, particularly his anti-Semitic remarks, has reinforced my opinion.

The jury deliberated for ten hours. I was sitting directly behind Sy, and I can still picture him when the jurors filed in. He was standing with his fear and grief hidden behind the blank expression on his face. Every person in that courtroom knew that Sy was a decent, caring public servant and an honorable man, and the *New York Times* noted that "even hardened court observers winced in sympathy" when Sy was pronounced guilty.

Sy's whole body shuddered as if he were having a mini-seizure, and he buried his head in his hands. Throughout the trial Sy had repeatedly told me that he had the bizarre sensation of living in the middle of a nightmare, and no matter how hard he tried he couldn't rouse himself from his terrifying dream. I think when Sy listened to the verdict he finally grasped the enormity of what was happening to him—that the life he had led for so long was over.

Reporters and television cameras were waiting for Sy and his family on the sprawling courthouse steps of Foley Square. I was behind Sy. His lawyer, Milton Gould, was ahead of him. A reporter asked Gould how he felt about the verdict, and he glibly replied, "You win some and you lose some."

His reply was the product of Gould's overblown ego. The seductive glow of TV lights shining on a lawyer like Gould can convince him that the trial had been about his agile mind and silver tongue, not his client's freedom. His glibness, while patently insensitive to Sy, was also bad public relations, because Sy would undoubtedly appeal the verdict. Gould should have continued his defense of Sy and blasted the judge for permitting the bogus photostat into evidence.

Naturally, Sy didn't appreciate Gould's comment. Turning from his lawyer and the gaggle of reporters, Sy craned his head back toward me and muttered, "Let's get rid of him. You handle my appeal, Stanley."

I accompanied Sy to his sentencing on August 8, 1972. Before Judge Gurfein handed down his sentence, Sy spoke for twenty minutes, fighting tears, his voice trembling as he professed his innocence to the hushed courtroom and begged mercy from the judge. After he finished, tears streamed down his face, and Gurfein ordered him to serve a year and a day in prison, and to pay a $10,000 fine.

It was lenient considering that Gurfein could have sentenced him to ten years, harsh when you feel that the crime Sy was guilty of was the puerile desire to prove to his wife and himself that the modestly paid public crusader had what it took to be a prosperous businessman. The sentence was the end of Sy's childhood dream. He would be disbarred and dismissed from his position as a judge.

Sy remained free pending his appeal to the Circuit Court of Appeals. Just prior to Labor Day, I filed a $52.5 million suit against Chemical Bank; the branch manager who had assured Sy that he would let him know if the Treasury Bills were legitimate; the Second National Bank of New Haven; and the Federal Reserve Banks of New York and Boston.

Sy held a news conference at my office on Lexington Avenue and told the press that any monies realized from the suit would go to charity. We were filing it in order to clear his name. My argument was that the bank manager and these institutions were negligent. They should have reported the securities as stolen. Had they fulfilled their responsibility, Sy wouldn't have been involved in the transaction.

On its merits, I had a case, but I was pretty sure that I was wasting my time. Once your client has been convicted in criminal court, it is nigh on impossible to win a civil suit for him related to the same matter. In ruling on my suit, the judge's opening line was "The plaintiff has a lot of *chutzpah*," and it went rapidly downhill from there. Needless to say, the suit was dismissed.

I thought I had a decent shot at winning the appeal. My main thrust was that the authenticity of the photostat was suspect. Some lower courts around the country had refused to deem photostats admissible evidence. I argued that since in Sy's case the disputed document was a photostat of a photostat, Judge Gurfein should have excluded it at the evidentiary hearing. The court strongly disagreed with me and denied the appeal.

The appeal process kept Sy out of jail for sixteen months, but on November 12, 1973, I got in my car, picked up Sy at his house in Forest Hills, and took the longest hour-and-a-half ride of my life to the federal prison at Danbury, Connecticut.

Driving along, I tried to bolster Sy's spirits, telling him that I would keep fighting to shorten his sentence. Sy had a heart condition by then, and I thought I could persuade Judge Gurfein that a medical parole was appropriate. Sy nodded, and he expressed his disbelief at his situation. Mostly, he peered out at the bleak, New England countryside, the bare trees lining the road framed against the gray sky with the empty fields of winter grass and the rocky brown hills beyond.

Sy surrendered to the authorities at the prison, and I watched as they handcuffed and shackled him. He maintained his composure until they locked him in a holding pen. Then he began to cry.

I stood there listening to his sobs, and suddenly the years rolled back for me so fast I was dizzy, and my mother was leading me inside the Brooklyn Hebrew Orphans Asylum and turning me over to a uniformed matron. An ungodly rush of sadness welled up in me. A sob caught in my throat, and then the past dissolved again into the present, and I was telling Sy to hang in there, be patient, I'd get him out, you can survive this, I know, because a person, even a four-year-old child, can survive just about anything.

I petitioned Judge Gurfein to release Sy due to his coronary condition. When I appeared before Gurfein I sensed that he was sympathetic to my presentation, but for reasons I couldn't pinpoint he denied my request.

Later, I was told that Gurfein was up for a promotion to the Second Circuit of the Court of Appeals, and I understood his reluctance to let Sy go. President Nixon would have to recommend him to the Senate, and Nixon leaned decidedly to the right when it came to court appointments. In addition, the justices sitting on the Second Circuit are, by and large, a staunchly conservative bunch, and I suspect that Gurfein was anxious to advance his career and wary of appearing too liberal in his sentencing practices.

Ultimately, I prevailed in having Sy transferred to a more sophisticated medical facility, the Correctional Institution at Lexington, Kentucky. He was released from there after serving nine months of his twelve-month sentence, and he spent the last year and a half of his life working at the Marbella Gallery on Madison Avenue, selling high-class art with his wife.

Sy Thaler died at home of his heart ailment in February 1976. He was buried, with hundreds of mourners looking on, in New Montefiore Cemetery in Farmingdale, Long Island.

In the last twenty-five years, scandals of immense proportions have become a permanent feature of America's political landscape. As scandals go, Sy's case was small potatoes. What hurts me about it beyond the toll it extracted from Sy is that the hoopla surrounding his conviction has obscured the importance of his real contribution, making New York a safer place to live, and so today few speak of the good Sy accomplished.

Illness has confined me to several critical-care units in New York hospitals. During some of the nights I spent in those high-tech rooms, I gazed at the equipment flickering and beeping around me and marveled at the excellent medical care that has prolonged my life. I often wonder if any of it is a result of Sy's crusade in the 1960s, his insistence that hospital administrators and doctors and nurses do everything in their power to save the patients under their care. I don't know the answer, but I like to think I owe a debt of gratitude to the crusading state senator from Forest Hills. At such times, I always like to remember Sy.

I remember him now.

CHAPTER 15

NOW YOU SEE ME, NOW YOU DON'T

In the early spring of 1974, my faction of the Liberal Party of Queens County had a decision to make. Alex was up to his old tricks, preparing to use Ed Morrison as a stand-in candidate for the governor's slot on the Liberal Party's primary ballot. After Howard Samuels faced Hugh Carey in the Democratic primary, Alex would then order Morrison to withdraw and give the slot to the Democratic winner.

From the outset of my chairmanship, my supporters and I had vehemently opposed this tactic, and that spring we were certain that we could field a candidate who could beat Morrison in the primary, thereby preventing Alex from filling the Liberal line with his personal choice.

Our man was Bill Baird, who was popular around the state as a pro-choice advocate on abortion. Bill agreed to enter the race, but the question facing my faction was, did we want to square off against Alex with all of the attendant bickering and battling at meetings, in the press, and most likely in court?

We chose not to debate the issue. This was an extraordinary exception to our standard operating procedure, which found us locked in mortal verbal combat over every issue from income redistribution to whether we should send out for moo shoo pork or pizza.

As an alternative to a debate, we rented a hotel conference room, and ninety of us wedged into it. No one spoke. We just voted. The final tally was forty-six against putting Baird in the primary and forty-four in favor of it. I'd cast my vote to run Baird, but a big segment of my young supporters had voted against the move. They'd had enough of Alex, and I was later told by Jerry Edelstein that a fair-sized group of them no longer had the heart to see me battered anymore. They had determined that it was time for me to get back to my family and to practicing law.

In July, I lost the county chairmanship to the candidate that Alex had backed, Stephen Mahler, an assistant district attorney in Queens. Following my loss to Mahler, I told my supporters that I would remain as the conscience of the Liberal Party and monitor its future actions, but as I spoke those words I keenly felt that my role as an active player was over.

I would continue to work in politics—once bitten by the bug it's hard to lose the habit—but I moved up to a higher level, confining most of my activities to the background and serving as a fund-raiser and an unofficial adviser to a wide circle of politicians— Governors Mario Cuomo and George Pataki; Senators Joe Biden, Birch Bayh, and Al D'Amato; New York State Attorney General Eliot Spitzer; New York State Comptroller Carl McCall and New York City Comptroller Alan Hevesi, both of whom are rightfully ambitious, the former for the governorship, the latter for mayor. (I predict that McCall will be the first African-American candidate for the governorship, and as such, Carl will have an uphill battle. Hevesi, a dear friend since the Sy Thaler days, will follow Rudy Giuliani to Gracie Mansion.)

Still, even though my days as a frontline player were over, every now and again there would be a faint, nostalgic echo of my bygone avocation.

For example, soon after my chairmanship ended, I introduced Hugh Carey, the then-Democratic candidate for governor, at my synagogue, Temple Gates of Prayer in Flushing, and then, one afternoon in 1974 I was contacted by an FBI agent who said President Gerald Ford had requested that the Bureau interview me.

"What for?" I asked.

"I'm not at liberty to discuss it over the phone," he replied. "But we must see you immediately."

I thought maybe it was some kind of joke, so I asked the guy for his name and number and said I'd call him right back.

I dialed, and before the second ring, a secretary at the New York field office of the FBI answered. I gave her the agent's name, and she connected me to him.

"Okay," I said. "Come on over,"

A pair of tall crewcut agents in polyester suits and black wingtips arrived at my office. This being the age of Watergate and rampant paranoia—especially for liberals—my first move was to check out their credentials.

After I handed them back their card cases, they sat down and one of them said, "President Ford is considering naming Governor Nelson Rockefeller as his vice president, and the president has asked us to talk to you. He understands that you might have a lot to say about the governor."

Oh boy, did I, and I proceeded to get six years of complaints off my chest. I told the agents that I considered Rockefeller an immoral man who had operated under the megalomaniacal delusion that he, a governor elected by the people, was in reality an emperor who ruled through divine right. I explained that Rockefeller had controlled the Liberal Party in conjunction with Alex Rose. He had butted into internecine political spats when he should've been paying attention to the needs of the state, and that such a man could be so close to the Oval Office was anathema to me.

It was relaxing, jabbering on for an hour, and when I was done the agents invited me to address a Senate committee that was doing the background work on the Rockefeller nomination.

It was tempting, but I recognized that I would be wasting my breath, that regardless of what I said Rockefeller would be named Gerald Ford's vice president.

I was relieved to be out of politics, personally and professionally, because by the summer of 1974, I was embroiled in a legal case that would at long last clear up my debts and define me as a lawyer for the rest of my life.

I got into the case through the side door, and ironically it wasn't one of the big shots I'd hoped to meet in politics who led me to the opportunity, but one of my young friends from the Liberal Party, Jerry Edelstein.

Back in 1970, while Jerry and I were at a meeting, he mentioned that two of his pals, Mel and Bobby Robbins, were looking to retain a lawyer. The Robbins brothers were co-owners of Robbins Mens and Boys Wear, a relatively small chain of New York City stores that specialized in closeouts, selling hats, shoes, and every article of clothing you might put on in between.

One of Mel and Bobby's stores was located on Steinway Street in Queens. Steinway Street was the borough's *goldeneh medina* of discount goods, with rows of open-front stores where every morning, seven days a week, the owners rolled up the metal gates and the shoppers flocked in, sifting through the merchandise piled high on the pushcart-type counters inside. It was the daily shopping that was responsible for the Robbins brothers needing a lawyer.

In 1970, New York City had a blue law on the books prohibiting street sales on Sundays. Women were pouring into the work force, and it was getting harder for the average family to do their shopping on days other than weekend. But the law, as frequently happens, hadn't been revamped to keep pace with the cultural shift, and the police had ticketed the Robbins brothers for rolling their clothing racks out on the sidewalk every Sunday for more than a year.

I met with Mel and Bobby at their Manhattan store on Lower Broadway. They were regular hard-working guys, and I liked them right away. Each ticket carried a hefty fine, and the Robbins brothers had more than fifty of them. To add insult to injury, the tickets had been written to them personally, not to their corporation, and hence a minor matter held the potential for costing them serious money. They asked me if there were any legal remedies available to them, and I said no, because they were in violation of a city statute. Yet sometimes a judge will substitute common sense for the majesty of the law, and I pocketed the tickets and took the subway over to court in Queens.

I spoke to one of the judges, pointing out that people had to shop and people had to earn a living, and couldn't he cut the Robbins brothers and the other store owners on Steinway Street a break?

Yes, he could, and he reduced the fine by 50 or 60 percent, and limited it to the corporation, not to the individual proprietors.

So I became a penny-ante hero to Mel and Bobby Robbins. Over the next year I handled a matter or two for them, nothing major, and I also, as a bonus, bought my clothes from them at half-price. Then one day Mel called me, saying that he and his brother had expanded their operation in Queens by moving Robbins Mens and Boys Wear into a much larger store at 30-88 Steinway Street, the former site of a Packer supermarket and now owned by Bohack. However, Bohack's landlord, Isadore Weinstein, had objected to the subletting of the lease. And now Izzy was suing his tenant, Bohack, and the undertenant, Robbins Mens and Boys, in civil court. Mel said that Bohack was being represented by its own attorney, Philip Waters, from the prestigious, politically connected firm of Hein, Bradie, Waters & Klein. Mel asked if I would represent Robbins Mens and Boys.

"Sure," I said, blissfully unaware that I was about to invest all my energies over the next five years in what would be, up until then, one of the largest bankruptcy cases ever filed in the Eastern District of New York.

By the early 1970s, Bohack was a publicly traded company with average annual sales in excess of $300 million. The late Charles Bluhdorn was the majority stockholder in the company, owning 21 percent of Bohack's common shares. Charlie was the then-chairman of Gulf and Western Industries. He acquired companies as chronically, and with the same single-mindedness, as Liz Taylor acquired husbands, and not infrequently with similarly unhappy results.

But more about Charlie later. Suffice it to say that he had pushed to expand Bohack; their bottom line had taken a dangerous beating; and in the mid-1960s the company started closing the unprofitable stores and hoped to turn a profit on its considerable real estate holdings, either by selling the land and stores outright or by subletting the long-term leases. Charlie Bluhdorn saw that it was essential for the corporation to hire somebody familiar with the New York real-estate market. So in 1967, he pressured the company's directors to appoint Franklin Knobel as chairman of the board and the chief executive officer of Bohack.

Frank Knobel was in his forties when I met him in 1971. Raised and educated in New York, Frank was street-smart, witty, and urbane, as though he had sprung to life through the joint efforts of Damon Runyon and Noel Coward. Frank's father had done well during the nickelodeon era by purchasing movie theaters. By the end of World War II, though, when Frank was discharged from the Navy, his father was nervous about the encroachment of the nascent television industry on the movies. So he sold off his theaters and entered the real estate business with Frank. After his father retired, Frank stayed active in real estate, both in New York and the Caribbean, but he was ready for some midlife adventure when Charlie Bluhdorn contacted him. Additionally, Frank had recently refinanced most of his assets and purchased half of Bluhdorn's Bohack stock, and so it made sense for him to oversee his investment by becoming the chief executive officer of Bohack. Besides the responsibilities of a CEO, Frank's main function was to direct the real estate activities of Bohack. They had dozens of empty or unprofitable stores around New York City and Long Island, and Frank set about recasting them into profitable investments. For example, he transformed one of the stores into a funeral home, and another into a movie theater, and gradually he stemmed the company's real estate losses.

About 1969, Bohack had merged with Packer's Supermarket, a smaller chain headquartered in Brooklyn. Packer's had been under the same financial strains as Bohack, but they had fewer stores. One of their markets that appeared profitable was their big store at 30-88 Steinway Street. It had been this location, and Packer's customer base, that had interested Bohack in the merger. Bohack was soon operating Packer's thirty-seven stores, including the one on Steinway Street. However, Bohack's management had not properly analyzed the shoppers who converged on the bargain paradise of Queens. On Steinway Street, no one paid full retail, not for shoes or Wonder Bread. In the Bohack store, the shoppers seemed to possess a sixth sense about picking loss leaders and leaving every moneymaking item to gather dust. Before long, Bohack was losing almost $40,000 a month on Steinway Street.

Frank Knobel decided to close the store and sublet it to another business. Since Packer's had signed the lease in 1965, before Bohack had merged with them, their rent was fixed at five or six times below market. Due to the demand for commercial space and the rise in rents, Bohack stood not only to stop its losses, but to realize a handsome profit by subletting their lease, which ran until April 30, 1978.

The moment word leaked out that Bohack was seeking to sublet its store, brokers were phoning Frank with retailers interested in the space. Frank would work out a deal in principle with one of the parties, and then he would talk to Izzy Weinstein, Bohack's landlord on Steinway Street.

Izzy had owned a small chain of supermarkets before retiring to his little house in the Flatbush section of Brooklyn. He was a shrewd guy with a head for numbers that could put a computer to shame, and he had a reputation as one of the craftier landlords in the borough.

Izzy had no intention of allowing Bohack to convert their lease into a cash cow when he could do exactly the same thing. Whenever Frank phoned to run a potential renter by him, Izzy told Frank to forget about it, that he should cancel his lease, give him back the store, and Izzy would rent it to another company.

Izzy was able to scuttle Frank's arrangements because Izzy had been clever enough, when he'd signed the original lease with Packer's, to include a severely restrictive use clause. The clause stated that 30-80 Steinway Street was "to be used and occupied only as and for a supermarket, with the right to sell all products now or hereafter sold in chain supermarkets." Moreover, if the tenant ever sublet the premises, the subtenant had to abide by the restrictions in the use clause.

It was an unusual clause in its particulars, but as I said, Izzy was shrewd. From his experience in the supermarket business, he knew that markets come and go, and he had probably thrown in the clause to prevent any of his tenants from doing precisely what Frank was attempting to do.

Bohack had a large investment in their Steinway Street market, and Frank Knobel was as clever as Izzy. He devised a scheme for circumventing the use clause of the lease. Frank told his potential renters that, at no expense to them, Bohack would open, operate, and maintain a glass refrigerator in the rear of their store, where bread, milk, cheese, eggs, and several other "products sold in chain supermarkets" would be available to shoppers. That should satisfy Izzy's conditions and allow Bohack to lease their unused space.

Frank's idea scared away potential renters until a broker brought him Robbins Mens and Boys Wear. Eager to expand their clothing store on Steinway Street, Mel and Bobby Robbins were risk takers of the first rank, and they told Frank they were willing to give his scheme a try.

Now, instead of losing forty grand a month on Steinway Street, the supermarket chain was collecting a twenty-thousand-dollar profit in rent, a sixty-thousand-dollar swing. The Robbins brothers got their desperately needed room for expansion, and everybody was happy—except Izzy Weinstein.

Two days after the Robbins Mens and Boys Wear sign went up and the Bohack glass refrigerator went in, Izzy filed an action to dispossess in the civil court. Izzy claimed that Bohack had violated the "use clause" of their lease and Robbins Mens and Boys Wear should have to vacate the premises.

Frank Knobel had in-house counsel at Bohack, a decent fellow named Morty Frankfort, and together they went shopping for a lawyer, finally hiring the law firm of Sydney Hein, the Republican leader of Queens. Izzy Weinstein retained the equally prestigious firm of Tenzer, Greenblatt, Fallon & Kaplan, and in court he was represented by Edward Sadowsky, who happened to sit on the City Council.

As the hearing began, Judge Meyer Tobias saw the two lawyers and commented: "What do we have here? A political tug of war?"

Mel and Bobby Robbins, as the undertenant of 30-88 Steinway Street, had been named as codefendants in Izzy's suit. They had called me and explained the issues, and just prior to the trial Mel informed Frank that he would prefer for me to represent them. As chairman of the board and CEO of Bohack, Frank was more familiar with the big-name New York City firms. Naturally, he had never heard of Shaw and Levine. Yet Frank figured that he had nothing to lose. The whole deal had been a crapshoot from the start; if it worked out, it was found money for Bohack; and Frank told Mel that he was welcome to bring me in.

I showed up in court, shook hands with Frank Knobel and Morty Frankfort, and after a few hours of watching Philip Waters trying to convince the judge of the legitimacy of the defendants' case, I knew that Bohack and the Robbins brothers were going to lose. Waters argued that the use clause was not technically a restrictive covenant, and even if it was, Robbins Mens and Boys was using the 30-80 Steinway Street space to sell food.

Waters was a good lawyer, but he was sticking too close to the letter of the law. This wasn't a major-league commercial case. A different argument should have been used, an argument based on broader issues, cultural issues, the changing times, new business approaches, something in that vein.

After all, it was obvious that Frank was abrogating the spirit of the lease. Izzy Weinstein wanted a supermarket in his building, not a discount haberdashery that peddled groceries to duck the strictures of a use clause.

During a break in the proceedings, Mel, Bobby, and I were standing in the hallway outside the courtroom, and they asked me my opinion of the trial.

I replied that Waters was blowing the case, which coincided with Mel and Bobby's estimate of the situation. Mel walked over and spoke privately to Frank Knobel and Morty Frankfort. Then Mel came back and said that everyone agreed I should be the lead attorney for both Bohack and Robbins Mens and Boys Wear.

Frank Knobel subsequently told me that he had no idea whether I could turn the case around, except he figured that he was on a sinking ship and he might as well switch and see if the other ship would sail. At that point, the trial was too far along for me to do much to affect the outcome, but I was confident that I would have a shot at beating Izzy Weinstein on appeal.

Judge Tobias ruled against Bohack and Robbins Mens and Boys, but, at my request, he stayed the vacate order and gave the Robbins brothers six months to convert the premises back into a supermarket.

This is a prime illustration of a common phenomenon in civil court—you lose the case, but win the order. In other words, Mel and Bobby would be allowed to continue running their clothing concern. They were making barrels of money on Steinway Street, and since I planned to appeal the verdict, Mel and Bobby would be sitting pretty for a while.

Meantime, Izzy Weinstein wouldn't be repossessing his building in the foreseeable future.

Critics of civil proceedings often say that the courtroom battles are nothing but a labyrinth of compound idiocies that profit no one but the lawyers getting paid to lead the interested parties around the maze. The criticism is generally unwarranted and owes much to the fact that petitioners and respondents invariably rush into a civil court believing that they are absolutely right and their opponents absolutely wrong. In civil cases, our legal system is more sophisticated. It recognizes that petitioners and respondents have their own self-interested perspective, and at its best the law is bound to disappoint both of them.

Therefore, it has long been my position that unlike criminal matters, civil law, and the expense of litigation, are tools for negotiation, a means of bringing parties together to save themselves time and money.

Personally, I thought that the differences among Izzy Weinstein, Bohack, and the Robbins brothers shouldn't have come to trial. It was a straight business transaction, not a legal matter.

Frank Knobel should have negotiated a settlement with Izzy. He easily could have offered him a percentage of the profit in rent he was collecting. With more money coming in every month, Izzy wouldn't have had any reason to feel like he was getting screwed, and he would have saved himself the trouble and expense of a lawsuit and returned to enjoying his retirement in Flatbush. But Bohack wasn't offering much, and Izzy was intent on winning.

Just after the trial, Frank Knobel called me and said, "Stanley, you did a hell of a job for us in court, and I know you'll do well on appeal. Do you think you could handle all of Bohack's litigation?"

"Frank, you told me you're paying Simpson Thacher & Bartlett a hundred and fifty grand a year to do Bohack's litigation. Simpson's a first-rate firm."

"I wanna retain you, too," Frank said. "I'll pay you twenty-five thousand a year."

I accepted on the spot, glad to have the work and the retainer, the largest I'd ever earned. My first action on behalf of Bohack was to appeal Judge Tobias' ruling to the Appellate Term, a trio of state supreme court judges who hear cases before they go up to the Appellate Division.

I geared my brief to a variation on the common-sense theme I had used to help Mel and Bobby Robbins get their fines reduced. My main thrust was that businesses are in a constant state of flux. In order to survive in the marketplace, they must stay current with the demands of consumers and create demands that consumers never knew they had.

Who should say that a supermarket cannot sell clothes or any kind of goods, especially if these added items made life easier for their customers? This is part of the successful marketing theory behind malls, the notion of one-stop shopping. With the fast pace of modern America, shoppers were apt to gravitate to stores that made their lives more convenient. Furthermore, all across the country, retailers were selling things unrelated to their primary business. In fact, I argued, this trend had gone so far that *The World Book Encyclopedia* claimed that nonfood items had become a notable feature of supermarkets.

I won the appeal, the judges stating in their decision that any ambiguity in the definition of supermarket "must be resolved against the landlord."

Izzy Weinstein then took his case upstairs to the Appellate Division, which promptly reversed the Appellate Term and reinstated the civil court judgment. Yet once again the justices stayed the vacate order for six months, so the Robbins brothers went right on raking it in on Steinway Street. Meanwhile, Izzy wasn't collecting a dime of additional rent.

Nor would he for some time, because I brought the case to the Court of Appeals. After another six months, the court upheld the ruling of the Appellate Division. Still, even though Bohack and Robbins Mens and Boys Wear had lost, Mel and Bobby were given another grace period to convert their store.

By now it was 1974, almost three years since the case first went to trial, and I scheduled a meeting with Izzy Weinstein. He was upbeat when I walked in. His good mood was presumably due to his mistaken impression that he was about to retake possession of 30-80 Steinway Street.

"Izzy," I said, "Mel and Bobby are ready to reconvert the store."

Izzy almost fell out of his chair. He said, "Whatta ya mean?"

"I mean that the Robbins brothers are going to pull out their clothes, turn the space into a supermarket, and lease it to somebody else."

Izzy said, "But then I'll get my old rent back."

"Right."

"That's no good," Izzy said.

"Not for you it isn't," I replied. "Maybe you should talk to Frank and the Robbins brothers."

As he should have done from the start, Izzy sat down with Frank Knobel and the Robbins brothers and cut a deal that brought him a nice monthly check. Robbins Mens and Boys remained where it was, and Bohack received the lion's share of what it had originally sought.

I don't recall the precise date that the agreement was hashed out, but I do remember it was on a hot weekday evening in late July that Frank called me at home. I had just finished dinner with Doris and the children. I thought this was one of Frank's typical calls to discuss some modest legal matter that had come up or to tell me a particularly good joke.

I was wrong, and I knew it the moment I heard Frank's voice. He sounded worried when he said, "I'm with some people at Joe Binder's house."

Binder was the president of Bohack, and he lived in Oceanside, Long Island. I had handled a variety of cases for the company, but nothing dire enough for Frank to call me from Joe Binder's house. I knew that for Frank to be at Binder's in the middle of the week something serious was going on.

"What's up, Frank?" I asked.

"We've got some problems," he said.

"What sort of problems?"

Frank said, "You've heard of Charlie Bluhdorn?"

I told Frank all I knew about Bluhdorn: He was the chairman of Gulf and Western; he had a ton of Bohack stock in his personal portfolio; and he was reputed to be half maniac, half genius.

Frank laughed.

I asked him what other problems he had besides Bluhdorn.

Frank didn't answer right away. Then he said: "You know anything about bankruptcy?"

"Bankruptcy?"

"Yeah," Frank replied. "Bankruptcy. Maybe you should come out to Oceanside now and we'll talk."

CHAPTER 16

A CHANCE TO GET EVEN

Inside Joe Binder's house, it was wall-to-wall Bohack middle management, and the first guy I saw was Lou Robustelli, a short, quiet man who was the treasurer. Lou looked about as happy as an undertaker presiding at his own funeral, and he was talking to Frank Knobel, who was about as grim as I'd ever seen him.

I remembered looking that way myself during my worst days with Schulman; I used to see it in the mirror every morning when I shaved. And not long after my experience with Bohack, I would come to recognize the meaning of this look on clients as soon as they shambled into my office. It was a combination of dismay and fear framed by what I would come to think of as the "Bankruptcy Pallor." It was usually most noticeable in those clients who, when their company had become besieged by a cash crunch, had stopped paying their corporate withholding taxes, since that is one debt it is impossible to avoid with a Chapter XI. The United States government is renowned for never failing to collect every nickel you owe them, and they will take it from you personally if your company goes under.

I said hello to Lou and Frank, and they filled me in on Bohack's current crisis. Late that afternoon, the checks that Bohack had recently written to its suppliers started to bounce like Spalding rubber balls, all of them stamped Returned for Insufficient Funds. Obviously, this had a disastrous potential for both the supermarket chain and its suppliers.

Without food stacked on the shelves, Bohack's revenue and—more important in the short term—its cash flow would drop precipitously. In this instance the situation for a majority of the suppliers was even more perilous. Bohack's needs required three thousand wholesalers of meat, produce, dairy and other perishables. Many of these wholesalers ran modest operations that depended on Bohack paying its bills in order to stay afloat. The bounced checks could force tens of thousands of people to lose their jobs.

Although the abrupt return of Bohack's checks was shocking, from my conversations with Frank over the past year I knew that the corporation's fiscal health had been declining for some time. Their operations had been hampered by a shortage of working capital and an inability to obtain sufficient credit to keep their stores well-stocked with merchandise, an absolute must if any supermarket is to succeed.

Back in May, the chain had obtained a $5-million line of credit from the Manufacturers Hanover Trust Company (commonly referred to as "Manny Hanny" throughout the corporate world.) The bankers at Manny Hanny hadn't had a sudden change of heart with regard to Bohack's fiscal future, but they had been pressured into granting what amounted to a huge overdraft to the company by Bohack's majority stockholder, Charles Bluhdorn.

In the mid-1970s, a decade prior to the front-page financial meltdowns of high-flying investors like Donald Trump, Charlie Bluhdorn was not the type of guy that banks said no to.

Charlie was the founder, chairman, and chief executive of Gulf and Western Industries, a multibillion-dollar conglomerate with over 100,000 employees that belonged to the select group of companies in the top 20 percent of the Fortune 500. Gulf and Western's corporate headquarters, a forty-two-story tower just off the southwest corner of Central Park at Columbus Circle, was a prominent feature of the New York City skyline, but not nearly as prominent as Charlie himself. Charlie had earned a reputation as a wheeler-dealer in Manhattan and Hollywood, since, among its other assets, Gulf and Western owned Paramount Pictures, the Madison Square Garden Corporation, and the publishing house of Simon & Schuster. That Charlie was also a certifiable madman was something the people gathered at Joe Binder's just suspected. However, Frank was convinced that Charlie was intricately bound up in Bohack's abrupt slide. How bound up he was in the failure of the supermarket chain would only become clear four years later, in the summer of 1978, when I got the opportunity to depose him.

In May, when Charlie had asked Manny Hanny to extend credit to Bohack, they were happy to oblige him, since G&W had recently switched from using Chase Manhattan as its lead bank to using Manufacturers Hanover. Manny Hanny had been happy to turn the $5 million that Bohack owed Chase into a line of credit. Five million dollars was spare change when compared to the sort of financing that Gulf and Western typically sought from banks. Thus, Manny Hanny not only accommodated Bohack's request for the credit, they threw in an additional overdraft facility because they were earning considerable profits by servicing Gulf and Western's financial needs.

Charlie had supposedly reminded the bank that G&W could easily cover any of Bohack's losses, which must have been, in the banker's eyes, equivalent to a personal guarantee on the loan, since, for all intents and purposes, Charlie was Gulf and Western. It also demonstrated the respect bankers had for Charlie, since Bohack's outstanding debt was in the neighborhood of $65 million (and in 1974 dollars at that, about $200 million in today's dollars). But perhaps the banks figured that Charlie was in the supermarket business for the long haul. He already owned 22 percent of Bohack, and in February 1972, Bluhdorn had directed Gulf and Western to make a tender offer for the Great Atlantic & Pacific Tea Company. The A&P had fought back furiously and rebuffed the hostile takeover, but G&W still held 4 percent of A&P's outstanding shares.

Every now and again, when I would be discussing business with Frank Knobel, he would casually allude to the part G&W's bid for the A&P had played in the sinking fortunes of Bohack. I didn't know the whole story then, though gossip about Bluhdorn's off-the-wall business practices was already hardening into legend. Furthermore, if Bluhdorn was interested in owning a viable supermarket chain, why would he let Bohack go down the tubes by not pressuring Manny Hanny to keep the overdraft active? The loan Bohack received in May was supposed to extend through the conclusion of their fiscal year, January 31, 1975. Now, though, just two months after the deal was completed, Charlie had, according to Frank and Lou, allegedly informed Manufacturers Hanover that he didn't care whether Bohack got its line of credit or not.

I asked Frank about it. He shrugged, saying that Bluhdorn and the bankers were a weird story. Frank said that he had been on a number of conference calls with Charlie and a bigshot loan officer at Manny Hanny. As usual, the loan guy had been haranguing Frank about getting Bohack to catch up with its delinquent payments to the bank. Bluhdorn would join in on the loan guy's side, yelling at Frank, asking him what the hell was going on, why wasn't Bohack paying Manny Hanny, and exhorting Frank to cut a check for the bank, on the double, and promising the loan officer that the money would soon be in his hands.

During the conversation Frank would be saying, "Okay, Charlie, okay," and when the banker got off the line Frank would tell Charlie that there was no chance Bohack could pay now. Charlie would answer, "Yeah, I know," and when Frank asked him how come he told the loan guy the money was coming, Charlie would reply, "Hey, I had to tell him something."

That evening at Joe Binder's house, none of us knew why Charlie Bluhdorn had suddenly decided not to keep Bohack afloat by continuing to intervene with Manny Hanny. Of course, Charlie had a well-deserved reputation for instantaneous changes of direction. Some said it was part of his genius. Others claimed his manic-depression was responsible.

From the moment Joe Binder had heard about Charlie's new position, he'd been frantically calling the board of directors, trying to see if they could prevail upon Bluhdorn to change his mind again. So far, that evening, Joe hadn't had any luck, and I could still see him in the corner, with his jacket off and his tie unknotted, dialing the phone.

Somebody at Bohack, either Frank or Lou, had already spoken to Manufacturers Hanover, but they wanted to get paid now and they weren't taking no for an answer. For all of their screaming and kicking about getting their money, Manny Hanny had known all along that Bohack was suffering from a serious cash shortage.

Remember, the line of credit that the bank had extended to the company was based on the amount of cash that Bohack poured into the pipeline every evening when they deposited the day's receipts from their stores. This gave the bankers a unique view of the chain's fiscal health. As the deposits fell off, the bank knew that Bohack's cash was drying up and the chain was in trouble. Yet it didn't seem to bother Manny Hanny until they believed that Charlie was no longer bankrolling Bohack. Once this became clear, the bank determined that it would be prudent to take another look at the company's balance sheet, which, according to Frank, wasn't a pretty picture. In loans and overdrafts Bohack owed Manny Hanny close to $10 million. The supermarket chain was so deeply in debt that they were paying interest charges in excess of two dollars a share, and Manny Hanny decided that they would begin applying all of Bohack's deposits against their corporate debt, which was why the checks had bounced.

I spoke to Frank about the situation for a while, mulling over the company's options. I recall that we discussed filing for a reorganization under Chapter XI of the Federal Bankruptcy Act. From the expression on Frank's face, I was pretty sure that he felt a Chapter XI was the one option that made sense, but nothing was decided at the meeting, not even that I would handle the filing if it came to that.

Still, after I said goodnight and left the house, I was convinced that I was going to get a shot at handling what I calculated would be an eighty-or-ninety-million-dollar matter, making it the biggest bankruptcy filing, up until that time, in the Eastern District of the State of New York.

I had two reasons for my confidence. First off, I had recently saved Bohack from a financial disaster. Upon reflection, I should have known at the time that the corporation was heading for serious trouble, but I was always impressed by the size of the chain and the scope of their assets, and it didn't occur to me that their lack of cash was squeezing them to death.

What happened was that one day Frank called me and said that Bohack had a little trouble out on Long Island. It seemed that a company that had sold the supermarket chain a variety of fixtures for their stores had suddenly filed for bankruptcy. Bohack owed this company close to $2 million dollars, and their lawyers had gone to court to demand that Bohack pay its debt.

"Stanley, We don't have the money," Frank said.

"Frank," I replied. "I know two million's a lot of money for most of us, but for you guys?"

"We don't have it," Frank said. "And we can't borrow any more. I want you to go to court and see what you can do."

Frank sent me the paperwork. I reviewed it until I found what I was looking for, and then went out to the court in Westbury. I appeared before Judge Redoyavich. The company had made several grievous technical mistakes in their filing. Maybe their lawyers were no good, or maybe they were just in a hurry, but I pointed out the mistakes to the judge, and he ruled in Bohack's favor. They wouldn't have to pay for now (and by the time the company refiled against Bohack, the supermarket chain was already in Chapter XI).

The second reason for my confidence was that Frank Knobel would have a significant say in who would do the filing for the Bohack Corporation. I had become friendly with Frank, talking to him on the phone several times a week. Like all of my clients, I'd given Frank my home phone number, and when he was in the midst of a legal hassle, I would literally put him to bed every night with a soothing discussion of the day's developments. I was also dealing with a host of legal matters for Frank, mainly involving his personal real-estate holdings. Frank was (and I hope he forgives me for this observation) a bit litigious by nature. He frequently found himself needing a lawyer by his side, and I knew Frank appreciated the way I dealt with lawsuits, employing a judicious mix of reasonableness and aggression. I called it: Litigate-Negotiate-Settle.

That July night, I remember standing outside of Joe Binder's, just looking around at the lights glimmering in the houses. Physical details seemed to jump out at me, and I noticed that the moon was shining on the leaves of the trees, casting silvered shadows across the neatly clipped grass, and the air was heavy and wet and still and scented with flowers.

I had the disconcerting feeling of time slipping backward, and I recalled those childhood summers of standing on the screened rooftop of the orphanage and looking out at the sky shimmering above Brooklyn and wondering why my parents had left me in that lonely brick and iron place.

I had no answer for that question in the 1930s, and forty years later, standing on a deserted front lawn in Oceanside, Long Island, I could only dimly perceive my parents' reasons.

Though they never mentioned it, the sadness and sense of failure they must have felt giving up their three young sons had to be heartbreaking. How difficult it must have been for Mother and Louie to live with the persistent friction in their marriage eroding any chance either of them had for happiness, especially given the desperation of their meager income and the long, hard hours they had to work during the downhill tumble of the Depression.

Yet all I clearly understood at that moment alone in the darkness on the moonlit lawn was that somehow my parents' motives didn't matter much to me anymore, thanks to Doris and Jeffrey and Lisa, and now, perhaps, to the financial hardships of the Bohack Corporation.

Glancing back at Joe Binder's house, I took a deep breath, still too excited to get in my car and drive home.

Maybe it was my turn, I thought, and promised myself—and Doris and the children—that this time I would do it right, no wild bets with hustlers like Marty Schulman. I still had a mountain of debt to pay off, and this case might provide me with the resources to get even. Furthermore, a successfully handled bankruptcy case in the eighty-to-ninety-million-dollar range could bestow upon an attorney a national reputation and make his career, bringing him the high-powered clients that most lawyers only dream about.

I was forty-five years old and had been waiting two decades for this opportunity. It sounds overly dramatic to me now, but as I stood in the humid darkness with a thousand thoughts whirling through my head I felt like the aging pitcher who has spent his career praying for a shot at playing in the World Series, and then suddenly the manager taps him to start the seventh game.

I looked over at the front door for a couple of minutes, wanting some company, eager to talk about the potential case. No one came out of the house. Then I got in my car and drove home.

CHAPTER 17

THE FILING

The English word bankruptcy has its origins in medieval Italy and reflects humanity's long-held prejudice against debtors. During the Middle Ages, when an Italian tradesman couldn't pay his debts, it was a common—and in my view, irrational—practice to destroy his workbench. This not only punished the tradesman for his inability to settle his bills but also removed any likelihood that he would do so in the foreseeable future. In Italian, this practice was known as *banca rotta*, literally "broken bench," and it is from this expression that our word bankruptcy derives. (In fairness to medieval Italian lawmakers, I should add that as harsh as losing a main tool of your trade must have been, citizens doubtlessly figured that a wrecked workbench was an improvement over the treatment of bankrupts during the Roman Empire, where supposedly debtors were dismembered and every creditor was awarded a pro-rated slice of his body.)

You can dismiss the treatment of medieval Italian debtors as belonging to a less enlightened epoch of history, but a century after the Middle Ages, bankrupts were no better off in merry old England than they had been in sunny Italy. Henry VIII was king when the first English bankruptcy laws were passed in 1542, and Henry had about as much patience with insolvent debtors as he did with his wives. A bankrupt was judged a criminal and treated like one, usually sentenced to prison and sometimes put to death. Either way, the creditors went unpaid.

Generally speaking, prior to the nineteenth century, the rules and practices of bankruptcy were intent on punishing the debtor and lacked the pragmatic remedy of attempting to keep him working so he could pay off his creditors. It wasn't until the 1800s, in the United States, the land of second chances, that bankruptcy laws were separated from the moral sphere and included common-sense provisions for the discharge of debt. Up until 1898, these federal statutes were primarily reactions to downward spirals in the economy. For example, the first federal bankruptcy law came about in 1800 because a pack of land speculators went bust. The second bankruptcy law was a response to the Panic of 1837, and Congress passed another law in the wake of the economic upheaval that followed the Civil War.

The Bankruptcy Act of 1898 was the first to provide distressed corporations with a means to be protected from creditors and to continue operations with the hope of regaining fiscal balance. The company could be put in an "equity receivership," which in my mind represents the birth of modern bankruptcy, an arrangement aimed not at social retribution or moral chastisement, but rather the financial rehabilitation of debtors.

The reorganization provision of 1898 was significantly broadened and formalized during the 1930s. As one would expect, the Great Depression yielded a rush of legislation, such as the Bankruptcy Act of 1933 and 1934, and the Chandler Act of 1938, which included substantial measures for the reorganization of struggling businesses.

From the Second World War until the summer when I became involved in the Bohack case, the laws didn't change much. With a few exceptions, America's economy was climbing steadily; inflation and unemployment were at record lows; and bankruptcy was seldom a topic in the news. As far as I can recall, by the 1970s, only two corporate bankruptcies had caused anything resembling a stir in the press: the Penn Central Transportation Corporation in 1970 and the W. T. Grant Company in 1975.

Over the next fifteen years, personal and corporate bustouts of the great and near-great would be headlined like World Series scores in both the financial pages and tabloids, and since there was such a glut of high-profile financial failures it has become difficult to remember when this wasn't true.

Yet to understand the Bohack matter in its historical context, it is important to know that during the early 1970s bankruptcy law was an issue of legislators replacing outdated views about business failures with attitudes more appropriate to a capitalistic society. Back then, we had the Bankruptcy Act, an incomplete series of laws when compared to what we have now, the Bankruptcy Code. In fact, it wasn't until December of 1977, while I was buried deep in the middle of the Bohack case, (which had been widely reported in *The Wall Street Journal* and the *New York Times*), that federal lawmakers finally decided hearings on the bankruptcy statutes were needed, and as a result I was called to Washington to testify before Congress.

I'm getting a bit ahead of myself here, but my point is that since bankruptcy law was in its infancy and bankruptcy filings were rare, the practitioners of this type of law were limited. The legal profession appeared to have deemed the practice of bankruptcy law an inconsequential subspecialty of business law, a perception that was underscored by the fact that for a long time judges didn't even hear the cases. That supposedly undistinguished assignment was left to referees, lawyers who would oversee the process for a modest fee and who would be supervised by a district court judge.

Additionally, it wasn't easy to find established law firms willing to take on bankruptcy matters. In New York City, as I recall, there was just one major firm, Levin & Weintraub, who took bankruptcy cases on a regular basis. The rest of the work was performed by attorneys whose reputations were often akin to ambulance chasers, bottom feeders who would do anything for a buck, earning negligible profits from minor misfortunes.

While the laws were instituted and redrafted over the years, it seemed that regardless of how the statutes were transformed by Congress and state legislatures, bankrupts continued to be morally tainted, as though by definition these unfortunate souls were dishonest, and this false and patently unfair perception rubbed off on any attorney who helped them with their difficulties.

Although you would have been hard-pressed to locate a white-shoe lawyer to take your bankruptcy case, you could find plenty of small-timers willing to assist a hapless debtor. All you had to do was look behind the musty, dog-eared stacks of books, briefs, and journals in one of the dark, cell-like law offices on Court Street in Brooklyn. Here you would find lawyers who were frequently struggling to make ends meet, and they would take on your troubles and do a decent job for you, all the while earning the undying disrespect of their allegedly higher-tone colleagues. Thus, in New York City, decades after these practitioners were dead and gone, referring to any attorney as "a Court Street lawyer," became an attack on his professional reputation, and because the majority of these attorneys had been Jewish, an anti-Semitic slur as well.

Underneath the quasi-moral objections that numerous lawyers had to getting involved in bankruptcy matters, I suspect that many of these attorneys were frightened off by the very real financial risks of handling a bankruptcy. Prior to the passing of the new Bankruptcy Code, the sole payment lawyers were permitted during a bankruptcy case was a retainer paid at the start. After your initial payment, regardless of how long the case dragged on, you went on the creditor list like everyone else and the debtor was barred by law from paying you until he was in the black again.

This presented a pair of distinct challenges to an attorney. First, you had to hope that the creditors and the judge approved your plan for coming out of Chapter XI in a timely fashion because if you couldn't win their approval and you allowed too much time to elapse, you would have invested a lawyer's most valuable asset—his time— in a losing venture, and you would shortly find your own practice in financial trouble. Secondly, you had to make sure that the plan you helped your client put together was realistic enough that his company would come out of bankruptcy. Otherwise, if he failed to emerge with a new and viable entity, you wouldn't see a dime.

I can easily understand lawyers shying away from this type of risk, but the truth is that I was attracted to it. Early on in my practice I saw that working purely as an attorney I would never get rich. There weren't enough billable hours in a day for me to earn the kind of money I wanted to earn, the kind that buys you freedom from worrying about money. That was the reason I'd gone into business with Schulman. However, as the Bohack drama played itself out in the press, I realized that bankruptcy work in general offered an attorney a unique opportunity. He could trade all or some of his fees for stock in the new entity that he helped create and wind up owning a valuable piece of a company.

Beyond the potential rewards, I was itching to dive into the game because handling a sizable bankruptcy was about as close as you could get to gambling without going to the track or calling a bookie. If you won you got a substantial fee for your work; if not, you went home broke. Except I was sure that if I got the shot I wouldn't lose, and what better animal to bet on than yourself?

It was during this period that I came to see a striking similarity between Louie and me. Without question, my father's gambling had been the bane of my early family life. Yet Louie's impulse to risk it all was alive and well within me, and I fervently believe that I could have become a degenerate gambler. But I was luckier than Louie. I became a bankruptcy lawyer instead.

On July 26, 1974, Frank Knobel phoned me and said that some of Bohack's produce suppliers were holding a meeting to discuss the chain's current status among its creditors. An attorney for the New York Produce Association, which operated out of the Hunts Point market in the Bronx, had gone so far as to try and pressure Bohack by revealing to reporters the reason for the meeting. The attorney stated that one hundred-plus members of his association were meeting to see how many of them were owed money by Bohack and to discuss the corporation's ability to pay its creditors.

Frank said, "Their lawyer's been calling Binder's office all day. Joe isn't returning his calls."

"Can't say that I blame him."

Frank said, "There's worse news," and then he told me that another lawyer, Harvey Goldstein, a partner in the firm of Finkel, Nadler & Goldstein, had been trying to get in touch with Binder, and Joe was avoiding him as well. Goldstein announced to *The Wall Street Journal* that his firm represented a number of "very substantial food suppliers," and some of his clients hadn't been paid since last May. When the reporter asked Goldstein how much money was outstanding, Goldstein replied, "We are talking about millions, not [hundreds of thousands]. Bohack is a force in the food industry in the New York metropolitan area and they've weathered many storms. We're interested in talking to them to find out how we can help. It would be a bad scene in this industry if Bohack went down."

I said to Frank, "Sounds like your creditors either want to get paid now or they want you in Chapter XI."

"That's what I figure," he said. "I hear Bohack's the number-one topic of discussion at Hunts Point."

I said, "It makes sense. A lot of people are worried about getting hurt. They think you're dead. The AMEX isn't even trading your stock anymore."

Frank was quiet for a moment. At last, he said, "Stanley, can you come out here and talk?"

"Sure, Frank."

As I packed up my briefcase to leave, I told my partner, Jesse Levine, that he better close his open matters and clear his desk, because I thought we were going to get the Bohack filing and he would be busy for the next year or two. My estimate proved woefully short. It would take five years to dispose of the case, and it would require Jesse and me to work day and night. As a result, he'd gain fifty pounds, and I'd wind up with a scar on my heart.

I went out to meet Frank at Bohack Square, the supermarket chain's sprawling thirty-seven-and-a-half-acre complex of offices, warehouses, and trucking and maintenance facilities that ran along the Brooklyn-Queens line. Frank was sick and tired of hanging around his office so we took a walk. In the summer sunlight, his Bankruptcy Pallor was especially pronounced.

Frank said, "Stanley, you figure you and Jesse can do this filing? You, you're gonna be negotiating till you drop, and Jesse's gonna get buried under a mountain of paperwork."

I felt my pulse quicken. "Don't worry, Frank. We'll take care of it."

Frank said, "Technically, we can file in Brooklyn or Queens. Where do you think we ought to file?"

I said, "Do you have a coin?"

"What?"

"A coin," I said. "A nickel, a dime, a quarter. You know, a coin."

Frank dipped into his pants pocket and handed me a quarter.

Tossing the quarter into the air, I called out, "Heads it's Brooklyn, tails it's Queens."

The coin landed on the sidewalk, rolled for moment, spun slowly and finally fell flat.

We bent over it: Tails. We'd file in Queens.

I picked up the quarter and gave it back to Frank. He said, "You're going to need some upfront money."

I nodded.

"How much?" he asked.

"Seventy-five thousand," I said. It was the first number that popped into my head. I probably could've gotten twice that amount, but I didn't want to appear greedy in the wake of Bohack's misfortune, and seventy-five was the biggest retainer that I'd ever been given. It would also be terribly inadequate to cover my costs. Naturally, I didn't know that yet, and at the moment it seemed like an awful lot of money.

Frank said, "I'll have them cut you a check when we get back to the office. But now we got one more thing to kick around."

"Go ahead, Frank."

He said, "I spoke to Bluhdorn, and from what he says I don't think he wants us to file for a Chapter."

I thought Frank had lost his mind and stopped dead in my tracks. "What the hell are you talking about?" I said. "Charlie cut off your money from Manny Hanny. He's responsible for your goddamn cash crunch."

Frank laughed. He said, "Stanley, have you ever seen the Gulf and Western Building?"

"Yeah, Frank. I've seen the Gulf and Western Building."

"Well, then listen, Stanley. Bluhdorn's ego is bigger than the Gulf and Western Building. You understand? He hates to lose. Charlie doesn't like stories in the papers about him being a big stockholder in a company that's about to fall on its ass."

I shook my head. Charlie definitely sounded a bit nuts, but maybe you had to be to start out with nothing and wind up creating a corporate empire like Gulf and Western. But Bluhdorn's reluctance to give his blessing to a Chapter XI filing presented me with a critical tactical hitch. Bohack needed the approval of its board of directors to file, and Charlie controlled the board through a solid network of financial and personal relationships.

As the majority stockholder in the company, Bluhdorn had been on the eight-member board until February 1973, which was when Gulf and Western made its unsuccessful tender offer for the Great Atlantic & Pacific Tea Company. At the time, Bluhdorn had placed his 256,393 Bohack shares in a trust with the company's president, Joe Binder.

Binder, however, had no say over the votes represented by those shares. Bluhdorn bestowed that honor on another Bohack board member, a longtime friend, Don Gaston.

In late July of 1973, after the A&P had beaten back Bluhdorn's takeover attempt, Charlie didn't retake his seat on the Bohack board. He didn't need to. Along with Gaston, the board included Roy Abbott Jr., a senior vice president of Gulf and Western, and Joel Dolkart, a senior partner in the law firm of Simpson, Thacher & Bartlett, which represented G&W.

These three guys, according to Frank, would stop us from filing simply because Bluhdorn didn't want his name publicly connected to a financially troubled venture. I thought about that for minute and revised my earlier opinion of Charlie. A bit nuts was too generous.

I said to Frank, "You don't think you can convince any of the three?"

He sighed. "You know, Dolkart's not a bad guy. Both of us used to belong to the Inwood Country Club. Before I invested with Bohack, Dolkart invited me to lunch at the club. I didn't know him very well, just to say hello to in the locker room or the bar, and I was surprised by the invitation. So we got together, and in the middle of lunch, he says, 'Frank, don't go into business with Charlie Bluhdorn. I'm his lawyer, and I'm telling you to stay away from him.'

"I had no idea what the hell was going on. Charlie had agreed to sell me fifty thousand Bohack shares from Southwest Holdings, which was the investment company he ran. I thought Charlie figured the shares were about to jump in price and he didn't want to lose the profit, so he sent Dolkart to scare me off. But that wasn't it. Dolkart was sincere; he was trying to give me some good advice. I should've listened to him. I've got almost everything I own tied up in Bohack, and I'm not gonna come away with much, am I, Stanley?"

I knew what Frank was going through, and I felt sick remembering that feeling I'd had when Schulman walked into my office to tell me we were broke.

I said, "It gonna be okay, Frank. I promise."

Frank said, "Charlie would be happy to let Bohack flounder on forever, taking the banks' money without any hope of ever paying them back. It's got to be over with, Stanley. It's not right. As things are now, we're carrying too much debt, and there's no way Bohack can get back on its feet. I can't be involved with this anymore. I feel like everybody's getting screwed. Me included."

"We're gonna file," I said. "Charlie Goodell is on the Bohack board, isn't he? He's a straight shooter. Call him up, explain things to him. And who's the other board guy you mentioned?"

Frank said, "John Timothy Collins."

"Does Bluhdorn control him?"

"Maybe not," said Frank. "He's always been square with me, and he doesn't owe Bluhdorn any favors I know about."

"So talk to him," I said. "Explain what's going on, that Bohack's going under unless they reorganize. When Binder spoke to these two guys they didn't want Manny Hanny lending you more money. Maybe it wasn't because Bluhdorn was breathing down their necks. Maybe it was just good judgment. Line up Goodell and Collins. That's two votes, you and Binder are on the board; Joe's with you, so that's four votes, and then you have Marvin Lerner. Will he go with you?"

"Probably," Frank said.

"Terrific," I replied. "Get a board meeting together tonight, I'll come along, and we'll make our pitch to file for the Chapter."

Frank said that he would phone Goodell and Collins and arrange a meeting of the board as soon as he got to his office.

"But what about Dolkart, Abbott, and Gaston?" he asked. "You don't know how it is, Stanley. I'm chairman of the board, except I might as well be serving the coffee and cake. Those three are Bluhdorn puppets. No kidding. When the board meets it's like their mouths move, but it's Charlie's voice coming out, and it intimidates people. They don't vote like they should, but like they think Charlie wants them to."

"Don't worry about those guys," I said. "I'm not sure how much longer they're gonna be on the board."

Frank said, "You got a plan."

"Sure, I got a plan, Frank. That's what lawyers do. We make plans."

Frank smiled. "What kind of plan?"

"I'm going to insult them," I said.

By the time I arrived at Bohack Square for the board meeting, Frank had Charlie Goodell and John Timothy Collins lined up behind him. Frank introduced me to the board, and I did my spiel about Bohack's current financial distress, pointing out that a Chapter XI would remedy their most pressing hardship, that being their crushing debt load.

Once you file, I explained, all of your debt goes up on the shelf, and your creditors, even the State of New York, to whom Bohack owed $600,000 in sales tax, are stayed from collecting any monies due them. You can go back into business and try to come up with a plan that can keep you alive long enough to settle with your creditors for a percentage of what you owe, meanwhile turning your operation into something worth keeping or selling to another company.

Predictably, the instant I finished, Bluhdorn's puppets—Abbott, Dolkart, and Gaston—began their protest. I don't remember their specific objections to the filing, but initially I responded politely by asking them to present a viable alternative. Without mentioning Bluhdorn's name, I added that while some people involved in Bohack might find a voluntary petition of bankruptcy embarrassing, the chain's debt was so overwhelming that the creditors could easily force Bohack into Chapter, which would look even worse on the financial pages of the newspapers and perhaps as a lead story on the local TV stations.

Abbott, Dolkart, and Gaston acted as though I hadn't said a word and continued to lodge objections to the filing without offering any other options save for going on with business as usual, which was ridiculous, since at best it would be only a matter of weeks before the creditors would have no choice but to push Bohack into bankruptcy.

I looked over at Frank. Then I turned on the three men, replacing the polite tone in my voice with as much contempt as I could muster. I don't recall the precise details of what I said to Abbott, Dolkart, and Gaston, but my guess is that it had been a while since anyone had spoken to them in just such a manner. I probably used the words "ignorant, stupid, sloppy, childish, ridiculous, dishonest, criminal," and a bunch of other related adjectives, and I think it was Dolkart who got so angry that he jumped out of his chair and tendered his resignation on the spot. The other two weren't far behind him, and suddenly Charlie Bluhdorn had lost his backers on the Bohack board.

The following evening, at an emergency board meeting, the remaining five directors voted unanimously to file for reorganization.

On July 30, 1974, the Bohack Corporation filed a petition for reorganization under Chapter XI of the Federal Bankruptcy Act in the U.S. District Court in Queens. The company claimed that nineteen months of "the most difficult period for the supermarket industry" had robbed them of their working capital, a situation that had been exacerbated by a "destructive price competition." In the petition, Jesse and I wrote that the company had made numerous good faith efforts to cut costs, and we presented an outline of a plan for Bohack to return to health; improving its data processing to maintain higher levels of inventory turnover and improved cash flow; reducing the size of its work force; and continuing to shut down unprofitable supermarkets.

On the petition, Bohack listed its creditors, and the amount the corporation owed was staggering. Its fourteen biggest creditors were due $24.5 million, and there were four banks among them, never a good sign, because in the 1970s banks, unlike business creditors, were generally less willing to settle a debt for less on the dollar. The Manufacturers Hanover Trust Company was Bohack's largest debt, $9.8 million, followed by the National Bank of North America, $3.8 million; the Security National Bank, $3.8 million; and finally Hartford's Connecticut Bank and Trust Company, $1 million. Other creditors included the Consolidated Edison Company, $400,000, the Long Island Lighting Company, $440,000, and over a thousand food suppliers.

Charlie Bluhdorn released a statement through a Gulf and Western spokesman claiming that he was surprised by Bohack's filing for protection under Chapter XI. From the disinterested nature of the statement one could get the impression that the matter hardly concerned him at all, but although I didn't know it then, nothing could have been further from the truth.

The most pressing item on my Bohack agenda was to prepare a presentation for an unofficial creditors meeting. Since the company owed money to hundreds of businesses, both small and large, we anticipated a tremendous turnout and scheduled the session for one of the ballrooms at the Waldorf-Astoria Hotel in Manhattan. Although nothing binding would be determined at that meeting, it was obvious to me that if I couldn't convince the audience that they would get a fair portion of the funds they were due, all of Bohack's assets would be liquidated at fire-sale prices.

Jesse and I worked seventeen hours a day, huddling with the Bohack people, crunching numbers and cobbling together the makings of an operational plan to keep the supermarket chain alive. I was spending so much time at Bohack Square that I was given my own office. As I was preparing for my pitch at the Waldorf, I was grateful that I'd been through a career in politics, because in this instance I saw my basic job as being closer to that of a candidate than to an attorney. At the Waldorf, I was going to have to stand up in front of an audience—most of whom were nervous and many of whom were angry—and attempt to persuade them that if they would trust me, I'd help straighten out this mess, and they would wind up better off than if they forced Bohack to cease operations. At bottom, I was doing nothing more than asking people for their vote.

Ironically, right before the meeting, I got a surprising blast from my political past. Donald Manes, who was then serving as president of the Borough of Queens County, phoned and asked me if I'd come see him at his office. With Bohack paperwork piling up on my desk, I didn't really have an hour to spare, but I'd always liked Donny, and as I said earlier, I never lost my appetite for politics and even the most trivial glimpse behind the scenes could amuse me for weeks.

So I met with Donny. It was good seeing him again, and we had a cup of coffee and made small talk. Then Donny said: "Congratulations, I hear you're gonna be taking care of the Bohack filing."

I swelled up with pride, glad that Donny had heard about it. However, if I hadn't been out of front-line politics for a couple of years, I would have seen where Donny was heading and cut him off. But I was rusty, and at that moment, a tad too pleased with myself.

Donny said, "Yeah, everyone says it's gonna be a big case. What kind of fee do you figure you'll get?"

That got my attention. A politician talks about money, you better make sure your wallet is safe in your pocket. I said, "Depends how things shake out. If I can't get a plan approved by the creditors and the court, I get *bupkes*."

Donny said, "I hear it's gonna be a lot of work for you and Jesse. Maybe you could use some help?"

"We'll be fine," I said.

"No kidding, Stan," Donny said. "I know a law firm that wants a piece of this action."

I said, "I'm sure you do, but they're not getting any."

Donny said, "That's not the way things are done. You're trying this case in Queens. You gotta give out a taste."

"No I don't" I said, furious with myself, because I hadn't seen this coming.

I tried to change the subject, but I gave up when Donny wouldn't quit trying to steer me to another firm.

Finally, I left, sadder and wiser, and promising myself never to forget the uglier side of politics.

The unofficial creditors meeting at the Waldorf-Astoria was standing room only, but as I stood at the microphone and spoke about Bohack's real possibility for recovery, my attention was focused on the first row of chairs, where representatives from seven banks were seated.

It was no secret that if I couldn't persuade the bankers to let their loans ride for a while we were dead in the water. Beyond convincing them to wait for their money, I was in what seemed like an impossible position with Manufacturers Hanover. I was not only going to have to prevail upon Manny Hanny to hold off on the $10 million that Bohack owed them, but I had to convince the bank that it would be in their best interest to continue lending Bohack money so they could operate.

I spoke for over an hour at the Waldorf, and while none of the creditors was thrilled with the situation, I did manage to instill a measure of hope in them, at least enough for them to vote for the half a dozen or so people who would serve on the official Creditors' Committee, approving or disapproving of Bohack's operational plans until the corporation had successfully moved out of Chapter XI. Eventually, Harvey Goldstein and Conrad Duberstein (now Chief Bankruptcy Judge of the U.S. Eastern District Court of New York), became the attorneys for the Creditors' Committee.

I wasn't sure how I had made out with the bankers—those folks could stay deadpan at the circus—but for the time being they weren't going to force Bohack out of business, and I made an appointment for the next morning to meet with a representative from Manufacturers Hanover.

The guy I had to talk to at Manny Hanny was one of the bank's directors and their senior attorney, Al Christy. Al was an older gentleman who dressed in the elegantly somber style of British nobility, and in banking circles he was referred to as the "White Fox."

In essence, I told Al that if Manufacturers Hanover, Bohack's biggest creditor, refused to extend the chain credit, no one would have any confidence in Bohack's recovery, credit would be impossible to find, and the company would never get out of Chapter.

On the other hand, I said, if the bank did make funds available, the suppliers would follow suit, and I believed that Bohack would have a real shot at paying off an appreciable portion of its debt.

Al sat behind his cherry-wood desk and studied me while I spoke, saying nothing, his eyes narrowed in concentration. When I was done, he said, "Son, it's not companies that pay you back, it's people. I trust you, and we'll lend you the money. However, I want you to make sure we get it back."

I was flattered, but they didn't call Al Christy the White Fox for nothing. He agreed to extend Bohack credit at a hefty interest rate; I believe it was 12 percent; and he wanted a kicker at the end, a bonus payout or stock in the new entity that would be created when Bohack came out of Chapter.

Bohack had no other reasonable choice but to accept the terms, and although I took Al Christy's faith in me as a compliment, the truth was that Manny Hanny was in a rough spot. They could have let Bohack go under, but then they would have had to kiss their

$10 million good-bye. Given the conservative corporate rules of banks—rules that require employees to be held strictly accountable for decisions that go sour, odds were good that some people would lose their jobs for lending Bohack such substantial sums in the first place.

I learned an important lesson about dealing with banks during the Bohack case, a lesson that would be borne out repeatedly during my career as a bankruptcy attorney: If you owe a bank $10,000, then it's your problem. If you owe them $10 million, then it's their problem.

By mid-August, *The Wall Street Journal* was announcing that Bohack had been advanced $2.5 million of a new $5 million credit line, the purpose of which was to induce the reopening of credit from suppliers. The remaining $2.5 million would be given to Bohack as trade credit became available. Furthermore, the bank agreed that it would allow Bohack the opportunity to work itself out of debt. This was reassuring to suppliers who were now confident that they wouldn't get burned by advancing Bohack goods, only to have Manny Hanny swoop in and grab everything before Bohack had paid them. No other bank was willing to lend Bohack money, but as I anticipated, once Manufacturers Hanover signed on, the suppliers fell into line.

CHAPTER 18

A FORCED REST

As I mentioned, until the 1980s bankruptcy was considered by many in the legal community to be work reserved for bottom feeders, and nowhere was this more apparent than in the selection of the site of the Bankruptcy Court for the County of Queens. Originally, the court was located in the Jamaica section of the county, in a rundown firetrap of an office, right above a furniture store and just below a methadone clinic. The bankruptcy court was eventually forced to abandon the locale when drug addicts, who were singularly unimpressed by the majesty of the court, began increasing their earning potential by regularly mugging attorneys and legal secretaries within sight of the courthouse.

Owing to the tireless efforts of Judge C. Albert Parente, who was in charge of the Bohack Chapter XI and who was soon to be the chief U.S. bankruptcy judge for the Eastern District of New York, the court was relocated to a building in a safer part of Queens, though the trappings of the court itself were not greatly improved. Judge Parente's chambers consisted of a small open space for his desk and library, and another small space was reserved for the clerk's office. The courtroom was a large, rectangular area with a scuffed floor, peeling walls, and grimy windows with cracked panes, and it looked as if it had formerly done time as the storage room for a discount carpet warehouse. It did have a raised podium for the judge's bench and a witness stand, but otherwise it was empty save for the rows of plastic molded chairs, the kind of chairs you might sit on in any reasonably well-decorated school cafeteria.

Judge Parente was responsible for every bankruptcy case filed in Queens County, which at the time had a population of two and a quarter million people, and a substantial number of businesses. Before the Bohack case landed in his courtroom, Judge Parente had approximately three hundred other cases on his calendar, and his ability to juggle his responsibilities was an act of dexterity that is probably unparalleled in legal history.

At the first hearing for the Bohack Chapter XI, the creditors had to wedge themselves into the courtroom. Dozens of issues were raised, both legal and practical, but each one had at its heart the same questions: What was the jurisdiction of the bankruptcy court? How extensive was Judge Parente's power to defend Bohack against the claims of the creditors? Which cases could be decided in Queens? And which ones had to go to the district court for a ruling or to state court?

Since bankruptcy had long been a neglected aspect of the law, the answers to these questions were frequently unclear. This lack of clarity over jurisdictional matters provided seemingly unending opportunities for the creditors' attorneys to try to collect money for their clients. Any time a creditor was seeking quick relief that should have been denied him due to the protection provided by a Chapter XI, his lawyer would march into Judge Parente's courtroom and raise a jurisdictional issue.

Now, I would not only have to argue against this creditor's original claim, but try to persuade Judge Parente that he was the one who should hear the case. Meanwhile, Judge Parente would have to make a complicated ruling even before a hearing on the merits of the original case could proceed. This ate up enormous blocks of time and made my life, and the life of my partner, Jesse Levine, impossible.

The creditors' attorneys freely pursued this strategy, unrestrained by the Bankruptcy Act. Their actions were chiefly responsible for the fact that there was a staggering number of proceedings during the course of the administration of the Bohack case, about five hundred of them. Four hundred and thirty of these were adversary proceedings commenced in the bankruptcy court, and there were an additional forty-eight other contested matters. This is a conservative estimate because it doesn't include those cases that came back two or three times before the court on various motions. Furthermore, at the direction of Judge Parente, Jesse and I had to litigate about seventy-five additional Bohack matters in other courts.

The foundation of the creditors' strategy rested on the perception that Judge Parente was the friend of the debtor, so they attempted to seek other forums for the sole purpose of receiving what they perceived to be a friendlier hearing. In my view, it was a misperception: Judge Parente was no friend of Bohack; he was simply doing his job by protecting the supermarket chain from creditors.

Thanks to the widespread bankruptcy experience of the 1980s and the transformation of the Bankruptcy Act into the Bankruptcy Code, the frantic reaction that occurred during the Bohack case would never happen again. Today, creditors and their attorneys are far too sophisticated about the legal protections provided by a Chapter, and creditors rarely waste their resources attacking such a company. But back in 1974, the Bohack filing was an unfamiliar and confusing experience, and everyone was scared so everyone was scrambling. As soon as Bohack filed, several large creditors commenced reclamation proceedings, attempting to recover goods that had been delivered to Bohack shortly before the filing of the bankruptcy petition. It sounds like a reasonable response by creditors. Except the goods they were trying to recover were, by their nature, impossible to reclaim. Missouri Beef Packers, for example, instituted a claim for $900,000 and tried to win the court's permission to retrieve the beef it had shipped to Bohack. Even if the court had granted Missouri Beef permission, what was the company going to do? Order their lawyers to march up to the meat displays in the supermarkets and start pointing at wrapped packages of hamburger and steak and say, "That's our client's!" and then grab it?

Hardly.

Yet Missouri Beef did file in court, which chewed up a fair amount of time, and believe it or not, as ridiculous as their claim was, they probably spent considerable money in legal fees.

In almost every case, the jurisdiction of the bankruptcy court to preserve and protect Bohack's assets was challenged by the creditors. One of their most popular strategies was to go into state court to enforce liens against the supermarket chain's property. Thus, for openers, Judge Parente was forced to determine, at least on a temporary basis, issues of jurisdiction relating to liens under the Uniform Commercial Code. He was required to do this only with the aid of a volunteer legal assistant, a very limited library, and no support staff to help him conduct hearings. The small clerical staff that he did have was tied up doing the daily business of the bankruptcy court, pushing the paper on the other three hundred cases that Judge Parente had to deal with during the first year of the Bohack Chapter XI.

Even when Judge Parente ruled in favor of Bohack, we found that his power to enforce his rulings was curtailed by law. At one point, an auctioneer deliberately conducted an auction of Bohack's property in violation of a restraining order issued by Judge Parente. Knowing that the contempt power of the bankruptcy court was limited to the ability to levy a small fine, the auctioneer said, "I've done this before and I haven't gone to jail yet."

During the summer and fall of 1974, the main squabble I got into with creditors was over the leases that Bohack held on its buildings. Many of these leases were financially burdensome, especially the ones on stores that Bohack had closed, and the supermarket chain needed to terminate these leasing agreements if they were going to reduce their overhead, a necessary step for them to come out of Chapter.

Naturally, the landlords wanted to be paid before allowing Bohack to cancel the leases, and they went to court to force the payment. There were over one hundred of these cases, and it was extremely frustrating work. Both sides had to present their arguments to Judge Parente, and he'd have to do the legal research. The biggest complicating factor in his research was that several new decisions regarding leases of a company in Chapter XI had been handed down by the Court of Appeals, and Judge Parente, without the assistance of a law clerk, was forced to do an exhaustive investigation of the case law to interpret these rulings.

One day, outside the courtroom, a frustrated landlord began shouting at me, accusing me of being a shyster crook who was helping Bohack renege on its responsibilities. I ignored the guy until he took a swing at me, and Frank Knobel was forced to break up a fistfight right in the hall.

Leasing was also an issue with regard to the fixtures—such as refrigerators and freezers—that Bohack used in its stores. The corporation owed over $5 million to various equipment leasing companies. The companies threatened to reclaim their property and pull them out of the supermarkets, which would have closed Bohack down. Obviously, this was a priority issue for Bohack, and I handled the situation through negotiation.

I met with the representatives of the leasing companies all at one time. I explained to them that if they reclaimed their equipment and tried to sell it on the open market, they'd get pennies on the dollar. However, if they left the equipment in the stores, Bohack would not miss a monthly payment, and the leasing company would come out ahead on their bottom line. The representatives grumbled about it, understandably, and a couple of them threatened to go get their equipment, but when all was said and done they left their equipment where it was and collected their payments.

Perhaps my biggest headache during the five-year course of the Bohack bankruptcy proceedings revolved around labor relations. If Bohack was going to emerge from Chapter XI, the chain was going to have to reduce its overhead, and so in successive stages they shut down their warehousing and trucking operations. By early July of 1975, Bohack had terminated these operations and turned to wholesalers or other supermarket chains with extra space in their warehousing facilities, and these other companies acted as purchasing agents and distributors for Bohack.

As a result of these cost-cutting measures, Bohack was forced to lay off their warehousemen and drivers. I made the rounds trying to negotiate with these groups, meeting their leaders and the rank and file at bars around New York. I tried to keep it out of court, but the issues were too complex and a substantial amount of vigorous litigation ensued. Two of the more prominent legal issues that were raised, and which reached the Court of Appeals, were the questions of severance pay and the right to arbitrate under a rejected bargaining agreement.

The warehousemen claimed that they had a right to severance pay as an administration expense because their jobs had been cut during the Chapter XI. Judge Parente had to investigate and found that Bohack was obligated to pay the severance because of a decision in a Second Circuit Court case. However, in a different case, the First Circuit reached an opposite conclusion, which was eventually sustained by the First Circuit Court of Appeals. Bohack, being bound by the Second Circuit decision, applied for certiorari to the Supreme Court but the corporation was denied that review.

If this sounds confusing, then you have an idea of how I felt while we were thrashing out these disagreements. It would have been far simpler had bankruptcy judges possessed the status to which they were legitimately entitled. I believe that the Supreme Court refused to hear the case because of the Justices' lack of familiarity with the practical problems of administering a Chapter XI. And the higher courts' general reluctance to heed the views of bankruptcy judges is simply because the law refuses to grant them the prestige they deserve.

The next major labor issue centered on the power of the bankruptcy court to enjoin a strike that began after Bohack let its Teamsters go and applied to the court for permission to reject the contract of Local 807. *Bohack v. Local 807* highlighted areas where the need for the expanded jurisdiction of the bankruptcy court was obvious. First, under the Taft-Hartley Act, the bankruptcy court was held to be without the authority to stop a strike, even though in the *Boys Market* case the Supreme Court had decided to the contrary. The district court, which by statute was charged with the responsibility of overseeing Judge Parente, ruled that only they could enjoin a strike, regardless of the merits, and that the bankruptcy judge did not have that power as an adjunct of the district court.

The injunction ordered by the district court threatened Bohack's existence, because it cost the company funds that it desperately needed to continue operating. The position of Local 807 was that their strike was legal because Bohack refused to comply with an arbitration award that had been made by a local joint council, despite the fact that the council was held in contravention of the Bankruptcy Act itself, and Judge Parente should have been empowered to make this ruling. But he wasn't, and Bohack wound up spending money it could not afford to spend.

Another labor problem arose that would have been comical if it didn't involve the subject of discrimination. During the Chapter XI the New York City Human Rights Commission sought to force Bohack to institute an affirmative action program just as the supermarket chain was laying off hundreds of workers. Now the company was supposed to hire minorities when it lacked the capital to hire anyone at all. Eventually, Bohack consented to a lifting of the stay of suits to negotiate this matter, but again the bankruptcy court should have been able to intervene. Yet, as with the Teamsters, Judge Parente's hands were tied.

By virtue of the fragmentation of legal jurisdiction, the Bohack bankruptcy began to seem like a round of ceaseless bickering, and it was enraging. I began to feel that if Congress, state legislatures, and the federal judiciary simply wanted financially troubled businesses to shut their doors, then Chapter XI protection should be revoked. However, once this protection was extended to corporations, the bankruptcy judge should have been given the necessary clout to enable the company to survive.

By July of 1975, Jesse and I were holding our own against the tidal wave of secured creditors and their lawyers. Although once a company is in Chapter XI every penny of the old debt goes up on the shelf and stays there, this fact didn't discourage the Creditors' Committee from trying to rush us to create a payment plan, however detrimental to Bohack, so the unsecured creditors could receive some money. I can't say that I blame the lawyers. Bankruptcy law in 1974 was not a work of art, and had I been a lawyer for a creditor, I might have tried the same thing.

Manufacturers Hanover Trust was not as rabid as these creditors, but the bank was certainly worried about the millions that they had on the line, and Manny Hanny required frequent assurance that Bohack was doing everything possible to cut costs and increase profits, and would be able to emerge from Chapter XI as some sort of viable financial entity. In order to reassure the bank, we had to prepare periodic presentations. I was usually in charge of the show, and one of them I'll never forget because I had to be carried into it on a stretcher.

Doris and I had gone to the Catskills to see Jeffrey at summer camp. She had become increasingly concerned about how hard I was working, and so on the Friday night before visiting day, we checked into a motel and I tried to get some rest. By Saturday morning, though, I was sick as a dog with a wicked headache, terrible chills, a high fever that aspirin didn't touch, and finally blood seeping from my ears. I was rushed by ambulance to the hospital in Liberty, New York, and admitted. Doris went off to visit Jeffrey, while the doctors examined me and discovered that I had a serious ear infection, which they treated by ordering me to stay in bed and pumping me full of antibiotics. Bohack had a presentation to Manny Hanny scheduled for Monday, so I called Frank Knobel in New York and told him about my sudden illness and that it didn't look like I'd make it.

Frank said, "Stanley, you have to make it. We screw this up and Manny Hanny cuts off our money and Bohack is history."

I said, "The doctors don't want me leaving the hospital."

"What about an ambulance?" Frank asked. "Will they let you come down in a plane with a doctor and nurse?"

"They might," I said.

"Find out," Frank said. "I'll pick up the tab."

Doris was skeptical about the idea, but the doctors agreed. I was scared, and fortunately the day of my flight the small airport nearby was fogged in, so the orderlies loaded me into the back of an ambulance, and in the company of a nurse, I rode down Route 17, with the lights flashing and the siren screaming, to Bohack Square, whereupon I was carried into the conference room, got off the stretcher, helped make the presentation, and then was taken home and put to bed.

I recovered quickly, which was fortunate, since there always seemed to be more work than I could do when it came to Bohack. Given the bankruptcy laws of the time as well as my own obsession with making the most of this opportunity to further my career, handling the Chapter XI of such a large corporation was, to say the least, a demanding task. My typical weekday began around seven in the morning. I'd shower, dress, grab a cup of coffee, and check in with Jesse. Because I was now zipping all over the city on behalf of Bohack, the company was kind enough to assign me a driver and a car, and he'd pick me up at my house around eight (a convenience that spoiled me, so right up until today I continue to use a driver.)

More often than not, I'd start out in Judge Parente's courtroom in Queens, answering the latest motion or filing one of my own. I'd generally finish around noon and go over to my makeshift office at Bohack Square, where I would spend the next five or six hours putting out fires, helping to decide which bills could legally be paid, talking to angry creditors and their screaming or smooth-talking lawyers, and occasionally advising Frank Knobel on a host of cost-cutting measures.

Following a fast dinner, I'd be driven to my law office on Lexington Avenue to go over the day's events and the upcoming court appearances with Jesse. I'd work in Manhattan until nine or ten, and then be driven back to my house in Flushing, where I would get on the phone with Frank and Joe Binder and outline for them where Bohack stood. Finally, I'd read briefs until after midnight and fall asleep wearing my glasses with the documents spread out around Doris and me on the blankets.

Weekends were hardly distinguishable from the weekdays. The only difference was that I didn't have to be in court, and I mainly worked at my law office and at home, spending hours on the phone with Bohack's officers, reassuring them that their supermarkets would be able to make it into the next week.

After a year of this pace I was beat, and I missed seeing Doris and the kids. However, I had also never been happier practicing law. It was thoroughly exhausting, but it was also exhilarating, and strangely enough, the exhaustion seemed to feed the exhilaration. I was living on adrenalin and walked around slightly high, safe and secure in a bright and merry twilight zone that was lit with the facts and figures of the Bohack Chapter XI and resounded with dozens of courtroom voices.

It might have gone like that until the conclusion of the case, but I was forty-six years old, an unwise age to be burning the candle at both ends, and so one Saturday morning in late May, while I was reading a brief on the living-room couch, I told Doris that I needed to head upstairs and take a nap.

For some reason, she seemed alarmed and asked me what was wrong.

"I feel sluggish and my stomach hurts," I said, going up to our room.

In bed, I tossed and turned, but couldn't fall asleep.

Pretty soon, I heard Doris walking up the steps. Then she was standing in the doorway and asking me if I felt any better.

"Not really," I said. "Maybe a little worse."

"Why don't you let me call Murray," Doris said, referring to our family doctor, Murray Safrin.

I didn't want to alarm Doris, but I was relieved when she suggested contacting Murray. For a few minutes I'd started to feel

With Congressman Allard Lowenstein.

The charismatic Mayor of New York, John V. Lindsay. He hugged me the night I helped him win Queens, but during my battle with Alex Rose, he didn't return the favor.

Comptroller Abe Beame and Paul O'Dwyer, president of the City Council.

With Governor Nelson Rockefeller, the man who perfected the art of arrogance.

The Honorable Arthur Goldberg was one of the most distinguished men in America, and during his run for the governorship of New York, Alex Rose did his best to humiliate him.

With Vice President Hubert Humphrey.

With Attorney General Ramsey Clarke at Liberals for New Politics event.

With Senator Charles Goodell at the Queens County Liberal Party dinner.

At Pete's Tavern in New York City with United States Senator George McGovern during his campaign for the presidency, 1972.

On vacation in Monte Carlo. Left to right: Doris, Helen Licitra, Sandi Meyerowitz, me, Joseph Licitra and Lenny Meyerowitz.

A LIBERAL FACTION PICKS OWN SLATE

Anti-Rose Unit Here Holds Separate Convention

By JOHN DARNTON

In a challenge to the leadership of Alex Rose, a dissident faction of the Liberal party held a convention of its own yesterday and approved its own slate of candidates for Mayor, Controller and City Council President.

The move by the anti-Rose forces, a group called Liberals for New Politics, opened up the prospect for the first citywide primary in the party's history.

With talk of "fighting bossism" in the air and not a single cigar in the room, the group presented three candidates and nominated them all "by acclamation" after a round-robin of seconding speeches.

Lawyer Tries for Mayor

J. Stanley Shaw, a 43-year-old Manhattan lawyer who is the Queens Liberal chairman and a prime figure in the anti Rose movement, was nominated for Mayor. He accepted with brief speech in which he sa he agreed to run, at a "sac fice" to his law practice a family life, to give the 000 enrolled Liberals a "t choice."

The candidate named for Council President was Joan Slous, a 24-year-old student at Brooklyn Law School.

The nominations followed a long, friendly discussion over whether to offer a "name" candidate or someone from the group's own ranks whose ideological loyalty would be beyond question.

Liberals for New Politics, which is similar to the ...

Candidates' Day

THE NEW YORK TIMES MAY 16, 1973

NEW YORK

THE CITY POLITIC

BY MICHAEL KRAMER

MR. ROSE SHOWS SOME THORNS

J. STANLEY SHAW MAYOR

Splinter Liberals pick Shaw for mayor

By HOWARD REISER

J. Stanley Shaw, Queens Liberal Party chairman, was designated yesterday as the mayoral candidate of the city-wide Liberals for New Politics in the party primary June 4.

The LNP is the reform caucus within the liberal party.

The 43-year-old Flushing resident, who has served as Queens Liberal Party chairman since 1968, was elected unanimously by the more than 100 delegates in hand vote in the Green Room of the New York Hilton Hotel.

Nominated for comptroller was Melvin J. Feit, 41, of Flushing, a lecturer and writer on city taxes and finance. Designated for City-council President was Joan Slous, 24, of Brooklyn, who will graduate from New York Law School in June.

FOLLOWING the designation for the "unprecedented" Liberal Party primary Shaw vowed to reform the city administration and the Liberal Party "if I am elected."

"We're in the primary race to win it," Shaw told the cheering delegates. "We have positive answers to the problems of the city."

He said the city is a "progressive town and promised to "make people proud to be Liberals again."

BEAMING from ear to ear, Shaw outlined to the press two major campaign objectives involving party reform and "answers to issues."

"In party reform we intend to see that the 90,000 Liberal enrollees in the City of New York are not disenfranchised when the time comes to choose candidates to run our city," he said. "I believe in one-man one-vote but do not believe that one man should have all the votes of all the enrollees. I have confidence in each and every Liberal enrollee and I know they will repudiate power politics, down to the basics of progressive, clean government."

Shaw Bids Rival Repudiate Rose

A section of the flyer we distributed when I ran for Mayor.

Me and Frank Knobel during the Boback bankruptcy.

The Boback group: Back row, left to right: Jesse Levine, Frank Knobel, Lou Campanelli. Front row: Joe Licitra, Lou Robustelli, Joe Binder and me.

Charles Bluhdorn, head of Gulf and Western Industries. Charlie had a well-deserved repu-
tion for instantaneous changes of direction. Some said it was part of his genius. Others
claimed his manic-depression was responsible. When I finally deposed Charlie, he stopped
e in the middle of my questions and asked the judge for permission to throw me out
f a window.

Lisa and Lon's wedding, March 1988.

Johnny Ma and me from my days at Community National Bank.

Stanley —
You are
one of the really
"good guys". Thanks for sticking with me

Joe
198?

With United States Senator Joseph Biden.

The Gross Family: Left to right: Aunt Shirley, Uncle Willie, Grandma Dubbie, Mother and Uncle Phil.

Shaw family Top row (L to R): Uncle Frank, Stepgrandfather Morris Slate, Cousin Teddy, Uncle Leo, Uncle Simon, Cousin Florence, Uncle Jack.

Middle row (L to R): Uncle Manny, Aunt Esther, Grandma Shaw (Slate), Mother, Dad

Bottom row (L to R): Cousin Sylvia, Aunt Ruth, Me, Aunt Adele, Aunt Lilly.

Louie during World War I.

Sol during the Second World War.

Me during Korea.

Louie in his coffee shop at 14th Street and 8th Avenue, New York City.

The Shaws at my brother Eli's wedding.

The Meyerowitz Family: Left to right: Me, Lenny, David, Betty, Sandi and Doris.

Our wedding: May 28, 1955.

Honeymoon catch at the Fort Montague Hotel in Nassau.

Golden wedding anniversary of my in-laws Betty and David Meyerowitz. Front row: Dad and Mom Meyerowitz and Lisa. Back row: Jeffrey, me and Doris.

Fishing with my Uncle Harry off Montauk.

Alex Rose, the tall, broad-shouldered father of New York's Liberal Party and a legendary figure in city politics.

Me, Doris and Isidore Levine upon my becoming chairman of the Liberal Party of Queens County, 1967.

*Me and Jerry Edelstein,
my political mentor.*

*Left to right, top row:
Congressmen Lester
Wolf and Joseph Adabbo.*

*Bottom row:
Congressman
Benjamin Rosenthal
and me.*

Left to right: A young Alan Hevesi and me with State Senators Emanuel Gold and Seymour Thaler.

With United States Senator Jacob Javits.

faint pains in my chest. Still, I figured it was probably nothing but anxiety and overwork.

Doris phoned, but she only reached Murray's answering service. I told her not to worry and said I would get some sleep. She went downstairs and kept trying Murray. I managed to doze off, and when I woke up, I felt better. Then Doris was in our bedroom again, saying that Murray had been outside reading the newspaper and she'd finally gotten in touch with him.

Doris said, "Murray says we ought to take a ride over to his office so he can check you out. What do you think? It can't hurt, and I'd feel better if you went."

I felt okay, but Doris had a point: it never hurt to be careful. "Sure," I said. "Let's go."

I recall walking downstairs, going outside into the warmth of the afternoon sun, and getting into the front seat of the car while Doris sat behind the wheel. She turned the key in the ignition, and I remember the engine turning over.

Then I was in pain.

It was almost indescribable. The closest I can get to it is to say that it felt as though somebody was striking my chest with a sledgehammer. Tears suddenly sprang to my eyes, and I was lying back in my seat, not really gasping for breath but winded from the pain, and I said to Doris, "You better hurry, honey, because I don't know if I can take too much of this."

We were heading to my doctor's office, Doris driving down Main Street in Flushing. The instant I told her I was in pain she hit the gas like the first driver off the starting line at Indy. She leaned on the horn and ran every light. People were honking at us, and a few of them had some unkind words to say, but none of it bothered my wife, who kept the pedal to the metal. When a cop tried to pull her over for about eighteen or nineteen moving violations, Doris calmly put down her window, pointed at me and shouted, "Booth Memorial Hospital!" and the cop drove ahead of us, red dome light whirling, to lead the way.

Doris was frightened, but I think she enjoyed the ride. She had always been a daring driver, and this was the first time in her life she really got a chance to show her stuff.

I remember being helped into the emergency room and lying on a stretcher. Doctors and nurses gathered around me. Overhead lights were shining in my eyes as the pain spread through my chest. I will never forget the pain. I can't forget the pain, or Doris standing next to me, holding my hand, even when they wheeled the stretcher into the elevator, and we went up to the Cardiac Care Unit. And all the while I was thinking that this was ridiculous because it was a sunny summer day, and I was in the middle of the biggest bankruptcy case ever to hit the Eastern District of New York, and I was only forty-six, much too young to confront my mortality.

That afternoon I was told that I did indeed have a heart attack, the plain vanilla kind, an inferior wall myocardial infarction. I was going to survive, for now, but according to my doctor and to Doris, I was going to have to make some serious changes—exercise regularly, watch my diet, and reduce the stress in my life that was related to my work. I could handle eating white-meat chicken and vegetables and running on a treadmill, but this last requirement sounded impossible.

First of all, who the hell ever heard of work-related stress? I grew up during the Depression, and the way I saw it a man was supposed to work hard. If you were tired at the end of the day, and upset about a few business matters, that was only natural. I remember when I was a kid working for my parents in their coffee shop, Louie used to tell me that hard work wouldn't kill you. Of course, he didn't mention that it could give you a heart attack. Besides, except the Rockefellers and their moneyed ilk, who else had the choice but to work as hard as they could?

My two weeks as a patient at Booth Memorial Hospital remain blurry, a kaleidoscope of flourescent lights and winking machines surrounding me while I drifted in and out of sleep. I vaguely recall waking up one morning, looking outside my glass-walled room in the CCU, and seeing a young man in a white lab coat sitting in a chair and crying.

I called to him, and he came over and sat by my bed and I asked him his name. He was Dr. Somebody-or-other, and he told me that he was a first-year resident and had been at the hospital for less than a month.

"What's the matter?" I said.

"I lost my first patient," he replied, wiping his eyes.

"Did you do everything you could for him?"

"Yes," the young resident said. "Yes, I did."

"Then okay," I said. "That's all you can do. You have to learn to be a good doctor the way I learned to be a good lawyer. You understand?"

He nodded, and I think I patted him on the arm, and fell asleep. I'm relatively certain that this conversation occurred, but there is a possibility that I dreamt it. My clearest memory of my stay in the CCU is the day that I woke up from a midmorning nap and heard somebody making a ruckus outside my room. One of the voices seemed vaguely familiar, but I couldn't place it, so I figured I was dreaming and drifted back to sleep until a nurse came in.

"I'm sorry to bother you," she said. "But your brother and his wife are here from Philadelphia, and he insists on seeing you. I told him no one except Mrs. Shaw was allowed to visit, but he won't leave and says he drove a long way and couldn't he just come in to see you for a minute."

I was pretty tired and not in especially good shape, and I looked at the nurse like she was nuts.

"I don't have a brother in Philadelphia," I said, thinking that maybe I was still dreaming.

The nurse said, "Well, according to the gentleman outside you do, and would you please let him say hello because he's driving the nurses crazy."

I nodded, and the nurse left, and in walked Joe and Sylvia Binder. I was laughing so hard that my whole body ached.

Joe looked over at the bed, turned to Sylvia, and said, "That's him. Let's go," and then he left.

That was my one amusing moment at Booth Memorial Hospital. They discharged me after a couple of weeks with instructions to relax at home for a month. I felt like I'd been sentenced to prison, but with Doris watching me like a mother hawk I had no choice but to follow doctor's orders.

I had always wanted a patio in the backyard, and I called my friend Joe Ferrara, who was in the ready-mix concrete business. Joe sent over one of those old Italian contractors, a terrific guy who did beautiful work. So I had my patio, and I sat outside in the sun every day with newspapers and books, and worried about my mortality.

CHAPTER 19

TAKING MY CASE
TO CONGRESS

Despite the assurances of my doctors that I had come through my illness with a minimal amount of damage to my heart, I was convinced that I was going to drop dead at any moment, and I was angry about it.

I still had too much that I wanted to accomplish in life, and it felt unfair that I wouldn't get my shot. The bar had been set higher for me than for most. I had passed much of my childhood in an orphanage and foster homes, and before I could really get going as a lawyer I did my schmuck-with-a-fountain-pen routine and got myself in debt up to my eyeballs. Hell, by the summer of 1975 I hadn't even finished paying off the debts that I'd accumulated during my association with Schulman, and the idea that I would leave Doris and the kids in such a rough financial situation was unbearable to me.

Sunning myself on my new patio, it occurred to me that every life was a story broken up into chapters. When you die, somebody sums up those chapters in a eulogy, and then they bury you along with your story. Unless you've accomplished extraordinary things, nobody remembers you. Sure, every once in a while your name will come up at a party or family gatherings and they'll say what a great guy you were, but that's it. When you go, you're an orphan forever.

Since I was now certain that this was going to be my fate sooner rather than later, I became depressed. Doris noticed my mood and invited our doctor, Murray Safrin, over to the house to chat with me. I told Murray about my fears, and he said that they weren't unusual for someone recovering from a heart attack, and he urged me to go talk it through with a psychiatrist who was experienced at helping patients cope with this kind of anxiety. When I agreed to go, Murray suggested a Dr. Rudoy, who had an office on Grand Central Parkway.

I took a break from my nice new patio, which truthfully was not a difficult thing for me to do since I was losing my mind out there in the sun, and I went to see Dr. Rudoy. He was an older, nondescript-looking fellow who sat across from me in a high-backed chair.

"What I can I do for you?" he asked.

"I just had a heart attack and I'm afraid I'm not going to make it and I can't even imagine having to leave my family."

"Quite understandable," he said. "Tell me more."

"Well, my wife, Doris, she wants us to move to Florida so I can sit on a chair and live till I'm a hundred and seven. I'm not ready to do that, but I'm also not ready for death."

Dr. Rudoy said, "What choice do you have, Mr. Shaw? At some point, everyone has to be ready to die."

Beautiful, I thought. Like I'd come to his office for a biology lesson.

I said, "Let me ask you a question, Dr. Rudoy. Are you ready to die?"

"I believe so," he said calmly. "I've tried to do as many enjoyable things as I can. For instance, as a young man I wanted to play the violin. But college and med school got in the way, and then work and family life. My children are grown now, and so recently I've had the opportunity to learn how to play the violin. It's been very rewarding, and it made me feel as though my time has been well spent."

Dr. Rudoy asked me if I would like to hear him play the violin. To be polite I said yes, and he played for a few minutes. Then we talked for a while longer, but I can't say that I found the music or his violin-playing anecdote overly comforting. Yet I knew that I needed to talk to somebody, and I made another appointment for a few weeks later because Dr. Rudoy was going on vacation.

When I showed up for my session, however, there was no Dr. Rudoy. He had died on his vacation.

Good thing, I thought, that he had learned to play the violin before he heard the angels sing. And his death did teach me an important lesson, namely that there is very little you can do about your mortality and so you might as well live right up until the end. For some, that meant playing a musical instrument; for others, it meant work, and plenty of it. Since I was a member of the latter club, I figured it was time for me to get off the patio and back to my office.

But I continued to be scared about dying. I'm still scared today.

Some time ago, Winston Churchill observed that nothing is more invigorating than to be shot at without result, and I can echo the same sentiment regarding my heart attack. Once I'd regained my physical strength and recovered from the fear that every ache and pain was an announcement that I was about to keel over, I had the feeling that I'd better live each day to its fullest because the sun was moving westward in the sky and you never knew when it would set.

Doris, however, had no intention of allowing me to resume my precoronary schedule. She said that she was too young to be a widow, and Jeffrey and Lisa needed me. When I told her that I had no choice but to put in seventy or eighty hours a week, she insisted that along with my changed eating habits and exercise classes, I had to find some arrangement to make my work easier. Otherwise, she was going to hijack me to Florida and chain me to a chaise lounge.

My solution was Joe Licitra. Joe was an attorney with his own practice in Ozone Park. He handled just about any legal matter that didn't require him to be a litigator. I first met Joe at Roosevelt Raceway. I would see him there often, sitting at a big table in the clubhouse with his friends. Joe Ferrara, who was friendly with both of us, made the introductions, and over the years Joe Licitra would use me on occasion to do his firm's litigation.

I had dinner with Joe Licitra at Roosevelt Raceway shortly after I'd finished my month of recuperation and asked him about his plans for the future. He had none, other than trying to expand his practice, and I suggested the we merge our firms. Joe was the most organized guy in the world. He had files for his files, and he was conservative with money. Since these were not my strongest suits, I thought Joe should be the managing partner and I'd be in charge of litigation. He agreed; we wrote up the terms of our agreement on a napkin; and the firm of Shaw, Licitra & Levine was founded, renting space at 1050 Franklin Avenue in Garden City.

Next to my marriage to Doris, this was the smartest partnership I've ever made. Joe was a first-rate manager and a sweetheart of a guy. (He and Joe Ferrara had a wonderful relationship with the Boys and Girls Club of South Queens, giving lots of their time and money to the young people. After Joe Licitra passed away, Joe Ferrara kept up with the youngsters, giving more time and money and serving as chairman of their board.) Anyway, Joe Licitra was a meticulous man. He used to keep his work area so neat it looked like a museum. Every paper clip had its special spot on his desk, and sometimes, just for fun, Joe Ferrara and I would sneak into his office and mess up his paper clips to get a rise out of him. At the time, the most immediate reward for forming a partnership with Joe was that with him now managing the daily business of the firm, I was completely free to concentrate on the Bohack Chapter XI.

Looking over what I've written about Bohack, I see that I have left the impression that the work was unrelentingly grim. While it was true that there was constant pressure on Jesse and me to deal with the constant round of lawsuits, the case itself did provide me with some comic relief, particularly when it involved working directly with Frank Knobel. One of my responsibilities during the Bohack Chapter was to assist the corporation in collecting funds they were due. A fellow in San Francisco, a Mr. Dumaini, had promised to lend Bohack hundreds of thousands of dollars to expand their real estate operations, and now, he was refusing to give them the loan. Bohack sued, and when it was time for the trial, Frank and I flew to California.

Mr. Dumaini was an arrogant little man who was convinced that he was entitled to stiff Bohack on the principle that he simply preferred not to pay. His arrogance was almost palpable, and as I approached the witness chair to question him, I decided to shake him up. Given his arrogance, rattling him was an easy thing to do, and I did it by continually mispronouncing his name.

"Now Mr. Dumane," I would say.

"Dumaini," he would correct me.

"Sorry," I'd reply. "Okay, Mr. Duman—"

"Du-main-i!" he'd nearly shout.

On and on I went, like I was performing a comedy routine, and Frank joined in the fun, writing Dumaini on a sheet of yellow legal paper and holding it up whenever I mispronounced the name, which was often. I think I even got a laugh out of the stenographer. In the end, I know I got some money out of Dumaini. Bohack settled with him for a quarter of a million dollars.

Frank was pleased with the settlement, and to celebrate we went out for a drink at one of the bars near San Franciso's Union Square. The singles era was in full swing, and the joint was loaded with men and women on the make. I sat at the bar and ordered a scotch, and an attractive young woman sitting next to me introduced herself, said she was a stewardess, and asked me what I was doing in town.

Before I could answer, Frank spread out a few fifty dollar bills on the bar and said, "We're Treasury agents, and we're looking for counterfeit fifties like these. Have you seen any?"

No, the stewardess hadn't seen any fifties, but she called over the bartender and explained the situation. Next thing I knew, the bartender was scooping his fifties out of the cash register and handing them to Frank, who studied the bills as if he knew what he was doing.

Within minutes, word spread around the bar that two federal agents were checking for counterfeit money. Patrons drifted off the dance floor and out of their seats and over toward Frank, offering him fifties to inspect.

I'm not sure why everyone believed that we were feds. Perhaps because we were a bit older than the average patron or were wearing trench coats. But as soon as I could I caught Frank's attention and dragged him out, informing him that his government took a rather dim view of people impersonating federal agents. So dim, in fact, that the government considered it a felony.

"Okay," Frank said. "It's a felony. But it's also a lot of fun."

So was going gambling in Lake Tahoe, which was what Frank wanted to do after he was done playing Treasury agent.

We flew up there and parked ourselves at a crap table for a while. I took a break and went to the bar for a drink. As I was sipping my scotch, an attractive young woman sat down next to me and we started a conversation. She was friendly and seemed very intelligent and I asked her what she did.

"I'm a hooker," she said.

"Oh," I said, and the conversation paused for a minute or two until Frank showed up.

"Who's your friend?" he asked.

"She's a working girl," I said, hoping that Frank wouldn't tell her he was an FBI agent investigating prostitution.

"Everybody has a job," Frank said. "A job's a job. Let's take her to dinner and talk about it."

The woman said she would be delighted to eat with us, and during the meal Frank questioned her about her work like a sociologist researching his dissertation. And so it was in this manner that I learned quite a bit about a profession to which mine is often compared.

If hanging around Frank Knobel was a sure path to comic relief, it was also a way to encounter relatively complicated legal situations. By nature, Frank is a risk taker and enjoys walking closer to the edge than most, and when we returned from California he found himself facing a serious tax problem.

To buy his Bohack stock from Charlie Bluhdorn, Frank had used his real estate holdings as collateral and a basic deed-in/deed-out arrangement to avoid personal liability. He assigned the buildings to his own corporation, and the corporation reassigned the deeds to him. Now, years after the fact, the Internal Revenue Service was claiming that the money Frank had raised from mortgaging his holdings represented a profit on which he had to pay taxes.

Frank was beside himself, and he asked me to help him. I had him give me his power of attorney and went to battle with an IRS agent, who wouldn't budge an inch on the original ruling. Our last option was the IRS appeals process, and I filed an appeal on Frank's behalf.

The notice of the hearing arrived at my house, and Doris, who has always handled our money, thought it was a personal matter so she opened the letter, which was signed by a Mr. Mamoon.

"That name sounds familiar," she said that evening at dinner. "Never heard of him," I said.

"I read it in the temple bulletin," she said. "I think he belongs to our temple."

A few days later at Yom Kippur services I saw Murray Safrin sitting across the aisle. I got up to wish him *Gut Yontif* and asked him if he knew a Mr. Mamoon who belonged to the temple.

"Sure," Murray said. "You're sitting right next to him," and nodded toward a man in a white suit.

I went back to my seat, said hello, told the man in white my name, and asked him if he had a relative at the IRS.

"That's me," he said. "I'm the one who's going to hear your appeal. It's my last case before I retire."

"You know my client, Frank Knobel, is on the level. He doesn't owe you guys a dime."

We chatted briefly, and after services, we talked a little more. He told me to submit my brief, and he would see me in a week. Then he wished me a happy New Year.

Two weeks later, Mr. Mamoon's decision arrived in the mail. Frank received a zero assessment.

After finishing up my business in California, I returned to New York to discover that the Securities and Exchange Commission was investigating Bohack and the role of Peat, Marwick, Mitchell & Co., in connection with the accounting firm's audit of the supermarket chain for the fiscal year that ended in January of 1974.

The SEC was hoping to determine whether Bohack had reported misleading financial information about its inventories and business operations. The SEC was demanding that Touche Ross & Co., another accounting firm, surrender any of its documents that related to the Touche Ross review of the Peat Marwick audit for Bohack. Touche Ross refused, stating the documents were confidential and irrelevant to the SEC inquiry.

Touche Ross came into the picture when it was retained to do the review by National Bank of North America. The bank had loaned Bohack $3 million based on Peat Marwick's certification of Bohack's 1974 financial statement. The bank reasoned that if it could prove that Peat Marwick didn't conduct its audit in accordance with generally accepted auditing standards, the bank might have a cause of action against Peat Marwick. What the bank was really looking to do was to cut the losses it had incurred when Bohack was unable to pay back its loan.

A major part of the SEC investigation focused on the overstatement of Bohack's inventory, which was uncovered by S. D. Leidesdorf & Co., an accounting firm appointed during the Bohack Chapter XI to certify that Bohack's financial statements were accurate on the day of its filing. Bohack had claimed total assets of $93 million, and $83.8 million of that was supposed to be in inventory. As it worked out, another inventory was taken and Bohack came up $5 million short. I told the company to report the shortage to the SEC, which they did in November 1974, stating that due to an unexplainable breakdown, their inventory records could no longer be relied upon.

This development was potentially disastrous if Bohack was ever going to confirm a plan and emerge from Chapter. The Creditors' Committee would be reluctant to approve any plan if they felt that fraud had been involved. I promised the Creditors' Committee that I would conduct an independent investigation into the causes of the inventory shortage. After several months I believe I found what had happened. To conduct the inventory, Peat Marwick would randomly select seven or eight Bohack supermarkets and go in and count the inventory and then they would apply their findings to the other sixty or seventy stores. This apparently was an acceptable accounting practice, but somehow someone at Bohack was able to determine which stores Peat, Marwick was going to inventory. Those stores would be stocked to the max, while the shelves on the other stores went empty. Thus, when the accountant applied their numbers across all of Bohack's markets, the figures multiplied out on the high side.

I never discovered which Bohack store managers learned about the intentions of Peat, Marwick, but I did find evidence that a ledger existed that would have helped in figuring out Bohack's true inventory. Yet I couldn't produce this ledger, and this part of the story has a somewhat ominous but amusing end.

In 1980, a year after I was done with the Bohack bankruptcy, I took Doris and the kids to Israel to celebrate our twenty-fifth wedding anniversary. We toured the country, and one afternoon we went to Jerusalem. I had gone up to the Western Wall with Jeffrey to say a prayer, and as my son and I were walking back up from the Wall, I saw the side room, more like a cave really, where the Hasidim sat with their books beside the Wall. Jeffrey and I kept walking, and then I noticed several men in American business suits approaching me.

Suddenly, as they passed, one of them jostled me hard and said, "Where are the books?"

I thought he was referring to the religious men who sat near the Wall studying Talmud, so I pointed toward it and said, "Over there."

"No!" he said. "Where are the books?"

"I told you," I replied, pointing again to the location.

"No! The Bohack books," he almost shouted, probably referring to the missing ledger. Then he walked past Jeffrey and me.

In its heyday, Bohack had operated 324 stores, but I don't recall that any of them were in Israel, and I never found out the identity of that man or how he knew who I was.

One cause of Bohack's troubles that became clear during my investigation was that the supermarket chain had been the victim of a price-fixing agreement. So under the authority of Judge Parente, we filed an antitrust suit against Iowa Beef Processors, the world's biggest meat company; Ira Waldbaum and his supermarket chain; and C.P.S. Sales and its president, Walter Bodenstein, who was an agent for Iowa Beef. In our suit, we alleged that there had been a conspiracy among the defendants to fix the price of boxed beef sold in the New York City area for the benefit of Waldbaum's and to the detriment of Bohack. We were looking to collect damages in excess of $15 million.

In response, William Heubaum, general counsel for Iowa Beef, denied to *The Wall Street Journal* that Waldbaum had "received any preferential treatment that violates the law or that Bohack suffered any injury by sales to Waldbaum. How can Bohack blame us for failure to properly manage its business?"

The Waldbaum management and Walter Bodenstein couldn't be reached for comment. I wasn't surprised. A couple of years back, *The Wall Street Journal* had reported how Iowa Beef and its co-chairman, Currier J. Holman, had conspired with a Mafia figure to bribe their way into the especially profitable New York City market. Bodenstein happened to be the son-in-law of Moe Steinman, who had previously confessed to bribing supermarket executives and officials of the butchers' union.

I was relatively certain that we would win our antitrust suit, though I was unsure about the damages that Bohack would collect. My confidence about winning was based on the evidence we had turned up along with the statements that Iowa Beef's general counsel made to *The Wall Street Journal*. Heubaum denied any illegality in the current case, but he stated that "he had been concerned for some years about possible antitrust violations." When Iowa Beef was first trying to enter the New York market, he said, "Mr. Holman promised the company's first customer, Waldbaum, that it wouldn't raise prices. But as costs rose and other New York customers were signed up, the other customers soon were paying more than Waldbaum."

Even though I'm an attorney, other lawyers occasionally enrage me with their tap dancing. It is as though they can admit to a crime, and then say that it's not a crime because they're admitting to it. For example, Heubaum went on to tell the newspaper that Iowa Beef had tried, without success, to talk Waldbaum into paying the standard price. Heubaum claimed that he went so far as to tell an Iowa Beef official who was going to meet with Mr. Waldbaum that it was "unlawful for a seller to discriminate in price between different purchasers of similar commodities, where the price differential cannot be attributed to efficiencies in the cost."

In other words, as we had charged in our suit, Iowa Beef and Waldbaum's had been guilty of price fixing.

Meantime, that summer, Judge Parente ordered Bohack to auction off its remaining supermarkets and other assets. Bohack's credit had been drawn down to the limit from Manny Hanny; continuing operations were impossible; and the creditors wanted their money. Therefore, Bohack had no other choice but to liquidate. My major contribution to the auction was to make sure it was public and that all of the supermarket chains were invited. By nature, the people who run supermarkets are very competitive, and I felt the owners would hate to be outbid by a competitor in public. That was how it played out, and Bohack raised millions of dollars because the bidders kept trying to one up each other, much to the benefit of Bohack's creditors.

On December 13, 1977, I appeared before Congress to testify on the difficulties I had encountered during the Bohack case due to the insufficient status and power of bankruptcy court judges. Congress was considering elevating these judges to Article III status, placing them on a par with federal judges, and I, along with other attorneys, had been summoned to Washington to present our views.

There was an ironic twist to the witness list. Testifying right before me, representing the American College of Trial Lawyers, was Judge Simon Rifkind. Judge Rifkind was a senior partner at the prestigious New York City law firm of Paul, Weiss, Rifkind, Wharton & Garrison. One of that firm's top litigators was Arthur Liman, a brilliant lawyer who passed away in 1997, a decade after becoming a familiar face to millions of Americans as the Senate's chief Iran-Contra counsel, the man who forced Lt. Col. Oliver North to admit that he had shredded secret documents. During his career, Liman was a specialist in white-collar crime. He defended such well-known clients as Dennis Levine, a central player in the Wall-Street insider-trading scandal; junk-bond financier Michael Milken; John Zaccaro, a real estate developer married to former vice presidential candidate Geraldine Ferraro; corporate raider Carl Icahn; and financier Robert Vesco.

It was in this capacity that I came to know Arthur Liman, because in November of 1977, a month prior to my testimony before Congress, Arthur had been retained by Charlie Bluhdorn to defend him against a suit that I had filed on behalf of Bohack, requesting $86 million in damages. The suit charged that Gulf and Western (meaning, Bluhdorn, several of his associates, and his outside law firm, Simpson, Thacher & Bartlett) had used Bohack to pressure the management of the A&P supermarket chain, which Bluhdorn was trying to acquire. As the majority stockholder in Bohack, Bluhdorn had a fiscal responsibility to the corporation, and he breached it by engaging in a vicious price war with the A&P, a war that led to the cash crunch at Bohack and forced them into Chapter XI.

Bluhdorn seemed to be offended by my suing him, and while he retained Liman, he was also busy trying to convince Judge Parente to remove me as Bohack's counsel, citing my former financial difficulties. This approach hadn't worked for Alex Rose; it didn't work for Bluhdorn.

Judge Rifkind testified that he and the American College of Trial Lawyers opposed the elevation of bankruptcy court judges because the vitality of the federal courts depended on the district courts having general jurisdiction so the judges would be well-rounded. Rifkind predicted that if bankruptcy cases were adjudicated in separate courts, it would dilute the knowledge and prestige of district court judges.

Furthermore, Rifkind stated, if this separation were to be sanctioned by Congress, bankruptcy law would become insulated from the general body of law and would create a specialized coterie of bankruptcy attorneys.

And finally, he said, if bankruptcy court referees were transformed into judges, then they would ascend to the federal bench without undergoing the same appointment process required in all other federal judgeships.

Frankly, I believe that the objections raised by Rifkind as spokesperson for the American College of Trial Lawyers were self-serving nonsense.

For openers, let me say that the knowledge any judge has of law is limited only by his own efforts and his willingness to pore over law journals and books of new case law. Secondly, how bankruptcy courts would rob district courts of prestige is beyond me. Does the existence of the Supreme Court rob them of prestige? Do the circuit courts rob them of prestige? Of course not.

As for bankruptcy courts creating specialization among lawyers, how in the world could Rifkind object to that? The practice of law had been specialized for decades. For example, any individual charged with a serious felony would be best off with a criminal defense attorney instead of someone with a background in estate planning. Rifkind was being disingenuous. He knew that I was about to face Arthur Liman on the Bluhdorn matter, and Liman was considered a specialist in his field. So why shouldn't a corporation facing a Chapter XI seek out a lawyer well-versed in the minutia of bankruptcy law?

Rifkind's last point was almost too silly to address. To make certain that bankruptcy court judges adhered to the same selection process as other federal judges all Congress had to do was require them to do exactly that.

When all was said and done Rifkind merely reflected the legal profession's longtime prejudice against bankruptcy, as well as an unforgivable ignorance about the complexities inherent in a modern Chapter XI.

I spoke to the congressional committee immediately following Rifkind and detailed for them the waste of time, money, and effort that was involved in the Bohack Chapter because of the jurisdictional conflicts that arose, conflicts that would be eased enormously if bankruptcy judges were elevated in status.

One of the final points I made was solely for Arthur Liman and Charlie Bluhdorn's benefit, but I figured it wouldn't hurt to let Judge Rifkind pass it on to his partner, Liman.

I said "Perhaps the gravest issue that the Bankruptcy Court was powerless to deal with [were charges of] unlawful conspiracies [one of which] is now being maintained by Bohack against a large conglomerate, of which Bohack was considered a subsidiary, and the individual who was Bohack's largest single shareholder [both of whom] caused directly the filing of the Chapter XI petition."

In effect, I proceeded to argue to the congressional committee that Judge Parente should be fully empowered to decide this case, even if criminal charges against Gulf and Western and Charlie Bluhdorn were warranted. I wanted Judge Rifkind to pass the word to Arthur Liman that I was going to pursue Bluhdorn by every means at my disposal, and should Congress vote to extend those means, that would be Arthur Liman's client's very tough luck.

I flew home from Washington, gratified by my appearance before Congress. After all, I had started out in life as a poor kid from Depression-era Brooklyn, a true believer in the American dream, in love with President Franklin Roosevelt and convinced that politics could be a powerful impetus for what was good and right. That beautifully appointed committee room, with the polished wood tables and chairs, and those wide, high hallways of the Capitol held an overwhelming magnificence for me, a symbol of the majesty of my government.

After a tough, protracted debate on the floor, Congress did vote to elevate the status of bankruptcy judges in 1978. However, in *Marathon Pipeline Company v. Northern Pipeline Construction Co.*, a district court held that giving bankruptcy judges Article III status was unconstitutional. I was flattered that the district court judge at least saw the problems with the reduced powers of bankruptcy judges and cited my testimony before Congress.

The case went directly to the Supreme Court, and I went to complain to the Bar Association of the City of New York, perhaps the most powerful association of its kind in the country.

My complaint centered on Chief Justice Warren Burger. While Congress had been considering the new legislation, Justice Burger had gone to visit his friend Richard Nixon at the White House and campaigned for the president to veto the bill if Congress passed it. Nixon declined, but I felt that since the issue was now before the Court, Justice Burger should recuse himself as he was already on the record as vehemently opposing the law. How then, I argued to the bar association, could Justice Burger be impartial?

The committee didn't disagree with my point, but they told me in no uncertain terms that they wouldn't ask the Chief Justice of the United States to recuse himself from a case.

So I wrote Justice Burger a letter, making my argument as to why he should recuse himself.

I never received a reply. But Justice Burger apparently held off on voting until the other Justices had weighed in with their decisions, which held that the elevated status of bankruptcy judges was unconstitutional. Evidently, after learning that a majority of the Justices would hold that the statute was unconstitutional, Justice Burger dissented from the majority opinion and voted that the statute should be constitutional. Maybe he read my letter.

Thus, it would be years before significant changes were made to bankruptcy law, and by then pragmatism forced Congress to act, since most of these changes came on the heels of the big-time corporate bustouts of the 1980s.

Of course, I was glad to see these changes. They were long overdue.

CHAPTER 20

CLOSING CIRCLES

The late Charles Bluhdorn, the founder, CEO and chairman of the board of Gulf and Western Industries, had many faults, but being stupid wasn't one of them. In my opinion, he was the premier wheeler-dealer of his day, a shrewd, smooth-talking, cigar-smoking hybrid of the Wild West and Wall Street.

If Charlie had a single great failing it was, like his talents, larger than life, and put him in the company of mythological Greek heroes. For Bluhdorn's greatest weakness was his pride, which led him to believe that he would prevail in any business confrontation because he was smarter than the rest of us, more clever, more willing to crawl further out on a limb. At times, Charlie was correct, and thus he built an impressive fortune starting from scratch.

At other times, though, he was dead wrong. As the Bohack Chapter XI dragged on and the Creditors' Committee continued to urge me to investigate the causes of the collapse, I discovered that Bluhdorn's pride had gotten him in over his head, and he wound up causing immeasurable harm to Bohack and the thousands of people who depended on the supermarket chain for their livelihood. This was the reason I wound up suing Charlie, his company, and several of his employees, board members, and his corporate law firm for $86 million.

The story begins in the mid-1960s, when Charles Bluhdorn acquired 256,393 shares of Bohack stock, approximately 22 percent of the corporation, and began to involve himself, as was his habit, in the major business and financial decisions of the company. However, given Charlie's temperament, it was only a matter of time before he set his sights higher. Bohack was merely the second largest supermarket chain in the New York City area. The biggest supermarket chain was none other than the venerable Great Atlantic and Pacific Tea Company.

Since the early 1960s, Gulf and Western had acquired ninety-two companies using methods questionable enough to warrant investigations by federal agencies. Then in January of 1972, Charlie decided to explore buying number ninety-three, the A&P. Certainly, it would have been satisfying to Charlie's ego to acquire A&P, but owning such a large chain would also give Gulf and Western a highly profitable outlet for the products of its numerous subsidiaries. So Charlie ordered his people at G&W and his law firm to examine the financial state of A&P, and they quickly determined that A&P shares were artificially deflated, and the company was ripe for a takeover.

It was then, in my view, that Charlie and his cohorts embarked on a scheme to obtain a controlling interest in A&P in a fraudulent manner, disregarding both the rights and interests of Bohack and the public at large. First, they employed the brokerage firm of Kidder, Peabody to acquire A&P shares without revealing that it was Bluhdorn buying the stock. Otherwise, his intentions would have been clear, and the stock price would have soared. Between February and September of 1972, Charlie purchased approximately one million shares of A&P stock, about 4 percent of the company. Meanwhile, to soften up A&P shareholders, who would have to vote for his eventual takeover, Charlie devised a public relations campaign to discredit the current A&P management.

In 1972, A&P had instituted a program to attract customers by lowering prices, in some cases below cost, and the program drove down retail supermarket prices in the area. Other chains tried to match the prices and lost money. In just the third quarter of that year, Bohack lost $415,000. A&P was also losing money on their program, and so Bluhdorn directed Joseph Binder, who was then president of Bohack, to hold a press conference attacking the management of A&P for its program.

The arrangement of the conference and Binder's statement were handled by Gulf and Western's PR department, and Bluhdorn was so anxious for the statement to accomplish its goal that he personally reviewed and revised it. The press conference was held on September 13, and indeed it served its true purpose, embarrassing the management of A&P for the program losses and its predatory pricing, which were in direct violation of Federal Trade Commission rules and federal statutes.

When it came to nerve, I'd have to say that no one was ever in Charlie Bluhdorn's league. Shortly after his tender offer for A&P stock at twenty-five dollars a share on February 1, 1973, Gulf and Western launched a preemptive strike, commencing an action in the United States District Court for the Southern District of New York against A&P, trying to enjoin their management from defending against his takeover. Bluhdorn specifically objected to allegations by A&P officials that he had undertaken a surreptitious scheme of acquisition of A&P stock to gain control of the company and replace its management.

This, of course, was precisely the path Charlie hoped to take, but during his deposition on February 7, he stated that he was simply making a passive investment and that Gulf and Western had played no part in the September press conference. To his credit, the district court judge didn't believe Bluhdorn. He found that the defendants could not demonstrate the passive nature of the investment and further held, based on statements made by Bluhdorn, that G&W intended an active role in A&P management. "It appears incredible," the court finally ruled, "that Bluhdorn would put $90 million in A&P stock merely as a passive investment."

Even though the tender offer was ultimately withdrawn, Charlie Bluhdorn was too sharp an operator not to realize that A&P would retaliate. My position in the lawsuit against him and his co-conspirators was that as the ostensible head of Bohack, Charlie had the responsibility to protect the corporation. Furthermore, he was duty-bound to inform Bohack's board and stockholders of his plan due to the potential risk of retaliation by A&P, and what it would mean for Bohack. Charlie never mentioned it. Instead, he chose to use Bohack as a stalking horse for his A&P takeover, and when that failed Bohack was left exposed.

The counterattack by the management of A&P was swift and devastating for Bohack. Frank Knobel and Joe Binder became aware of it within two weeks of Bluhdorn's tender offer. Joe and Frank were working at Bohack Square when they got a call that a representative from the meat company Armour was downstairs and wished to speak with them.

The rep, whose name Frank remembers as D.J., didn't have an appointment, and when Binder joined Frank in his office, they knew it was trouble.

When D.J. walked in with his ten-gallon hat and cowboy boots, Binder said to him, "You just passing through Brooklyn?"

"Yeah," D.J. replied. "I'm just passing through Brooklyn."

Chewing on his cigar, Binder said, "Did you have much trouble tying your horse to the pole outside?"

D.J. was not amused, and he got right to the point of his visit. He said that Armour would now require Bohack to stay current on its bills. A&P paid as soon as they received an invoice, and Bohack would be expected to do the same. In other words, he was cutting off Bohack's credit.

Frank said, "We've had three weeks credit with you guys forever. We do maybe twenty million bucks a year with you. And we run a monthly balance of three or four hundred grand."

"Not anymore," D.J. said, and turned around and walked out.

Other suppliers, at the request of A&P, followed suit, and soon Bohack was being pressed for payments from suppliers with whom they had longtime extended-credit arrangements. To apply further financial pressure, A&P brought its money-losing WEO program into Brooklyn and Queens, Bohack's stronghold. This cut into Bohack's gross sales receipts and severely drained their cash flow at a time when the chain needed every available dollar to finance its new stores.

Prior to that time, Bohack had primarily used retail outlets of no more than ten thousand square feet in urban locations. Bluhdorn had ordered Bohack to build larger stores of up to fifty thousand square feet in suburban areas. This was known as the "Village" concept, and vast capital expenditures were needed to put it in place. Because Bluhdorn was responsible for the Village-store program, and in fact had cited it as proof of his sound management skills when compared to the managers of A&P, he was aware of the cash requirements to put the program in place. Thus, Bluhdorn had a fiduciary duty to Bohack to avoid this conflict of interest, but he and his cohorts chose to ignore that at this juncture Bohack would be particularly vulnerable to a price war. A&P counterattacked, causing the Village stores to fail, and this failure led to Bohack's filing for Chapter XI.

I got my chance to depose Charles Bluhdorn on July 26, 1978. During the deposition I was able to bring out the story of his scheme to take over A&P, but I knew that proving it in court and getting an actual cash judgment would be a tougher trick. Charlie was as clever as I'd expected, and as evasive, but I did manage to annoy him enough that at one point he requested to go off the record and said to Judge Parente, "Would it be okay if I threw Mr. Shaw out the window."

Judge Parente said no. He was the owner of the building, and he didn't want to get sued. After that brief injection of humor, I returned to thundering away at Charlie. I really did feel that he was responsible for the Bohack bankruptcy, and I wanted to make him pay for it, but Arthur Liman was a hell of a lawyer and he realized that he had Bohack over a barrel, because by the time I deposed Charlie Bluhdorn, I had found a potential buyer for Bohack.

As a major stockholder of the company, Bluhdorn was entitled to file a notice of appeal when I tried to confirm my plan. Such a notice would have delayed the process for months, and I risked losing the buyer.

So not long after concluding the deposition, Arthur Liman asked me to have a turkey sandwich with him at his office, and Bohack settled with Bluhdorn for a little under $200,000. I comforted myself with the fact that I recovered another $90,000 from the law firm of Simpson, Thacher & Bartlett, because their lawyer Joel Dolkart personally cashed Bohack checks that he shouldn't have, and I seem to recall that he ultimately got himself in some legal trouble for this misstep.

Ida and Louie had been at odds for the first quarter century of their marriage, but as time went on, and with the grace and resiliency that long-married couples seem to develop, they managed to transform their last years together into a far happier arrangement. For the record, I consider this indisputable proof, divine proof if you will, that if you stick with a marriage long enough you can make it work.

My parents' biggest battle had always centered on Louie's gambling, and even though he never lost his interest in betting with the bookies, going to the racetrack, and playing cards, his compulsive wagering had, to some degree, been integrated peacefully into their relationship.

It didn't hurt that during the late 1950s and early 1960s, Louie earned a decent living at his last luncheonette on Eleventh Street and Third Avenue. For a while, my Uncle Frank was a partner with him in the place. That's one of the reasons I know Louie was still betting every chance he got. One evening, according to Uncle Frank, the subways weren't running because of a strike. Louie and Frank took a hotel room, intending to stay in the city until the trains were operating again.

Yet, as soon as they checked into their room, Louie said, "I gotta go now. I'm going out to Roosevelt Raceway. To see the trotters."

My Uncle Frank asked, "How are you getting there?"

"Don't worry," Louie said. "One of the guys works at the post office is borrowing a truck. He's gonna take me."

Louie returned at three o'clock in the morning a winner, woke up Uncle Frank, showed off his wad of cash, and asked him if he would open the luncheonette for breakfast, which as a rule was Louie's job.

Annoyed, Uncle Frank said, "No, you wanted to go to the races, you open the store."

Louie opened the luncheonette that morning, but he was older now and the late nights didn't leave him with enough energy to put in a full day cooking and filling orders, and he began to consider selling his business and retiring. In 1963, Uncle Frank bought out his interest in the coffee shop. Louie had actually made a few good investments in other restaurants, money he handed over to his partners before he could bet it on a race or a poker hand, and with help from Doris and me, my parents were able to buy a nice spacious apartment in a twelve-story co-op on the boardwalk in Brighton Beach. They also vacationed in Florida every winter and lived out their lives surrounded by a serenity they had never known.

Louie played cards every day with his pals in the Liberal Party club that met downstairs in their apartment building, and Mother walked the boardwalk with her women friends. Age had not only slowed Louie physically, it had also curbed the stakes he was willing to wager. My guess is that Louie, in his later years, never gambled with more money than he could afford to lose, and thus Mother was no longer worried that she would wind up homeless and hungry. Also, strange as it sounds, despite all of my parents' problems I always felt that they loved each other, and in their old age Louie began to express his love for mother openly, to say the words and act affectionately toward her in a way that I had not seen before. It was wonderful to watch, and to see my parents happy together was enough to make anyone who had known them beginning in the1920s believe in miracles.

About 1971, Mother was diagnosed with circulatory problems and rheumatoid arthritis, and she lost both legs to amputation. Louie took care of her like a child right up until she died five years later. At the funeral home, I put a deck of cards and a bottle of scotch in her coffin so when she reached the other side, she could have a drink and play a game of *tablanette* with Dubbi.

We buried Ida Gross Shaw in the New Montefiore Cemetery in Farmingdale, Long Island. Before she died, Mother had ordered a bench installed nearby, so when we went to pay her a visit we could sit and think for a while.

After more than two decades of sitting on that bench and visiting silently with Mother it occurred to me that she was, whatever her faults, a courageous woman. She never looked back, never mentioned that unhappy time when she sent Sol and me to the Brooklyn Hebrew Orphan Asylum and a series of foster parents. With no education, growing up in the meanest sort of poverty, Mother simply did what she could to protect her children and help her husband with his business.

I feel sad when I consider what the Shaw boys missed during their childhoods, but I know that Ida missed more than we did, and I comfort myself thinking about the small joys that Mother had with Louie in the latter part of her life. They were the simple pleasures that so many people take for granted, but I knew Mother appreciated every moment, and perhaps comforted herself with the knowledge that she had always done the best she could.

CHAPTER 21

CONFIRMATION

Frank Knobel has led an interesting life. Like many people whose lives do not follow a predictable line, Frank has undergone his share of hardship. Perhaps his worst, and best, moment occurred during the Bohack case, when the plane on which he and his family were passengers crashed in the Caribbean. At ten o'clock on the morning of September 2, 1978, Frank Knobel, his wife, Lisa, and Lisa's thirteen-year-old son, Chris, boarded a seaplane on the island of St. Croix for a day trip to St. Thomas. The plane was part of the fleet of Antilles Airboats and it was being piloted by Captain Charles Blair, who happened to be married to the actress Maureen O'Hara. Along with Frank and his family, there were several other passengers, and as the plane was flying smoothly over the sparkling blue sea, an engine blew.

Suddenly, the plane was descending toward the water. Frank had no time to think as it crashed into the sea, splitting into two, with the water rushing in and people sinking and gasping for air. Frank is a strong swimmer, and he managed to pull a few people to safety, but tragically the pilot and some of the passengers died in the accident. Frank and his wife and stepson survived, but both Frank and Lisa were badly injured, and once they were stabilized they were flown to New York City for treatment.

Frank wound up in the hospital, and since he can't stand to miss work, he returned to managing Bohack's affairs from his bed, which was how I came to receive a call from him early one morning.

"Stanley," he said, "Bohack needs to hire a new financial guy. The doctors got me on so many pain meds I'm not sure my judgment is what it should be. Why don't you come over here and keep me company while I do the interviews. I could use a second opinion."

I went to Leroy Hospital, where, it turned out, Frank was not only a patient but chairman of the board of directors. He was propped up in bed, ready to work, and for the next couple of hours a parade of accountants marched through the door. Frank interviewed them and sent each one right out again, unhappy with the answers they gave to his questions.

"I got the patience for about one more of these," Frank said, and when the next guy came in, Frank, kidding around, asked him, "How much is seven plus five?"

The fellow replied, "How much do you want it to be?"

Frank and I laughed.

"You're hired," Frank said.

With a new financial person onboard and Frank definitely on the mend, my main concern at the moment was finalizing my deal with a young man I had only recently met, Chris Jeffries.

In the fall of 1978, Chris Jeffries was a twenty-eight-year-old lawyer working for Key International, a privately held company based in Southfield, Michigan. Chris had grown up in Flint, Michigan, the son of a telephone linesman, and he had first come to New York City ten years before to attend Columbia University on a basketball scholarship. The city seemed strange to him, impersonal and too fast-paced, and he was terribly lonely, so he had gone back to Flint, married his high-school sweetheart, and then returned to finish college.

After graduating, Chris attended law school at the University of Michigan and then accepted a job with a prestigious Detroit law firm. One of Chris's clients at the firm was the Keywell family, who had made their fortune in the scrap metal business. Their company was now being run by Joel Tauber, a son-in-law of the company's founder, Barney Keywell. Barney had three daughters, and he was getting older and wanted to sell his business, which was valued at $25 million.

Joel Tauber wanted to buy the corporation, but he didn't have the cash, and he hired Chris away from his law firm to help him figure out how to raise the capital. What Chris figured out would later be referred to as a leveraged buyout, and so Joel Tauber bought his father-in-law's business, and Chris ultimately wound up with a substantial amount of stock and a seat on Key International's board of directors.

Now Key International had a problem, a very nice problem but a problem nonetheless. For something like thirty or forty years, as scrap metal was acquired from national companies, it piled up in Key's storage yards. The metal shavings would eventually accumulate and be swept into shining, mountainous piles. Although Key was unaware of it for decades, it turned out that these shavings included tons of precious metals. The problem was that after Key sorted these assets and determined their probable value, they had to then list them on their balance sheet and would have to pay a whopping tax bill. The answer was to buy another company with losses that would offset Key's gains.

At that time, the Internal Revenue Service had a relatively liberal policy permitting a company to purchase another company for the purpose of utilizing its tax loss. However, the buyer had to be in either the same primary or secondary business as the company it was buying. Of all Bohack's assets, its $92 million tax-loss carry-forward was its most valuable. I had been trying to peddle it and did manage to sell an option on it to someone, but he wasn't ready to go through with the deal. Meanwhile, Chris Jeffries had heard about Bohack's troubles and phoned me. I set up a meeting with him and Frank Knobel.

I remember that Chris's hair was sticking up in back like Alfalfa from the Little Rascals, and within a couple of minutes of talking to him his agile mind, good humor, and essential decency were apparent, all of it framed by his gentle Midwestern earnestness. Key International, Chris said, had no intention of going into the supermarket business, but then I mentioned that Bohack was also in real estate, which was an undertaking that Key had been considering.

Discussions about Key International buying Bohack went on for months, and the particulars of the deal changed dozens of times. Finally, Key Land Development Corporation was formed, and they gave me a $100,000 check as a down payment to purchase the land and facilities at Bohack Square. I took the check over to the president of the Brooklyn Savings Bank, who held the mortgage. He told me that a buyer had already come forward and Bohack Square was no longer for sale. Later, I learned that an individual with a questionable reputation had bought the property, paying $3 million for real estate and warehouses and equipment that were easily worth $8 million.

As I looked around to work out another purchase, I, along with Frank Knobel, became deeply concerned that because Bohack was on the block, the people in management would lose their jobs. So Frank and I began looking for ways to place them in other businesses. Joe Binder wound up with several Bohack stores and turned them into a successful supermarket chain. Lou Robustelli and Lou Campanelli purchased three stores, and they ran them until they sold out and retired. Frank was eager to get back to his real estate business, and we managed to knock off two birds with one stone when I discovered that Frank was holding options on some property on Staten Island.

I had Frank assign his options to Bohack, and then I had Key Land Development Corporation buy the options from Bohack. It was beautiful, right? Now Key had some real estate and Frank was back to wheeling and dealing.

Suddenly, though, a fly appeared in the ointment, threatening the entire deal. A gentleman contacted me and said that since he had the court's permission to buy the loss carry-forward, Bohack couldn't sell out to Key.

I said, "But you won't put up any money, and you won't exercise your option. You have to make some kind of a decision, and I think I can help you. Bohack will give you a quarter of a million dollars for your option. You'll make money, and they'll be free to come out of Chapter."

He refused and went out and retained a crackerjack lawyer to represent him. Her name was Dorothy Eisenberg. (Dorothy would later become my partner at Shaw, Licitra, and then go on to become a first-rate bankruptcy judge.) Dorothy advised him to file a notice of appeal. It would have been a brilliant move, since it would have held up the sale of Bohack, and the company would have risked losing the Key deal. But Dorothy's client exhibited the sort of destructive stubbornness that lawyers occasionally suffer through with their clients and told Dorothy that he wouldn't file the notice. Instead, he wanted to sue. She advised against it, but he didn't listen and sued in state court. His case would later be dismissed by the Court of Appeals.

According to my calculations, if Bohack didn't finalize their deal with Key, they had about six more months before Judge Parente would convert the Chapter 11 to a Chapter 7, appoint a trustee who would do a final liquidation, and the creditors would wind up with nothing. Once Dorothy's client was out of the way, the biggest impediment to confirming a plan were the back taxes that Bohack still owed. If you don't settle up with the government, you cannot come out of Chapter, and then they will pursue the former officers of the corporation personally for their money.

I negotiated with the IRS in New York City. Tax issues of this variety were not covered by statute in 1979. Today, they are covered under the Bankruptcy Code, and a company can opt to take six years to pay its debt to the government. I asked for a fifteen-year spread for Key to pay off Bohack's tax liability, and the IRS guys looked at me like I was crazy. However, they signed the deal anyway. I figured what had worked in Manhattan would work in Albany, where I spent the next three days and nights negotiating around the clock with the unemployment and sales tax people. After a fair amount of screaming and stamping of feet, I got fifteen years from them as well.

Another chapter of the Bohack case closed when a jury agreed that the corporation had been the victim of a pricing scheme between Iowa Beef and Waldbaum's. Unfortunately, this became one of those situations where you win the verdict but lose the judgment. Damages were impossible to assess, and Bohack received no monetary award.

The deal was now done. Bohack issued 90 percent of its outstanding common stock to Key International. Key would then transfer to Bohack all of its assets, and the current stockholders of Bohack would own 1 percent of the shares; unsecured creditors would own 4 percent; and administrative creditors would hold 5 percent. The other 90 percent belonged to Key.

By then, I also had a nice souvenir in my basement. While doing some construction work at Bohack Square, one of Joe Ferrara's truck drivers had backed his vehicle into the stanchion that supported the Bohack Square street sign, pulling it out of the ground and knocking it over. Joe had been kind enough to preserve the sign and deliver it to my house.

On Thursday, December 13, 1979, *The Wall Street Journal* ran a short, unsigned piece under the heading of Company News: "The Bohack Corporation, one of the first of many supermarkets to file for bankruptcy in recent years, announced yesterday it had been discharged from Chapter 11 bankruptcy proceedings."

I read the article on the plane, flying to Ft. Lauderdale to join Doris for a week's vacation in Florida. The piece outlined the basic deal between Bohack, its creditors, and Key International, but my eyes kept returning to the phrase *"discharged from Chapter 11."*

Five and a half years had passed since that summer night I'd stood on Joe Binder's lawn in Oceanside, believing that if Bohack retained me to do their filing my whole life would change. I'd been right, but not in exactly the way I thought.

I was already receiving calls from potential clients that previously wouldn't have contacted me, and I was confident that there wasn't a bankruptcy I couldn't handle. I'd made some money and would make a lot more by holding on to the Key International stock that I'd been issued in lieu of my fee, and so my gamble that Bohack would get out of Chapter and I'd collect my fees had paid off.

It was also during the Bohack case that I, after more than a decade, settled the last debt that I'd incurred during my doomed partnership with Marty Schulman. I was at a meeting with a group of creditors when a representative from National Westminister Bank approached me. He said that my name was familiar to him, and I replied that was because I owed his bank money. He laughed, and I explained the situation, which he checked up on, and then informed me that the bank would release me from my obligation for a single payment of five thousand dollars. I gladly wrote out that check, and my Schmuck-with-a-Fountain-Pen days were behind me.

Judge Parente's final ruling on the Bohack matter was so laudatory that it could have been written by me. He began by stating that for him to expound on the specifics of "the extraordinary accomplishments of debtor's counsel in this landmark case would incur a decision of extreme length. Suffice it to say that debtor's counsel's indefatigable and fervent spirit overcame and prevailed over resistance of the flesh. Counsel's performance [exemplified] the quintessence of advocacy."

And, believe it or not, the ruling got even better: "The multitude and complexities of the issues engendered by this case can only be characterized as awesome," Judge Parente continued. "Various classes of creditors filed thousands of claims. The total claim debit was well over the one-hundred million dollar mark. The legal docket contains more than five hundred adversary proceedings, motions and contested matters. Two issues traveled the full appellate process reaching the United States Supreme Court. *Cert.* [leave for permission to appeal] was denied in both instances by a close majority vote of the justices, Were it not for the unswerving faith of debtor's counsel in consonance with superb legal ability, professional capacity and [timely] response to the almost daily problems of the debtor, this case would have aborted."

Then Parente moved on to assaying the value of our fee application. I had long since recovered from the shyness about fees that had plagued me back in the days when I had stood in Judge Babitt's courtroom, unsure of the compensation I should request for my services and hoping only to earn enough money to pay for Jeffrey's bar mitzvah. The Bohack bankruptcy had dragged on for nearly six years, so long in fact that during the proceedings I had to apply to the court to receive payments for costs and fees, a highly unusual situation back then, but one that is now standard operating procedure during a lengthy Chapter 11.

Still, I hadn't expected Judge Parente to grant my full request, and so I was stunned when he said, "Notwithstanding the seven figure amount of the fee sought, when viewed within the purview of the scope of services rendered by debtor's counsel, the fee requested is patently modest. It calculates to $55.31 per hour, well below the per hour norm or standard for a case of this magnitude.

"Accordingly, the attorneys for the debtor-in-possession are hereby awarded the sum of $1.85 million as the fair and reasonable compensation for legal services provided on behalf of the debtor. The distribution of said fee is reduced by the sum of $332,000 previously received, leaving a balance due of $1.518 million." The fee was eventually paid five years later, a full decade from the start of the bankruptcy.

With all of the outward signs of success that accrued to me because of Bohack, I expected to feel relieved after the case, to have a sense of safety, a feeling that I had, at last, arrived, and could slow down. My heart attack, however, had proved to me that life is not a dress rehearsal, that your time is short, and so you better cram it all in before the lights go out.

My plane landed at Ft. Lauderdale. Unbuckling my seatbelt and standing up, I still couldn't believe that Bohack was behind me.

Doris was waiting when I entered the terminal, and as I approached her a lump rose in my throat.

"It's over," she said. Her voice both asked a question and made a statement, and I knew she meant more than just my winning case. We had finally made it, crossed over into that place where we had, for so long, dreamed of going.

Nodding, I hugged her. Then, suddenly, I began to cry. My wife and I held each other, and I could feel the tears on her face, too, and we stood in the terminal, just holding on to one another until we weren't crying anymore, and then together we walked out into the Florida sunshine.

CHAPTER 22

A BLACK VELVET JACKET
AND A BANK OF ONE'S OWN

Mario Puzo once commented that after years of living in barely respectable poverty, borrowing from relatives to survive, and then finally earning himself and his family a measure of financial security by publishing *The Godfather*, he felt as though not having to worry about money was almost like not having to worry about dying.

My situation was slightly different than Puzo's, because by the time I completed my work on the Bohack case I was the not-so-happy owner of a heart condition. Yet when all the legal decisions were in, all the negotiations were done, all the papers were filed and signed, and the court was finished awarding my firm its fees, I was fifty years old and discovered that not only didn't I owe anyone a penny, I had money in the bank.

I thought I should go out and buy myself something, but I couldn't think of anything to buy. I didn't want a Ferrari or an estate with a view of Long Island Sound. Why bother? I don't like driving fast, and I always figured you could just sit on one toilet seat at a time. I don't recall Doris buying anything special for herself or Jeffrey or Lisa, though it was certainly going to be easier to pay our daughter's college tuition at Syracuse University.

My main pleasure was to look at my bank statements with that beautiful black ink and revel in the peacefulness of my newfound economic security. My reveling lasted for a week, maybe two. Then I got bored and discovered how much I had in common with Louie. I was truly the son of a gambler and, like my father, in love with very long odds.

I don't mean this too literally. I was never into the bookies like Louie, although I occasionally enjoy playing craps in Vegas and Atlantic City. It wasn't winning at the dice table that turned me on, but the never-ending action, and of course, the laughs. One night in Atlantic City with Joe Licitra, I must have been rolling for an hour straight and winning on almost every roll when Doris got tired and went up to bed. I said I'd be there in fifteen minutes, but I was still winning a half-hour later, and another woman, who had been betting with me, pleaded with me not to hand over the dice. She asked me what room I was staying in, and I told her, and she said she'd call Doris to explain. She got a house phone, called upstairs, and said, "Your husband can't come up right now. He's too hot."

So I stayed at the table for a while longer, and when I went upstairs to our room Doris gave me a quizzical look.

But again, that's not the kind of gambling that can hold my interest. The stakes aren't high enough if just money is on the line, something I began to understand as word started to circulate about my success representing Bohack, and other financially troubled clients called for my services. You had to be a betting man if you wanted to handle bankruptcies. If you didn't eventually confirm a plan with the court you wouldn't get paid except for the initial retainer, and the subsequent hours you invested would be unbillable. And that would be the least of it. Your clients, their creditors and their employees would suffer. Those are big stakes, and I enjoyed the pressure, the knowledge that I could win or lose it all.

Yet even lawyering seemed too safe now that I had some money. As devastating as my dealings with Marty Schulman had turned out to be, I can honestly say I fell in love with the excitement, with juggling the details of four or five deals, sweating out the financing, thinking about the profits. I had learned my lesson with Schulman, though. I was smarter and didn't sign papers. Besides, I had plenty of my own cash now, so instead of nursing my winnings, I couldn't wait to find another crap game, and I heard the sweet, unmistakable sound of the dice hitting the table when Teddy Broome phoned from Manufacturers Hanover Trust and said, "Stan, I got a guy here you should meet."

Teddy had been in charge of watching over the Bohack account for Manny Hanny during the worst moments of the Chapter XI. Back then, I had to speak to him nearly every day. He was tough and smart, and he kept his eye on the bottom line. So I knew he wouldn't call to waste my time, and I was half-sold on whatever Teddy had to say before the words were out of his mouth.

Teddy said, "Stan, I got Sal Ceserani here. Sal just won the Coty Award. You know what that is?"

I said, "Isn't that's the award for designing men clothes?"

"Exactly right, Stan. For designing the best men's clothes of the year. Sal just won it, and he wants to go into business for himself."

"Sounds interesting," I said.

Teddy said, "So come on up here and meet Sal."

Sal Ceserani was a sincere, lovely guy who didn't appear to have an inch of larceny in him. He had borrowed $100,000 personally from the bank, and he needed additional seed money to start his operation. I told Sal I'd think about lending him the money, and a few days later I had dinner with him and his wife. I told Doris I was considering making the loan. She didn't object. She didn't offer any opinion, since she figured I was in charge of making and losing money, and she was in charge of saving it, meaning that she had squirreled away enough of my Bohack fees that for the moment she wasn't worried about how much I could lose.

I wrote Sal a substantial check and became a 50-percent partner in a men's clothing company. I loaned the money to Sal's corporation so if the business went under I could write off the money on my taxes as a business loss instead of a personal loan. I told Sal that he didn't have to consult me about any decisions, just send me an interest check every month. That was fine with him, and for the first few months the checks arrived regularly. Sal would call me every now and again and ask if there was anything he could do for me, and I invariably said no.

Then one day we were talking, and I said, "Sal, you know, there is one thing I always wanted; a black velvet jacket. Could you make me one? Not on the house. I'll pay you for it."

I'm not exactly sure when I started desiring that kind of extravagant elegance, probably back when I was a kid and read some storybook about a prince decked out in velvet.

Sal said, "By all means. And no charge."

He came to my office and measured me, and pretty soon the jacket was delivered to my door. It was gorgeous, cut beautifully; everything was perfect.

And the price of that perfection was exactly what I loaned him, because before the year was up Sal was out of business.

I still have the jacket, though. I wear it on occasion, and if someone compliments me on it I tell them it should be nice, since it is the most expensive black velvet jacket in the world.

I just knew I would never be short of money again when Carmine Messano phoned, because I was going to be part owner of a bank. Hell, I felt like a fat guy about to buy an ice cream factory.

I had met Carmine during the Schulman years. He had been in charge of FHA loans at Manufacturers Hanover, and he had handled one of the loans I'd personally guaranteed and had to pay when Schulman and I lost our apartment houses. Since then, Carmine had moved on to a job at Community National Bank in Staten Island, and that was the reason he was calling. He said that the federal government—the Comptroller of Currency to be exact—had declared that Community National was $3 million short of cash to meet the federal capital ratio requirements, and the bank needed a cash infusion or the feds would close it down.

"The bank is solid," Carmine said. "We've been trying to sell stock privately, but nobody is buying."

"Why not?"

Carmine said, "Because we're in Staten Island and everyone thinks we're involved with the Mafia. We got a lot of Italians out here, so it's a good bet we got some wise guys with accounts in the bank. But everything is on the up and up. We're not laundering money or hiding accounts from the IRS."

"Hey, Carmine," I said. "Don't get me involved, okay?"

"The Mafia has got nothing to do with the bank," Carmine replied. "Just meet the president and see what you think."

I checked out the bank on my own, and then I had lunch with the bank president. He impressed me as a real sharp guy, and I promised to try and raise the money for him, adding that I'd also make a substantial investment.

Frank Knobel directed me to his good friend Herb Feinberg. Herb was a tough Brooklyn boy about my age who had been smart enough to buy the American rights to Stolichnaya vodka in the mid-1960s, and then make himself a fortune by selling his company to Pepsi-Cola.

I explained the deal to Herb, and he said, "I'll match what you put in. If it's good for you, it's good for me."

Swell, but I still needed more, and I contacted Arnold Burns (later to become first deputy to U.S. Attorney General Edwin Meese), who had helped us when Bohack butted heads with the SEC. Arnie had a lot of well-heeled clients, and he sent Herb and me to one of them, who lived in a castle in the Hamptons, and he took Herb and me for a nice long ride on his yacht so we could admire him and his art collection. He seemed interested, but then he passed, perhaps because he had some assorted troubles that ultimately got him thrown in jail.

I figured the bank was dead in the water until the president informed me that he found a fellow to put the $2.5 million into Community National. I met this fellow. He was in his early forties, and from the looks of things a couple of million to him was nothing but pocket change. He lived in a big, expensive suite at the Delmonico Hotel, and I never spotted him riding around in anything but a limousine.

Everything was set with the Comptroller of Currency, and yours truly was named to the board of directors, one of my prouder moments. However, we soon discovered that our new investor had invested in the bank with the bank's own money. On the surface, it appeared legitimate. He had put up real assets as collateral for a loan from Community National, but when the feds order you to shore up your cash reserves, it's not quite cricket to take in cash that was sitting on your own balance sheet.

The money had to be returned to the bank, and at an emergency board meeting I demanded that the president of the bank resign because this occurred on his watch. He hemmed and hawed, and then we promised him a modest severance package, and he was out the door. The investor was another story. He proved to be about a hundred yards shy of legitimate. He was involved in drugs and Russian pornography. We learned the nature of his livelihood when he either fell or got pushed from the window of his hotel suite and wound up dead on the Park Avenue pavement and in the tabloids.

I hadn't bargained for this level of excitement, but the mundane fact remained that the bank still needed capital. I became the attorney of record for Community National and convinced the district director of the Comptroller of Currency to give us some breathing space to locate an investor. I beat the bushes with my two friends from the board, both of whom had businesses on Staten Island, Jack Sedutto from Sedutto's Ice Cream, and Al Baron, who owned a paper company.

Nothing turned up until late on a hot Friday afternoon when I was driving to pick up Doris at the house so we could go to the Catskills for the weekend. Jack Sedutto called me in the car and said, "Stan, what're you doing?"

"I'm five minutes from home."

Jack said, "Well, turn around and come to the city."

"Jack, are you crazy?"

"No, Stan. It's just that I got a guy who wants to buy the bank."

I called Doris, saying what I had been saying for the last twenty-five years, "I'm sorry, honey, something's come up. I'll be a little late," and then I drove into Manhattan, to an apartment building downtown on Waverly Place, which ironically happened to be one of the buildings that Schulman and I had once owned.

Jack was waiting for me outside, and we went to a second-floor apartment and knocked on the door. The broker who let us in looked like a character out of B movie. I had the impression he had a habit of sleeping in his suits and showering only when absolutely necessary. There was hardly any furniture in the apartment, just a table, three chairs, a Telex, and a phone.

He said, "You want to sell the bank to my client?"

"Sure," I replied.

"Would you sell seventy-five percent of the bank?" he asked.

"For five million," I said. "Who's your client?"

"He's in Thailand."

I said, "Does he have a name?"

He said, "Mr. Wallob Tarnvanichul. But mostly everyone calls him 'Johnny Ma.' What kind of deal do you want?"

I explained it in broad strokes. The broker handed me a pen and yellow legal pad, and said, "Write the deal down, and we will Telex it to Thailand, and I will have an answer for you in half an hour."

I phoned Doris to let her know I'd be even later than planned, and I caught a minute or two of hell from her before hanging up and writing out the deal. Then the broker sent the terms of the deal through the Telex, and within a half-hour a reply came back through the machine: "Deal OK. We buy bank. We come to New York."

"When is he coming?" I asked the broker.

"Today is Friday, Johnny Ma will be here on Monday night."

"How do you know?" I asked.

"It always takes him four days," he explained.

The deal had popped up so suddenly, and the B-movie broker and the empty apartment had seemed so strange that the first thing I did Monday morning was try and find out if Johnny Ma was for real.

For all I knew, he could have been a fictional character created for the purpose of scamming Community National. Worse yet, Ma could have been a front for gem smugglers, drug dealers, or arms merchants looking to give their cash a shower and shave by running it through a small local bank. This isn't as crazy as it sounds. Rumors had been around for years that Community National was a mob bank, rumors that persisted even after John Amodio, a wonderful young man who was straight as an arrow, was named our new president.

The broker had mentioned that Ma's representative in New York City was Bill Yang, who worked in the international department of Citibank. I spoke to Bill, and from the conversation I gathered that Johnny Ma was supposed to be about the richest fellow in Thailand. That was welcome news, but by then I had been practicing law for a quarter century and had developed a healthy amount of skepticism. But it was possible that Johnny Ma could save the bank, so I dropped by to see the district director of the Comptroller of Currency and explained about our Thai angel. The district director stared at me like he thought I'd been smoking opium.

"Listen," I said. "You don't know me, I don't know you, but I'm telling you what happened."

He said, "When is your Mr. Ma arriving?"

"Tonight," I said.

"All right," he said. "But you call me when you have the money. And don't take too long."

That evening, Johnny Ma checked into the Waldorf Towers along with his son, Tinakorn, two Thai generals, his own chef and doctor, three valets, and his beautiful mistress, Betty. He took an enormous suite for himself and Betty; cases of fine wines were stacked up to the ornate ceiling; and his entourage seemed to occupy enough rooms to take up an entire floor of the hotel.

When I arrived, they were in the middle of preparing a Thai meal and celebrating their arrival with champagne. Johnny Ma was a short, conservatively dressed man with dark hair and eyes, a soft voice and open smile. He spoke English with a Chinese accent, and it was hard for me to understand him. However, he seemed to follow my English quite easily, as did his lawyer from Thailand, Professor Somebody-or-other.

Bill Yang was right: Ma may well have been the richest guy in Thailand. His lawyer handed a net-worth statement to me so I could submit it to the Comptroller of Currency. The statement claimed that Ma was worth somewhere between three and four billion dollars. He owned radio stations, ships, banks, office buildings, apartment houses, land, and a cache of gold bullion.

I asked Johnny Ma if he was ready to formalize our deal. Smiling, he replied: "You draw official agreement and give to my lawyer. He like agreement, we sign agreement. Deal all done."

I said, "We can't do it that way. The Comptroller of Currency has to see some money or he'll shut down the bank. If you're interested, give me a check for a million dollars against the other four million, and I'll deposit it in my escrow account. Whatever interest accrues is yours. You get the million back if we don't do the deal."

Johnny Ma looked me straight in the eye and said, "I like you. I do that." Then he turned to his lawyer and told him to wire one million dollars to my escrow account.

After confirmation of the wire transfer, I contacted the district director to let him know Johnny Ma was the real thing. He asked me to bring him by his office the following Monday.

The next week Johnny Ma and I stood before the district director and a board of fifteen people in a big, drafty room with an American flag in the corner. After I explained the plan for Community National Bank to meet the federal cash requirements, the district director said: "You understand there is a change in control here. This type of change must be approved by Washington. Furthermore, I should tell you that there has never been a change of control given to an individual Asian investor, only to foreign corporations or other banks, so you are breaking new ground here."

"So I'll break new ground," I said. "Whatever I've got to do to keep the bank open, I'm going to do."

"That's fine," he said. "But before you start, I must see the bank's agreement with Mr. Ma."

That afternoon, I drafted the formal deal and had it hand-delivered to the Waldorf-Astoria, where the Professor examined it and called in his change: Johnny Ma's real name had been misspelled in one place.

I wish the rest of the transaction had gone as smoothly. For the next fourteen months, I traveled back and forth to Washington trying to obtain permission for Johnny Ma to own a majority stake in the bank. I submitted his financial statements to the Comptroller of Currency and the FDIC, and he was cleared by the FBI and Interpol. At last, I thought we could make it official, but then the district director in New York decided that the stock transfer shouldn't be allowed.

I met with him and blew my cork.

"Johnny Ma is legit," I said. "He's worth billions. And you have the nerve to turn him down without giving us a reason? You can't do that. It's not legal. So if there isn't a single legitimate reason for denying his application we're headed for heavy litigation."

The district director said, "We don't know where his money came from."

"It came from the assets listed on the financial forms," I said. "The investigators told you they were aboveboard."

The district director said, "He lists a hundred and fifty million dollars worth of gold bullion, but he doesn't list the appropriate certificates for it. Where is the gold? And where are the certificates?"

"I'll let you know," I said.

That night, I phoned Johnny Ma in Thailand. I think it was the middle of the night over there. His voice was heavy with sleep when he said hello.

"Johnny," I said. "Your gold bullion needs certificates. "Where are they."

He said, "Gold?"

"The gold bullion."

"Hold on," he replied. I waited a few moments. Then he said, "I'm looking at the gold."

"Where is it, Johnny?"

"It under my bed," he answered.

I couldn't believe it. "All of it, Johnny?"

"All the bullion," he said.

I got some paperwork together to go along with his gold, explaining that it was a personal collection he kept in his home, and shortly thereafter Johnny Ma was approved by the government to become the first Asian individual to own a majority stake in an American bank.

For the next several years, Community National prospered, and I was proud that we were making our presence known again around Staten Island, helping businesses get started or expand or stay afloat through a tough period, or lending money to just plain folks for cars or houses or college educations. This is the role that community banks were designed to play, and we were doing it so well that the value of our loan portfolio shot up to the point that the Comptroller of Currency was constantly after us about the capital-ratio situation, and we were always adding to our reserves.

Johnny Ma was a delight as the major stockholder of the bank. He would visit New York with his entourage once a quarter and host an endless party in his suite. Once, he hired a fleet of limos to drive himself and his entire crew out to Garden City to see my offices. I took him to lunch with some of my friends and law partners. During the meal, someone raised his glass and drank a toast in honor of my birthday.

Johnny Ma listened to the toast. Then he narrowed his eyes at me and said: "You birthday?"

"Yes."

Suddenly, he seemed angry and raised his voice, saying, "You no tell me it your birthday."

"No."

He said, "No good. That no good." Reaching into the inner pocket of his suit coat, Johnny pulled out his pen and gave it to me. "Happy birthday," he said.

It was an extraordinarily generous gesture. The pen was solid gold and studded with diamonds. Then after Johnny returned to Thailand, he sent Doris an equally lovely gift, a necklace with rubies and diamonds.

My gift went straight into the vault, where it has resided for the last eighteen years. I look at it whenever I have occasion to go to our bank for some papers, and I remember Johnny Ma fondly and with some sadness, because a few years later he got into trouble, and I lost touch with him.

The exact story remains unclear, but it seems that in one of Johnny Ma's Asian banks there was a young man working for him who was either a thief or incompetent or both. Johnny caught this fellow in a financial irregularity and fired him. However, the young man was related to Thai royalty, and they looked with disfavor on the firing of their relative.

Next thing Johnny knew the Thai government was closing his banks, confiscating every one of his assets they could get their hands on, and accusing him of being a criminal. He packed up his family and entourage and all of the money and valuables he could get out of the country and fled to Germany, where he set himself up for the life of a well-to-do fugitive.

To live in comfort, he needed to sell his stock in Community National Bank, and when he called to tell me the situation and said he wanted fifty cents a share, which came to about $9 million. I replied that I would try to find someone to purchase his stock, half now and half next year.

I went to Jack Sedutto and Al Baron. They were not inclined to invest any more money in the bank, and neither was I. I started shopping for other buyers and spoke to Jerry Cardin, a banker in Baltimore. Jerry promised to come up with the money, but then he got hit during the S&L crisis. Unfortunately, Jerry became one of my clients, and I helped defend him against the scapegoating bureaucrats who seemed to be going after everyone involved with the savings and loans in Maryland.

I didn't have much luck after Jerry, but then, on a trip, Herb Feinberg was sitting next to Howard Curd in the first-class cabin. Howard was an investment banker, and Herb told him the story of Johnny Ma. Howard landed, got on the phone, and offered Johnny Ma sixty cents a share, which was accepted, and Howard wound up owning the bank. I stayed on the board, and everything ran smoothly until the years immediately following the S&L crisis.

The federal rules for required cash reserves kept growing more stringent, and the federal regulators continually forced us to pull more money out of our profits and hold it in reserve against our loans. Of course, this ultimately makes a bank unprofitable, which the federal government doesn't like, and in 1991 we were forced to close Community National, and the FDIC ordered Chemical Bank to take it over.

That heavy-handed action turned out to be completely unnecessary. The loans were good, the proof being that even the depositors who had over $100,000 in the bank and lost that federally uninsured part of their savings when the bank was originally closed, eventually collected a major portion of their deposits, and I believe they will eventually receive all of their money—because the assets were there to pay them. The closing of Community National was another sad example of the government moving in to fix what wasn't broken and scaring and inconveniencing people and destroying a bank that had been making a valuable contribution to the businesses and neighborhoods and families of Staten Island.

As for me, the bank proved to be a profitable venture. Although I lost my entire investment, from 1980 until 1991, Shaw, Licitra handled the legal work for Community National and collected very healthy fees.

Sadly, five or six years after Johnny Ma got his money from Howard Curd, he died in exile.

CHAPTER 23

THE LAW

During the Bohack case, Congress passed the Bankruptcy Reform Act of 1978, and in my view it was an enormous leap forward for bankruptcy practices. A fine business reorganization was born, and a far more powerful personal bankruptcy was created. As I expected, the legislation kicked off a round of bitter legal squabbles, and numerous amendments and judicial rulings have been handed down during the last two decades. In the main, the changes in the laws over the last twenty years have made it easier for businesses and individuals to file for bankruptcy and to recover from it. In some quarters this change represents a dark new chapter in the economic life of our country with some critics considering it a form of government-sanctioned permission to avoid obligations. But I have never seen bankruptcy in this cynical light. For me, the ability to file for bankruptcy is the essence of being an American. We are a nation bursting at the seams with people who came here seeking a fresh start, who wanted to wipe the slate clean and line up for a second chance, and bankruptcy protection is our government assuring us that it is permissible to hope—that no matter how badly you fall on your face the law will allow you to stand up and try again.

It has been said that you can't be a wise man until you've been a fool. I always liked that saying because it recognizes and celebrates the value of experience. It also has meaning for me, a former fool. The lessons I learned in the real estate business have been invaluable to me as a lawyer, since I can honestly tell my clients that I understand their problems: After all, I've been to that land of hopelessness when you consider yourself an abject failure and feel as though you haven't a friend in the world.

What follows, in no particular order, are some of the dealings I had with clients who felt just this way. Some of them recovered;

some of them did not. I am proud to have done my best to help them all.

When I met Bill Levitt in the mid-1970s he had already achieved legendary status as America's greatest, twentieth-century, suburban pioneer—the visionary builder of Levittown, Long Island. Immediately following the Second World War, his construction firm, Levitt & Sons, built more than seventeen thousand inexpensive, almost identical eight-hundred-square-foot houses on seven and a half square miles in Nassau County that Levitt & Sons had possessed the foresight to purchase before anyone else had figured out that a housing boom was on the horizon. Levitt's houses were made of prefabricated materials and could be built in a hurry. The starting price for the new homes was under seven thousand dollars, and with the acute housing shortage that occurred in the wake of our soldiers being mustered out beginning in the early summer of 1945, the homes sold like hotcakes to returning veterans and their growing families. Levitt & Sons also built projects on an equally vast scale in Pennsylvania, New Jersey, and Maryland, leading one urban historian, Kenneth T. Jackson, to observe that the Levitt family had the greatest impact on postwar housing of any construction company in the United States.

In 1968, Levitt & Sons was sold to the International Telephone and Telegraph Company for $92 million in ITT stock, making the Brooklyn-born Bill Levitt one of the wealthiest men in America. By the early 1970s, Bill was sixty-five years old. He lived with his beautiful, charming third wife, Simone, in a gorgeous thirty-room mansion on his estate, La Colline, in Mill Neck, Long Island, and sailed the waters of Long Island Sound on his own 237-foot yacht, *La Belle Simone*. Yet once a gambler, always a gambler, and despite all of his success Bill couldn't stay out of the game. His sale agreement with ITT mandated that he stay out of the construction business in the United States for a decade. So Bill broke ground on projects in Iran, Venezuela, France, Israel, and Nigeria. They didn't prove to be as successful as his American suburbs. Then ITT nosedived, and his stock lost most of its value, a disaster for Bill because he had used his stock as collateral for his building projects.

And so it happened that when I met Bill Levitt he was looking for financing just like any other ordinary builder. I was a board member of Community National and was serving as the bank's counsel when Bill applied for a $750,000 loan. He was planning to collateralize the loan with unimproved land as well as his wife's ring, which was set with an enormous glittering diamond that looked like it belonged under glass in a museum. The closing was at Levitt's office, and the bank instructed me to bring a gemologist. Right before we signed the papers, I said, "Mr. Levitt, do you mind if the bank takes a look at the ring?"

Bill wasn't a tall man, but he had an imposing, slightly intimidating presence. He looked at me hard for a moment and then handed over the ring.

I said, "Mr. Levitt, this is Mr. Jones, the bank's gemologist. They want him to appraise your wife's ring."

Bill seemed surprised, but said nothing, and my gemologist took the ring outside to inspect it in the natural light. Five minutes later, he poked his head back in the door and asked if he could speak to me privately. I went outside, and the gemologist said, "This stone is as close as you will ever find to a real diamond. I'm not even sure what kind of stone it is, but it is definitely not a diamond."

After returning to the office, I said, "Mr. Levitt, we have a problem here. The gemologist has taken the position that this isn't a real diamond."

Bill said, "What do you mean?"

"I mean we can't close the loan."

Bill said, "Why don't I take this ring and anyone you want to my gemologist?"

Although I hadn't raised my voice or become lawyerly with Mr. Levitt, I had for all intents and purposes accused him of lying, so I was willing to do anything I could to smooth this over. I said that would be fine; I would be available tomorrow. Bill promised to send a driver to pick me up.

His driver showed up the next morning, and we rode over to Levitt's gemologist. He inspected the ring and pronounced it a real diamond worth $850,000, more than enough to collateralize the loan. Then we drove over to the bank's gemologist, who reversed himself from the day before and said that this stone was a real diamond.

Bill later explained what had happened. On a trip to Las Vegas, thieves had broken into his hotel room and stolen just under a million dollars of jewelry. Since then, he had all of his wife's jewelry copied and left the real stuff locked in the vault. The copy had been brought to the closing by mistake.

Now that I had the real ring in hand, the bank made the loan. I never thought I would hear from Bill again, but I guess he liked the way I had dealt with the situation because a couple of years later he gave me a call and said he had a business proposition for me. Bill owned some enormous tracts of land in Florida, and he was hoping to turn the land into a kind of Levittown South, putting up twenty or thirty thousand houses. The day he announced his plans something like eleven hundred deposits flooded in. Bill was closing in on his eightieth birthday, and he was hot to build these houses and regain his fortune, most of which was gone. That was why he came to me. He needed financing to complete the project.

I interested some my friends and clients in investing some money, and so did my friend Herb Feinberg, who also spent the next year talking to his friends and business associates, trying to raise capital for Levitt, convinced, as I was, that Bill was going to make an absolute killing with these Florida houses. Eventually, Bill's name proved to be a liability for raising money. Investors backed out because his financial plight had been widely reported in the press.

Bill had always been straight up with me, never a dishonest moment. He even gave me a $150,000 donation toward a residence for the learning disabled in honor of my son Jeffrey, and the house was named after Bill. Of course, Bill was also accused by New York State Attorney General Robert Abrams of illegally taking money from a charitable foundation that the Levitt family had established decades before. To his credit, Bill repaid all of the money he had borrowed from the foundation, and I came to like and respect the man. Here he was, one of the giants of the century, slowly going broke, and he managed to maintain his dignity. It was heartbreaking to watch, especially after it became clear that Bill would never get his Florida project built and would have to refund all of the deposits.

By the mid-1980s, Herb and his associates had made a substantial investment with Bill, and Bill had put up his estate, *La Colline*, and the surrounding sixty or seventy acres of prime Long Island real estate, as collateral. When the loan came due and Bill didn't have the money to pay, Herb was legally entitled to simply take over the property. Yet he just couldn't do it. By then, the house and land were worth over $9 million, so he could have made more than $5 million on the deal, but he didn't have the heart to take the estate away from Bill and Simone and pocket the additional money. Instead, I put the house on the market for Bill and sold it for $9.3 million.

Herb made his money back, and Bill and Simone got the rest. I continued to do legal work for Bill until he died in 1994, and I still advise his widow, Simone, who is now a dear friend of our family. Bill was a remarkable man, and I wished I could have done more for him, but in all likelihood it would have been impossible to get him to retire from the real estate game. He loved it too much, and he was one of those restless and luminous people who never felt truly alive unless he was betting everything on the next spin of the wheel.

Sometimes what clients need is not the smartest lawyer in town, but one who is willing to do a little digging and then have the nerve to run with what he finds. This is what happened to my clients Anna and Abe, whom I represented in a bankruptcy filing. They owned a good deal of real estate, but because of a preexisting judgment of about $4 million, they wound up in a cash-flow bind and were being pressed by the judgment creditor who wanted to sell some of the real estate to satisfy his judgment. This is not an uncommon situation for real estate investors, and Anna and Abe only needed time to convert their sizable real estate assets into cash. They had filed for a Chapter 11 not to avoid their financial responsibilities, but in the hope that the court would give them a chance to get squared away and hold on to the investments they had worked a lifetime to acquire.

The first judge who heard the case wanted to liquidate their assets and appoint a trustee to dispose of their real estate. This was not only unwarranted, but the worst possible outcome for my clients. I told the judge that the value of the real estate more than qualified them for the court's protection and asked her to appoint an examiner who would look into the claim that, prior to filing the Chapter 11 petition, they had been fraudulently passing money to family members. The judge turned down my request, and we went to trial. After three months, the judge developed an appreciation for my point of view and called everyone into her chambers to say that she had changed her mind on appointing a trustee and had decided to appoint an examiner.

Terrific, right? You would certainly think so. But then the judge, after handing down her decision, announced her retirement, and another judge caught the case, Judge Edward J. Ryan.

During the course of my career, I had probably appeared before Judge Ryan on thirty or forty matters, and I always thought him to be an excellent judge, bright and practical with a decided lack of patience for any form of legal posturing. Except now, the instant I stepped before Judge Ryan in this case, he started snapping at me. For no reason I could discern, he seemed to be convinced that my clients were a couple of crooks, and from what I could tell nothing could have been further from the truth. Yet Judge Ryan was hell-bent on putting in a trustee to break up their holdings and pay off the creditors. I had already covered this ground with the first judge. I thought we had a decision, and the examiner should stay in place, but Judge Ryan was disinclined to hear my side of the story.

His stance didn't make a damn bit of sense until I did some checking around with my contacts and learned that Ryan's daughter was a lawyer who worked for a firm that represented the major secured creditor in the case. The firm was opposing me in the case solely for the purpose of having a trustee appointed so that my clients' real estate would be liquidated and the major creditor would get paid immediately. This would have prevented my clients from coming up with a reasonable reorganization plan, which would have permitted all of the creditors to collect their money over a period of time.

A couple of days later, I appeared before Judge Ryan. I mentioned that I knew where his daughter was employed and said: "Your Honor, I've known you for a long time as a fair and impartial man. But in this case, at this time, it is only appropriate that you recuse yourself. In so doing, I'm not claiming that you've been unfair, but it must not only be right, it must look right."

Judge Ryan refused to step down. However, my clients got a break. During the case, the opposing counsel for the secured creditor was a top-notch woman attorney who happened to be pregnant. At the start, she was three months along, and as the matter had dragged on, so did her pregnancy. As soon as I introduced my recusal motion, my opposition stood up and asked the judge if she could please have a minute. Judge Ryan said okay, and she walked over to me and said, "Stan, you SOB, my water just broke and I've got to leave."

I congratulated her and wished her luck with her new baby, and even sent her flowers when her daughter was born. The delay that followed gave me time to argue for Judge Ryan's recusal before the district court and later in front of the Second Circuit of the U.S. Court of Appeals. Although I couldn't get the appellate courts to rule in my favor, it is noteworthy that Judge Ryan was not reappointed, and the judge who replaced him allowed my clients' assets to remain in the hands of the examiner. Eventually, the properties were sold in an orderly fashion in favor of my clients, and my firm was able to collect our fees.

In late 1991, I received a call from John Torell, the former president of Manufacturers Hanover Trust. I had met John during the Bohack case, and he must have respected the work I'd done because he wanted me to help him with a problem. John was in Clearwater, Florida, serving as the chairman of the board of Fortune Savings Bank. Fortune was owed $25 million from Consolidated Minerals, Inc., the largest loan on Fortune's books, and John wanted the bank's money back. He would have gone to Fortune's general counsel, the largest law firm in Florida, Holland & Knight, but they couldn't take on the matter due to a conflict of interest.

Previously, Holland & Knight had represented CMI in the company's negotiations with Fortune Bank.

I retained local counsel to deal with the stacks of paperwork, and then I began traveling back and forth to Clearwater with a lawyer from Shaw, Licitra, my then-associate (and now partner) Roberta McManus. The negotiations were long and complex, as they usually are in such a case, but the pressure on all of the parties came from the fact that if CMI defaulted on the Fortune loan, it would have triggered a host of other defaults for CMI. I pushed hard with Bruce W. Griffin, executive VP of Fortune Bank, against Browne Gregg, the CEO and major stockholder of CMI, until I worked out a repayment plan that recovered a hundred cents on the dollar for the $25 million and reimbursed the bank for all of the outstanding interest and legal fees. Fortune obtained cross-collateral and cross-defaults of CMI's loan with Fortune, and as security CMI posted two commercial properties and one agricultural lot, along with all of the machinery, fixtures, and crops. I was also able to get Browne Gregg to make a personal guarantee on the interest payments on the loans, which came to $2.5 million a year.

We did a superb job, which took over twelve months and required more than a dozen trips to Clearwater. The fees we received were excellent, but the real payoff was that we became involved with Holland & Knight, one of the twenty largest law firms in the world. (At the time, they had two hundred lawyers around the globe; today, that number has grown to over a thousand.) It was John Torell of Fortune Bank who played matchmaker. By the end of the case John was asking me to set up a satellite office of Shaw, Licitra in Tampa. I rejected the idea, explaining that my firm had more than enough to do up north in Garden City. John then prevailed upon me to meet with Bill McBride, the managing partner of Holland & Knight, and the social and business friendship that I developed with Bill proved to be the biggest bonus of the case.

I discovered that Bill and I shared a strikingly similar philosophy when it came to managing a law firm, namely that each and every member, from the partners to the clerical staff, should be regarded as nothing less than family. That wasn't pure altruism. With so many people depending on us, it made waking up in the morning and getting to the office exciting and challenging. Over the years of my friendship with Bill, he introduced me to Chesterfield Smith, the former president of the American Bar Association, and founding father of Holland & Knight. Bill also introduced me to Michael Jameson, Parkhill Mays, and the entire board of Holland & Knight. I had hoped that I could persuade them that our firms should merge. Although the merger hasn't happened yet, my friendship with all of these people continues to this day, and we maintain a fine working relationship and together have served as co-counsel for major clients throughout the United States.

Nothing ever infuriated me more than to watch the little guy take a beating in bankruptcy court. My feelings were fueled by more than the fact that I invariably rooted for the underdog, having grown up poor and Jewish in Brooklyn during the Depression, or that as a young man I had been hounded by creditors. It was that I hated to see anyone lose their shot at living out a long sought after dream.

Two wonderful fellows facing just this situation walked into my office in 1991. The men had formed a partnership that since 1985 had owned the remarkable office building and national landmark, One Times Square, where the ball dropped every New Year's Eve. The building, which has been the centerpiece of so many illustrious photographs of New York City, was topped with a spectacular advertising sign and featured the famous news zipper that rotated around the exterior. The partnership had poured its resources into One Times Square over the years, its single asset, and the two men were waiting patiently for their ship to come in.

However, as frequently happens in the volatile New York City real-estate market, prices slumped, and on paper, at least, the value of One Times Square was now less than the mortgage, which was held by the Banque Nationale de Paris. It has been my experience that bankers know a good thing when they see one, and I am of the opinion that the Banque Nationale was not worried about receiving its mortgage payments, but they were eager to take ownership of the building, and then weather the downturn in prices and cash in the moment the market recovered its value.

I was glad to have the chance to represent the owners of One Times Square against the Banque Nationale, and the strategy I used was a long shot, but I felt that the courts had neither been logical nor fair with single-asset holders facing bankruptcy. The courts' position has always been that a single-asset bankruptcy was a no-brainer: The debtor can't pay, so sell his asset and divide the proceeds among the creditors. Since these cases usually involved real estate and a temporary downturn in the local market, I felt the courts were undercutting the purpose of bankruptcy—providing people with the opportunity to turn red ink into black.

My first move was to open up negotiations with the Banque Nationale and to sweeten the pot, offering the unsecured creditors another $1 million in order to give my clients enough time for the value of One Times Square to catch up with the mortgage. The bankers weren't interested, most likely, as I've noted, because they really wanted the building not their mortgage money, and they probably felt that they could make more than $1 million by eventually selling the property.

When the negotiations fell through I tried to break new legal ground by arguing to the court from the start—and throughout a lengthy appeals process—that the portion of the mortgage that was not covered by the appraised value of One Times Square belonged in a separate classification of creditors than the part of the mortgage that was secured by the current value of the building. I also argued that the creditors who rented space on the building to put up their signs belonged to another entirely separate class of creditors. In other words, I argued that Banque Nationale was partially an unsecured creditor and therefore belonged in a class along with those creditors who will accept less than they are entitled to in order to collect some money from the bankrupt party.

Had the courts accepted my argument, the owners of One Times Square would have been able to pay Banque Nationale a percentage of what the mortgage didn't cover and hold on to their building. But the courts rejected my position. The judge wouldn't permit me to establish another class of creditors, and so Banque Nationale eventually took over One Times Square. Interestingly, a few years after the appeals process had been exhausted, there were so many single-asset real estate foreclosures pouring into the legal system that Congress amended the Bankruptcy Code's treatment of these specific matters. Even after the amendment was added, however, I suspect that my clients would have lost their investment because Congress made it more difficult for owners to hold on to their buildings in the belief that the owners of single-asset properties had agreed up front that the mortgage holder could take the property if the owners defaulted on their payments. Congress did decide that if the property owners were receiving significant income from their building other than rentals the courts should offer them some protection from creditors. Although I had argued that my clients deserved this protection because of the rental payments they received on their signs, and the courts had not agreed, I continue to believe that the ruling was unfair, and someday we will see bankruptcy judges willing to protect single-asset holders.

An interesting side note to the case falls under the category of Divine Intervention, of God making things right—as far as my client list was concerned. The Banque Nationale recouped their money by selling the mortgage on One Times Square to another group of investors. These investors sold the property to Lehman Brothers, who turned around and sold it for a fortune, earning in the neighborhood of $50 million—money that Lehman ultimately invested with another client of mine, Willie Breslin, thus helping Willie realize one of his longtime dreams.

It is hard for me to talk about Willie without bringing up another friend and client, Chris Jeffries. Chris was involved with the company that took over the Bohack assets, and I received stock in this new enterprise, Key Land Development, in payment of my outstanding fee. When I met Chris he was a young man obviously headed places. However he had a conflict with his boss, and his first marriage was breaking up. Fortunately, I was in a position to lend him support; we became very close friends and I handled various legal matters for him. I also did quite well with the stock.

Chris went on to found Millennium Partners and become one of the most successful developers in New York City, building the notable Lincoln Square complex along with a host of other well-known residential and commercial sites not only in Manhattan but across the country. When Chris was seeking $1 million to obtain the option on the Lincoln Square complex land, he asked me to help him find someone to put up the million in exchange for a fifty-percent equity in the deal. I immediately sent the proposal over to Willie Breslin, who was too busy to focus on the project and had to pass.

Willie is also one of the most successful developers in New York, but he is more than twenty years older than Chris, and his area of operations was mainly on Long Island. I met Willie years ago when I was in the midst of suing five banks in bankruptcy court. (Prior to the bankruptcy the banks had stupidly refused a settlement and wound up losing most of their $65 million investment.) Wille was interested in the property the banks and I were battling over, so he stopped by to participate in the proceedings, making an offer on the property. He saw me in action and obviously liked what he saw because he called and we struck up a friendship.

Willie has the best qualities of a developer—hard-headed pragmatism coupled with the vision of a dreamer and the energy to work around the clock and then play tennis on Sunday. For a quarter of a century, Willie had a dream—to build a gigantic commercial and residential development in the Pine Barrens on Long Island. He bought approximately two thousand acres of land out there, and for years tried to put the deal together.

We used to discuss the problems involved in realizing his dream, and I'm sorry to say that there were a great many of them. Willie was subjected to more zoning hearings than anyone should have to endure. He faced environmental lawsuits and citizen groups who didn't know what they were talking about and the banks pulling out their financing. By then, Willie had millions invested in the project, and although he had been doing business with some of these lending institutions for decades and had a long, successful record as a Long Island developer, he was faced with the real possibility of losing his money and his dream.

All of these conflicts generated litigation. There was a mountain of work involved, but I found nothing more satisfying than helping my friend to pursue his sought-after star. I tried to put Willie together with Chris, hoping that Chris could provide the financing the banks had cut off, but it wasn't in the cards. Then Willie had a stroke of genius. He contacted Lehman Brothers and brought them in on the deal. Willie got the $60 million he needed, and I like to think that it was money Lehman earned from the sale of One Times Square.

As of this writing, I am happy to report that Willie has repaid Lehman, the project is well on its way to completion, and Willie will finally see his dream come true.

* * *

Joe Murphy is another of my clients who combines vision and courage and never backs down from a challenge. Joe is in his sixties now, a smart, self-made man with a distinguished mane of white hair. Joe's parents were Irish immigrants, and he grew up in modest circumstances in the Inwood section of Manhattan. He attended Iona College on a scholarship and after graduation worked his way up to become president of the Lambert Brussels Corporation and the Lambert Brussels Real Estate Corporation. He oversaw the $2.5 billion capital of Groupe Bruxelles Lambert, of New York, and I believe he became a member of the top echelon at Drexel, Burnham. I got involved as Joe's lawyer around 1990, when a property he owned, the venerable Hotel Syracuse in Syracuse, New York, filed for Chapter 11.

The City of Syracuse tried to remove Joe as the owner, claiming that he had breeched his lease when the hotel fell behind on its bills. Our position was that Joe had no lease because he had financed the hotel with bonds, and so the terms of his ownership were really part of a financing package. We litigated the issue in bankruptcy court. The judge agreed with us regarding the lease, ruling that the city had no right to evict Joe as owner, and thus new law was made.

Joe's biggest problem was that he had personally guaranteed the hotel's debt. His situation was the same as mine had been back in my days with Marty Schulman, except Joe had used his pen to take on responsibility for tens of millions of dollars in debt. Consequently, when the hotel went into bankruptcy, the creditors came looking for him. Stuart Gordon, one of the lawyers at my firm (and now a partner), handled a good deal of the work in Syracuse.

Our firm was able to help arrange the sale of the Hotel Syracuse to the Bennett Group. The sale cleaned up all of Joe's personal debt. Unfortunately, the major officers of the Bennett Group wound up being indicted for allegedly running one of the biggest pyramid schemes in American history and later filed for Chapter 11. The Bennett Group asked us to represent them in their bankruptcy proceedings, and we accepted. It was a complex and fascinating case with fees that probably would have run into the millions, except that we were suddenly displaced when someone in the bankruptcy division of the Department of Justice insisted that a former head of the SEC be appointed trustee for the Bennett Group, a position that generated millions of dollars in fees for him. I was annoyed, but I knew there was nothing I could do about it, even though the Bennetts opposed this appointment, since the bond between greed and politics is unbreakable.

Meantime, Joe continued with his career as an investor. Understandably, many people would have been soured on the hotel business after undergoing an experience like the battle of Hotel Syracuse, but many people aren't Joe. He is too tough and persistent and energetic, and he called us again in 1997 to help him with his new big idea, his plan to purchase the bankrupt Concord Resort Hotel in the Catskills. In its heyday almost a half century ago, the Concord was one of the gems of the Borscht Belt. By the1960s, though, the Catskill hotels began to lose their aging clientele to other vacation spots. By November of 1998, when the Concord finally closed, the majority of the other Catskill resorts were already gone.

Joe formed a limited partnership to purchase the Concord, and Joe's group, in conjunction with the Sheraton chain, is in the process of refurbishing the Concord, which they plan to reopen as the Sheraton Concord Resort Hotel and Convention Center. It is going to be a first-class hotel with close to two thousand rooms and beautiful golf courses and ski trails and indoor everything.

Of course, it wouldn't hurt Joe's investment one little bit if casino gambling were approved in that area.

However the deal works out, Joe deserves a lot of credit. Over a thousand people, many of them longtime employees, lost their jobs when the Concord closed. Now many of them will have a chance to be rehired.

When I was a young man, I used to wish that the day would come when I would be successful enough as an attorney that I could take down my shingle, pack up and sit myself in the Florida sunshine and retire in style. It was only a fantasy then, but now that I have reached that stage of my career and have the financial means to do it, I strongly resist the idea of retiring and find that I love practicing law and meeting the difficulties faced by my clients more than I did when I was first starting out.

To some degree, my attraction to the law is rooted in the fact that the law is a living and breathing representation of the shifting values in our country and the conflicts created by these changes. Being immersed in the practice of law is a way of living on the cutting edge of our culture and staying forever young mentally, physically, and spiritually. So of course when people I haven't seen in quite a while call and ask me how I'm doing, I can answer with a line I heard years ago and have admired ever since: "I'm doing the same thing I always did, but not as often."

Perhaps the biggest reason I continue to attack new problems with new clients can be found, like so much of my motivation, in my earliest years. Looking back at that part of my childhood from the comfort and safety of seven decades, I have concluded that the day Mother and Aunt Shirley left me at the Brooklyn Hebrew Orphan Asylum was the day I began to perceive myself as unworthy of love.

Luckily, with the passing of time and the good luck to live for so long with a loving wife and children, I have come to understand that the financial, cultural, and psychological forces that swept me off to the BHOA were far more complex than I could have possibly understood in the 1930s.

Still, I have learned that the cliché "Time heals all wounds" is not wholly accurate, and that there are wounds even time cannot heal. But we, in all of our flawed and splendid humanness, continue to try—don't we?

So today, after I solve a client's problems, I hope to hear the words "Thank you, for a job well done," and for a fleeting moment, I will have won the adulation and love I missed as a child.

CHAPTER 24

SUMMING UP

OR
MY RECENT THEORY
OF DIVINE INTERVENTION

Save me from the self-made man. I have heard that saying over the years, and yet I've never known exactly what to make of it. After all, the country I grew up in professed the notion that discipline and hard work and taking chances and refusing to quit no matter how bad a beating you took were the true roads to moral and financial righteousness. It was a vision that was drummed into your head in the classroom, and after school the lessons were reinforced on the blacktop with your boyhood friends and enemies.

This strict philosophy of self-reliance, which was really more a standard of personal honor, was tailor-made for my generation— we serious-minded, well-mannered children of the Depression, who knew we should be seen and not heard when in the company of our elders. We grew up with indelible memories of bread lines and Bing Crosby on the radio asking if his buddy could spare a dime, and bleary-eyed apple sellers on wintry street corners, and families shivering in the cold twilight, huddling together on sidewalks with their few pathetic sticks of furniture and staring up at the apartment house where they had lived until moments before when the landlord had evicted them for nonpayment of rent.

As the writer Caroline Bird so movingly points out in her study of the long-term impact of the Great Depression, survivors of those grim days bravely pushed on into postwar America, many of them making the most of the continuing economic expansion, only to find themselves afflicted with what Bird refers to as "the invisible scar." This lingering, painful reminder of that desperate past takes the form of a haunting insecurity that does not disappear, regardless of how much money you sock away.

In the case of my childhood, living on the thin ice of poverty was complicated by the thinner ice on which my parents chose to conduct their marriage, and even today, sixty-six years after I arrived at the Brooklyn Hebrew Orphan Asylum, I still feel sad and empty when I recall that sprawling brick Castle on the Hill with those colorless institutional walls and scuffed floorboards and the dim, late winter light in the high drafty hallway, with Mother and Aunt Shirley walking away from me for what seemed like forever. Thus, if you add my personal history to the tenor of the times it is obvious that if I hoped to avoid the sorrows of Mother and Louie I had no choice but to become a self-made man.

Still, when I began this memoir, I realized that there was wisdom in that expression about self-made men, a warning that one ignores at his peril. So many men and women who start life with scarce resources and achieve a measure of professional and financial success feel that they are solely responsible for their upward climb, an opinion that can only lead to the overweening pride that has laid people low since the beginning of time.

As an adult I understood that whatever I've accomplished would have been impossible without the love and security provided by my wife, Doris. I'm convinced that she literally saved my life when I had my first heart attack by rushing me to the hospital. Since then, her attentiveness to my emotional and physical well-being has made it possible for me to continue to practice law and generally enjoy my life despite my serious health problems.

Not that everything has been perfect between us, even though Doris is an unrelenting perfectionist. I frequently tell Doris that I'm going to buy her a barber shop and a diner because she constantly combs my hair to correct my barber's alleged mistakes, and because she has a lot to say about restaurants. I would also like to buy Doris the Diet Shasta ginger ale plant in San Francisco, since for the last forty-five years she has been carrying her own can of Diet Shasta ginger ale to restaurants, so she can use it as a mixer with her V.O. But it is difficult for me, even in jest, to be critical of the person who I believe has provided me with what I missed most in childhood, a loving, nurturing family.

From the beginning, Doris's parents treated me as a son, and her brother, Lenny Meyerowitz, and his wife, Sandi, seemed to welcome me like a long-lost member of the family. Since then, Doris has overseen what is really the bedrock of my emotional security— our son, Jeffrey, our daughter, Lisa, her husband, Lon Goldstein, and our wonderful granddaughters, Ashley-Lynn and Brittany-Lee, whom I think of as my little darlings, A and B. In fact, the only regret that I have in life is that I never spent enough time with my children. When they were toddlers, I was fighting to get even. After that, I was struggling to get ahead.

Yet as I reflected on my past to capture the shadings of its meaning and emotion in words, it occurred to me that ever since I was a child I had a sense of another presence in my life, a gentle, guiding hand, and I have always thought of that hand as belonging to God. For instance, to this day, forty-four years after marrying Doris, I still feel that a higher power was at work that summer I was waiting tables at the Riverside Hotel. Had Doris not pursued me, I probably would have wound up the well-kept, unhappily retired husband of my law-school girlfriend. Come to think of it, I have the same exact feeling about my stint in the Army and the general stepping in to rescind my orders to go off to fight in Korea because he liked the way I served his food at the Officers' Club and wanted to keep his personal waiter around. I don't mean to suggest that I have been singled out for divine preference. It is just that looking back and reflecting on my journey, I can't begin to imagine how I escaped my past and managed to build anything resembling a normal future. I certainly couldn't have done it alone, or even with only Doris, her loving family, and the children. The odds against me, like the odds against my brothers, Eli and Sol, were too great.

My brother Eli died a few years ago. He had retired from Bullards, a machinery plant, and still lived in the house he had bought outside Bridgeport shortly after the war. Fortunately, he married Ruth, who turned out to be as fine a wife as a man could ask for, and together they raised two terrific children, a son, Stuart, and a daughter, Donna. Eli remained a bright, energetic man until the end. Later in life, he learned how to do quite complicated tax returns and studied for and obtained a real estate license, so he earned money on top of what Bullards paid him in salary. Yet to some degree he seemed never to recover from the disappointments of our childhood and always carried an understandable bitterness about those years after our family reconstituted itself in the dreary, four rooms of a rented Coney Island bungalow.

I prefer to remember Eli when we first moved back with Mother and Louie, and Eli used to stand in his room playing "Stardust" on his trumpet with a happy, faraway look in his eyes, as though he were imagining his future in all its infinite possibility. He had not yet been forced to give up his dreams to work with Louie at his coffee stand, or to leave school because he found Lincoln High School in Brooklyn far less appealing than the clean, bright suburban schools of Lawrence, Long Island, where he had lived with our wealthy aunt and uncle and cousins. His frustration hadn't overwhelmed him, and he had not directed his rage toward Louie and fought him in the bungalow and spent the better part of a year in the psychiatric ward of Kings County Hospital.

Our brother Sol is still alive, but he walked the longest and hardest road of us all, and he required a kind of bravery that I find remarkable. Added to the sadness of growing up in foster homes with me, Sol was haunted by the anguished legacy of helping to clean up battlefields during the Second World War, and today he lives in a residence for disabled veterans near Northport, Long Island. His marriage to Evelyn ended in sorrow, but even after they were separated, Sol kept up with her as she moved from locked ward to locked ward and then died. His daughter Brenda and his son, Seymour, have required long-term care in managed facilities, but his daughter Sheila, the little girl I long ago helped to place in foster care, is a geneticist and the mother of two adopted children from Columbia. She lives in Seattle, and Doris and I speak to her frequently and see her on occasion. As hard as life has been for Sol, he has remained a loyal father and brother and spends almost no time ruminating about his past, building those sand castles of what-might-have-been. He has courageously accepted what the world handed him, without complaint, and he did his best. And I don't think you can possibly ask more from a human being.

How then, I often wonder, did I escape? Part of the impetus behind that question is survivor's guilt, the knowledge that life worked out better for me than for my parents and brothers. But for me there are philosophical issues involved as well. A statistician might answer my question by citing the randomness of circumstance, the chaos factor, the unpredictable workings of fortune. A psychologist would point out my place in the family and add a lecture on the genetic basis of character structure. I am not immune to the well-structured arguments of logic. Yet my answer to the question is found in the realm of the theological.

To this day I do not recall if, as a foster child, I prayed for deliverance from the grim, lonely regimen Sol and I faced during the two and a half years we lived with Mrs. Wind and her family in Bensonhurst. However, I am sure that the day Mother and Louie announced they were giving their marriage a second try and came to retrieve us from the Winds was an event that assumed a place in my mind on the order of Moses leading the slaves out of Egypt.

The less scientific among us would describe this development as just good luck. I never saw it that way and, with the passing of time, I have come to think of it as Divine Intervention, for I shudder to think how the rest of my life might have turned out had I been forced to shuffle between foster homes like the one run by Mrs. Wind. I thank God for those roaches and bed bugs that Sol and I were forced to share our room with at the Winds', for I believe that when I pointed them out to Mother she knew our situation had moved beyond desperate, and she decided that our only hope was for her to give her marriage to Louie another chance.

Now that I am approaching the end of this memoir, and I am struggling to weave the threads of my seventy years into a tapestry that has some discernible pattern, the one thread that seems to run through it all is my belief that so much of our lives rests in the hands of God. Whatever we accomplish, we owe not only to our own efforts, but to the will and grace of a higher power.

For me, it is this belief that saves me from myself, from the conviction that everything that has ever enriched me was purely the fruit of my own labors. I would have nothing without Divine Intervention.

Ever since I can remember, I have believed that with time and luck and the help of God, people have the power to change for the better, and no one proved it more than Louie toward the end of his life. After he and Mother moved to their co-op on the boardwalk in Brighton Beach and Louie retired from working in coffee shops, he was transformed into what he had never been, an attentive husband.

When Mother got sick with rheumatoid arthritis and became bedridden and finally had to have her legs amputated, Louie cared for her day and night. Unlike the earlier part of their marriage, even after they got back together, he always had time for her now, and whatever she needed Louie was willing to do. After Mother died, Louie adjusted. I have to hand it to him. He didn't ruminate or express regret for what he had missed; he just put his head down and continued with his life. He stayed on in the co-op for a few years, playing cards and socializing with his friends, and doing a little betting with the bookies. But he never had to ask me to pay his debts, and no shylocks were calling me at home or the office, so I assumed that Louie wasn't wagering beyond his ability to cover his losses.

Louie was gradually losing his sight, and I used to talk to him on the phone every day during those years when he was living by himself in Brighton Beach, checking up on him, making sure that he was remembering to eat his meals and swallow his daily rainbow of pills. By now, Doris and I were going to our apartment in Florida quite a bit in the winters. We would leave on a Thursday and return Sunday night. I would call Louie right before we boarded the plane, and then once or twice while we were down there, and again as soon as we came back to the house in Queens. On this particular weekend, I couldn't get him on the phone while we were in Florida. I didn't get really nervous, though, until we landed in New York, and I called him again from home. It was after 11 P.M., and there was still no answer.

I contacted the police and told them the story. I said that I was going over to my father's apartment with the keys, gave them the address and asked the desk sergeant if some patrolmen would meet me out front. I jumped in the car and sped over to Brighton Beach, and when I arrived two policemen were standing outside the building. We took the elevator upstairs, I opened the door, and one of the cops said that it would be better if I hung back until they checked out the place. They walked past me, then one of them called that I should stay out, my father was dead. I looked into the apartment and saw Louie stretched out on the floor. Feeling that I had to see him, I walked in and stood over Louie. He looked like he was sleeping, and I must have been standing there for a minute or two when I began to think that my eyes were playing tricks on me because I could have sworn that I saw Louie move.

"I don't think he's gone," I said to the cops, and then I bent down and gave Louie a light tap on the face.

He opened one eye.

Feeling my spirits rise, I said to him, "They had you dead, Dad. You're not dead."

Now, I realize that this may have been one of the only times in my life that I called Louie "Dad."

"No," he said. "I'm not."

The police radioed for an ambulance. Apparently, Louie had suffered some kind of minor stroke, and he had been lying on the floor, unable to get up, for a couple of days. I felt guilty about it, but Louie never reproached me. I have to hand it to him. For as long as I can remember, he was never a hypocrite, refusing to hold anyone to higher standards than he set for himself.

Louie spent a while in the hospital, and when he got out he was frail and almost completely blind, so Doris and I had to move him to the Hillside Nursing Home in Queens. Louie always made friends wherever he went, and he had a television set and could watch the ball games and seemed to get along well at the place. I still spoke to him every day and went to visit with him every Sunday, bringing him his favorite jelly doughnuts and cigars, which had always served as the two staples of his existence except for gambling, which I assumed he wasn't doing much anymore. For one thing, he didn't have easy access to money, since Doris was handling his finances by then. I also figured that most of his pals among the bookies would be as old as Louie, in their late eighties, if they were still alive, which was statistically improbable because given what I had observed over the years of Louie's contacts in the gambling world, being a bookie was a high-stress occupation that seemed to involve a lot of smoking and drinking and keeping very late hours.

I didn't ask Louie about his gambling. Those questions were never asked out loud in our family, and certainly not by one of his sons. So while Louie was at Hillside, I comforted myself with the knowledge that none of the nurses reported any bone breakers showing up at the nursing home to twist my father's arm for his losses. One nurse, however, did object to my bringing Louie his regular supply of doughnuts and cigars. She stopped me in the hall outside his room to explain that they weren't good for his health. She was probably right, but Louie was pushing ninety and I doubted there was too much damage he could do to his health.

"You have to be kidding," I said, and continued to bring Louie his treats.

One day while I was at the office, I received a phone call from Louie, and he told me that I had to come over to the nursing home right away. I only visited him on Sundays, and he had never made such a request before, so I got worried.

"What's wrong?" I asked.

"I just have to see you," he said. "Today."

I zipped over to see him and found Louie stretched out in bed in his bathrobe. I sat down, and he reached into the pocket of his robe and pulled out a thick wad of money and handed it to me. I was stunned. I was holding about three or four grand.

Then Louie said: "I just beat the bookies for thirty-five hundred bucks. I want you to keep the money because I'm done with those bastards. I'm not betting another dime with them."

Louie was true to his word. As far as I know, after all of those decades of compulsive gambling, of straining his marriage and busting apart his family, of taking money he shouldn't have from his mother and brothers and sons, Louie finally quit calling the bookies. He seemed to be awfully glad when he did, so proud of himself, and I often wondered if it had been a promise he made to Mother after she died or if he had simply decided he wanted to see if he could, at the end of his life, become the master of his own ship.

There is an old saying that goes something like "God may appear to work slowly, but He is always right on time." Maybe that was the case with Louie. Somebody has to be a gambler, and Louie was one of them right up until the moment came for him to stop. Although his compulsion turned my childhood upside down, it is

316 : *I Rest My Case*

only fair to observe that the impulse to take big risks, bequeathed to me by Louie, has served me well as an attorney and business-man. In that sense, I owe some of my success to his lifelong battle with his uncontrollable impulses.

Less than a month after Louie gave me his final winnings, he came down with pneumonia and was taken from the nursing home to a hospital. I received another call from him at my office, asking me to please come right away. He had sounded so sick and weak on the phone that this time I thought he was dying and hoped that I'd get there before he passed away.

Entering his room, I was greatly relived to see him sitting up in bed. After I said hello and sat down, Louie said, "I didn't want anybody to steal my watch and ring. You hold onto them for me."

I watched him as he handed me his rather ordinary wristwatch and a ring that looked as though it had a nice-sized diamond set in the middle of it. Of course, given Louie's gambling and his chronic shortage of cash over the years, I never thought the stone was real. Nor was I quite certain, as I visited with him in the hospital, whether he was concerned someone would steal his jewelry or whether he sensed that he wouldn't be here much longer and wanted to give me something, to let me know he appreciated all that I had done for him since Mother's death and perhaps for never reproaching him for the sad and ugly past.

Shortly after giving me his watch and ring Louie died at the age of ninety-three.The diamond was indeed real, worth over five thousand dollars, and I had it reset and I wear it now as a way of remembering Louie, of his wish to be a better husband and father. We buried him next to Mother, and I made sure to put a box of cigars in his coffin so he wouldn't be caught without a smoke on the other side. My Uncle Harry Miller used to say that people don't really die, they just change addresses, and I pray that wherever my parents are now residing they are enjoying the love and seren-ity in the afterlife that they enjoyed during their last years.

Good-bye, Louie. Take care of Mother.

I stayed close to my mother's sister and brothers until the end of their lives. My Aunt Shirley and Uncle Harry moved to Florida,

Harry remaining the bon vivant he had always been. He had earned a small fortune in the garment business, and the man had more talent for enjoying himself than anyone I've ever met. My aunt and uncle had been living in their luxurious apartment less than a month before Uncle Harry knew just about all of the other residents by name, and everybody who worked there. It was as though a party followed in his wake everywhere he went, and I wish that I had developed some of his talent for relaxing and enjoying life without work. I was sad to see them pass on, but their lives proved that some of my mother's family could prosper and lead what can only be described as a happy life, for this was not the case with her brothers, my Uncles Phil and Willie.

My boyhood hero, Phil Gross, suffered terribly and eventually died from Lou Gehrig's disease. Uncle Phil died broke, and he wasn't that close to his children, so before he passed away he asked me if I would look after his wife, Ethel. I was happy to have the chance to repay Phil for sticking with me through my worst moments back when I fancied myself a real estate developer, and for giving me those white bathing trunks when I was a child. Uncle Phil spent his last years in Florida, in a condominium that Doris and I bought for him. After he was gone, Ethel continued to live there, and Doris and I handle her expenses. It was the least I could do for Uncle Phil—the tough guy and ladies' man—who in my memory remains as the only constant bright spot of my childhood.

My mother's other brother, Willie Gross, also died broke, but he had a lot more fun getting there than most people. Willie had been a hell of a bookie in his day and had gone through all of his money. He probably counted on making more, but once the police had identified Willie as a Known Gambler—a KG in police parlance—he was forced to get out of the business or go on a lengthy trip to upstate New York, where he would pass the time making license plates. When Willie quit making book, his life seemed to go into a slide. He was a longtime widower who had become estranged from his children and grandchildren, and he lived alone in a small apartment in Coney Island. He had a girlfriend, God bless him, but I'm not sure how much time they actually spent together. As Willie got older, I became his surrogate son. One afternoon, I was talking to him on the phone. I could hear that he was a little blue and said, "Willie, anything that you want I can give you, you've got it."

Willie said, "I'd like to spend the winter in Florida. How's that?"

"I'd be glad to do it, Willie. You pick the spot, I'll take care of the bills and send you the plane ticket."

So for a few years Willie wintered in Florida. By the time he turned eighty-six, though, he didn't enjoy going back and forth any longer, and he kept to himself in Coney Island.

One day I get a call from Willie, and he said, "Stan, you told me that whatever I need you'd help me out, right?"

"That's right, Willie."

"Well," he said. "I need a new mattress."

"We'll take care of it," I said, and so I told Doris about it and she had a brand new mattress delivered to Willie in Brooklyn.

About a week later I walked into the house for dinner, and Doris said, "I just got off the phone with the mattress people. They said Willie sent the mattress back."

I called my uncle and said, "Willie, I thought you said you needed a new mattress?"

"I do, Stan," he replied.

"So why did you tell the deliveryman to take it back?"

Willie said, "Because I don't take bullshit off nobody."

"What was the problem?"

Willie said, "I told the guy I wanted a ten-year guarantee. He wouldn't give it to me, so I told him to take the damn thing back where it came from."

I didn't know whether to laugh or cry. Here he was, pushing ninety, and what he was worried about was the next ten years. I finally had the mattress sent back. I would like to say that Willie got his decade of use out of it, but he didn't.

Then all of Mother's immediate family was gone.

By 1981, Doris had had enough of taking care of the house, and we decided to sell the place and move to an apartment. We still had Jeffrey with us, but Lisa was getting ready to go out on her own.

We had heard that the developers Rose & Ratner were going to develop a matched pair of luxury high-rises right across from the

Throgs Neck Bridge in the Bayside section of Queens with a terrific view of the water and the New York City skyline. For years,
even after I began to earn a lot more money, Doris and I had lived
as we always had, a comfortable, upper-middle-class life, but being
sensible children of the Depression, we had avoided anything extravagant. Now we figured was the time to splurge, and we bought
two of the planned penthouse apartments and arranged to have
the developer knock down some walls to form a bigger living area.

Our new home turned out to be as beautiful as we had imagined, but by the time we moved in I was involved in a court battle
with the developers, a battle that, in retrospect, indicates that my
little theory of Divine Intervention comes awfully close to the Hindu
and Buddhist belief in karma or—perhaps more fitting because I
was born in Brooklyn—the expression one frequently overhears on
New York City playgrounds, "What goes around, comes around."

When Doris and I, along with twelve hundred other families,
purchased condos at the Bay Club, the developer gave us the impression that the health club he was putting into the complex would
be for the private use of the Bay Club owners. But then Rose &
Ratner, probably believing they had an untapped income stream,
tried to negotiate with New York City so that the health club could
become a public facility.

The condo owners objected, and I offered to represent them in
a suit against the developers for nothing—after all, these were my
new neighbors, why not make friends? I commenced an action
against Rose & Ratner on the grounds of fraud and false representation, collecting nearly180 affidavits in which the condo owners
claimed that the sales personnel had assured them that the health
club would be private. To keep pressure on Rose & Ratner, I notified the New York State attorney general of what had transpired.

Meantime, I came up with an idea to resolve the problem. I
had the residents of the Bay Club purchase the property next door,
a swim club, for $200,000, and we donated it to the YMHA on the
condition that it be opened up to the public while the Bay Club
facility remained private. I again notified the attorney general of
this plan. It was approved, and the Bay Club owners got their
$200,000 back from the developers, while our health club remained
private except for three mornings a week when we open it to senior

citizens, a plan I put together with my old friend, the late New York State Senator Len Stavisky.

I didn't see any divine handiwork until I appeared before a judge to help straighten out this mess. I was sitting there when I heard the court clerk call out, "Luigi Goldstein against the State of New York."

Luigi Goldstein is not the kind of the name that one easily forgets, and I remembered where I had previously heard it. Luigi Goldstein had run a food business that served the New York City schools. He had owed Bohack over a hundred grand, and during the Bohack bankruptcy I had tried to collect it. However, I hadn't succeeded, because I believe the owners of the food service had been involved in some fraudulent schemes and had gone to jail. Still, the state had owed them money, and when they got out of prison they filed suit, and they were in court on this day to have a judgment levied.

I dashed out of the courtroom and called my office to check the file. Sure enough, we still had an outstanding judgment against Luigi Goldstein. When I went back into court and heard that Luigi had won a hefty chunk of change from the state, I hit the food-service folks with subpoenas, and very shortly thereafter they handed me a check for $110,000, which I felt was God's way of telling me I had been wise to do the Bay Club work on the arm.

The cynic will tell you that no good deed goes unpunished. I have tried to maintain a different perspective, and collecting that long-overdue payment has only reinforced my view.

Then one evening in September, Jeffrey didn't come home from his workshop. It was shortly after we had settled into the Bay Club. I was about to pass the worst hours of my life. The panic was overwhelming. I have lived on the edge of financial ruin and undergone open heart surgery; but those experiences were a moonlight stroll compared to that moment Doris and I realized that Jeffrey was missing.

Jeffery was in his midtwenties. He would never rack up the traditional accomplishments that fathers brag about, but Jeffrey's courage was remarkable. He had struggled mightily against his handicaps, making enormous strides in his functioning, but if some nut had tried to grab him off the street or hurt him, it would have been beyond his abilities to know how to handle it. As the hours passed and he didn't arrive, a cold dread swept over me, and I felt encased in a fog of unreality, not believing that this could possibly happen, that Doris and I would have this terrible sorrow to bear.

We phoned the police and explained that despite his handicaps Jeffrey was able to function fairly well on his own. However, his ability to travel around the city was based on his sticking to a routine that he had developed with years of practice when we had lived in Flushing, and he had traveled back and forth to work in the sheltered workshop at the Cerebral Palsy Center that wasn't far from our home. Now that we had relocated to Bayside, Jeffrey's routine was different. For a couple of months, he had practiced riding the various buses back to Flushing with supervision, but he had been on his own this morning, and there was no telling where he might be.

Doris and I waited through an excruciating night and into the early morning hours. The police set up a command post in our apartment. Every radio car in New York City had his description. The police tried to retrace Jeffrey's route, questioned people and searched abandoned buildings, but they found nothing until a bus driver, pulling into the terminal in Brooklyn, saw him sitting alone in the back of the bus at about three o'clock in the morning. Jeffrey had boarded the wrong bus, but he'd had the presence of mind to take the identification he kept in his wallet with him that morning and show it to the bus driver.

My biggest concern was that Jeffrey had been kidnapped, and any minute I expected to receive a call or a note demanding a ransom. I don't recall exactly what prayer I uttered late that afternoon when I finally saw Jeffrey step out of the radio car that brought him to our local police station—perhaps the universal benediction for frantic parents—Thank you, God, for returning my child.

Jeffrey's getting lost proved to be a blessing in disguise. Ever since he was a child and we discovered that he was learning disabled, Doris and I had gotten him involved with organizations that would help him become more independent. His first group was ANIBIC, the Association for Neurologically Impaired Brain Injured

Children. Doris and I were very active in the organization and helped ANIBIC raise money to start up their residential care facilities. We brought in a substantial donation from Bill Levitt, and for my efforts ANIBIC presented me with a gold lapel pin that I wear every day as a way for me to keep my son, and those who struggle with similar handicaps, close to my heart.

Anyway, once Jeffrey got lost in the city, Doris, Lisa, and I decided it was time for him to move out and hone the skills he would need in the coming years after his parents were no longer around to protect him. It was a traumatic moment for all of us, Doris and I because to cut the umbilical cord a second time is never easy and we worried about Jeffrey more than your average child. The move was especially hard on Jeffrey because emotionally he was far younger than his twenty-six years, and it was difficult to explain it to him without making him feel rejected. Doris handled the challenge with her usual mix of pragmatism and compassion, and I marveled at her patience and skill with our son. After a thorough round of research, Doris found an organization, New Horizons, which ran a group home for the learning disabled in Ellenville, New York. It was a long ride for us to visit Jeffrey, but the care was first-rate and he made a good deal of progress and later moved to another New Horizons home nearby in High Falls.

By 1994, Doris, Lisa, and I were worn out from traveling back and forth to visit Jeffrey, and he had made enough headway in his development that we felt he could safely be placed in a group home not too far from New York City. The Association of Children and Adults with Learning and Developmental Disabilities was planning a residence in Farmingdale, Long Island, which would have been perfect for Jeffrey. Governor Cuomo had already approved money to purchase and staff that group home, and we put Jeffrey's name on the ACLD waiting list.

When Jeffrey's name came up on the list, Doris and I were thrilled that he would be nearby, but then we ran into a problem. The new governor, George Pataki, had campaigned on a platform of fiscal responsibility and immediately upon taking office he froze the state budget for funding new residences for the disabled. This move put ACLD's new group residence on hold, and I decided to write the governor to explain the situation. I knew him as a sensitive man, but I wondered if he would be too busy to get back to me.

The new governor proved remarkably responsive and compassionate. The next morning, I received a call from the executive director of ACLD that Governor Pataki had expedited the release of the funds that allowed ACLD to buy the house, and Jeffrey is now living in that wonderful home in Farmingdale.

As a lawyer I have passed the better part of forty-five years negotiating with people, but when Doris got sick, I started bargaining with God. I don't remember the precise terms I was offering—just about anything I'm sure—because Doris was diagnosed with cancer, a rare lymphoma of the eyes. The thought of losing her was unbearable. I had already lost my dear friend and partner, Joe Licitra, to cancer in 1987, and years later, another close family friend, Lillie Marmelstein, had died of lymphoma. Lillie and her husband, Jerome, had a son, Lewis, who like Jeffrey had a learning disability, and they were in the same class at school, which was how Doris met Lillie. Lewis actually was a bit less disabled than Jeffrey. He managed to complete college in seven years, and he now lives on his own and works with computers for the Defense Department. After Lillie died, Doris, in her typically generous way, added the Marmelsteins to our family, making sure they had what they needed, helping Jerome to open his own business, and becoming the surrogate mother to Lewis, a role she also played for another of Jeffrey's classmates, Colan McNeill, who lost his mother at a young age.

Who knew? Maybe God would count her extraordinary generosity of spirit in her favor. Then, too, I had started the Joseph Licitra Memorial Fund (which has given out forty college scholarships, over ninety thousand dollars, to youngsters in South Queens who did well in school and demonstrated exceptional character). Perhaps God would count that fact in my favor.

Doris was treated at Memorial Sloan-Kettering Cancer Center, and when we came through the front door I couldn't help but remember meeting the former director of the center at Rudolph Fluege's apartment back when I was starting out as an attorney.

Her physician was Dr. Burton Lee, who later became the personal physician to President George Bush. Beyond his obvious skill and experience, Dr. Lee was a compassionate man. He gave us reason to hope, which we did, along with my private negotiating, and I maintain that the combination helped Doris beat cancer.

Once Doris was in remission we discovered that the Shaws were going to require some more Divine Intervention if they were going to remain intact. This time, I had the problem.

I had been suffering with angina for a while, and one night I was having a great deal of discomfort. Doris tried to contact my cardiologist, Dr. Christodoulou, but he was on vacation. So Doris suggested that I go see another cardiologist, Dr. Stanley Shanies, who had been recommended to us by her close friend Anita Ovberg. However, Dr. Shanies was off that day, and his associate, Dr. Peters, told me to go right to Long Island Jewish Hospital for an angiogram. I got to the hospital and thought maybe I would be better off at New York Hospital. The next morning, Dr. Shanies returned, took one look at my record, and ordered me to stay at LIJ for the test. His timing couldn't have been more fortuitous because that night, I went into cardiac arrest. I was later told that they had to call for the crash cart, and for a moment they actually lost me before getting my heart beating properly again. As soon as I was stabilized, I underwent a triple bypass.

Ever since my heart attack, I had watched my health carefully, and on the rare occasions I slipped up, Doris steadied me. I joined a cardiac rehabilitation exercise class overseen by a nurse, Josephine Cruz, and I went (and still go) three mornings a week. Jo not only put us through our paces but also closely monitored us, which was lucky for me because she spotted the fact that I had developed ventricular tachycardia, an irregular heartbeat that can lead to sudden death. I immediately went over to LIJ and had a pacemaker put in.

By the time I was recovering from my surgery, my long days and late nights leading the rebellious Liberal Party of Queens County were well behind me. First off, I didn't have the energy or spare time to throw myself into campaigns and elections: I became the man in the joke you hear about bar mitzvahs: I'll attend the services and party and give the boy a check, but if I don't have to come, I'll send twice as much.

Secondly, my politics had changed. Some pundits have observed that as men age their politics shift to the right with each dollar they earn. I don't accept that view with regard to myself and other politicos I've known. Rather, what aging teaches you is that political problems are not black or white, and thus they are immune to ideology. Leaders only leave notable accomplishments behind them if they can sort through the endless shades of gray. During the last two decades I have voted for people of all political persuasions, and the deciding factor in my choice was simply that I thought he or she would take an open-minded, pragmatic approach to the challenges of the moment.

For instance, in 1994, Democratic Governor Mario Cuomo ran for a fourth term against the Republican challenger, George Pataki. During the early part of the campaign season, when the polls indicated that Pataki had no chance of unseating Cuomo, a couple of partners in my law firm, who are Republican, came to me and said they would like to put together a cocktail party to raise funds for Pataki. I had no objections; the man was running for governor and it would be interesting to meet him. Doris was certainly glad to hear about the party because she had been working on behalf of nonprofit organizations for the learning disabled for many years. She was president of New Horizons and she, along with the organization's executive director, had drafted a letter outlining the educational and fiscal needs of the learning disabled and why the state should support them. She handed me the letter with instructions to pass it along to the candidate. At the reception, I shook hands with Pataki and noticed that he was staring at me and smiling.

Finally, he said, "You don't recognize me do you?"

"I'm sorry," I replied. "I don't."

Pataki said, "I met you fifteen years ago during the Bohack case. I represented the apple growers and Borden's Milk Company."

We reminisced about Bohack, then discussed some of the issues facing the next governor. I gave him Doris's letter and told him about Jeffrey. I liked George Pataki. There was an openness about him, a passion mixed with pragmatism. Also, Senator Al D'Amato was backing him, and I had been a D'Amato supporter since his first run for the Senate. I know Al attracted his share of critics, but no senator has ever worked harder on behalf of all New Yorkers. Whether it was for funding for AIDS treatment or new economic initiatives, Al always made sure New York got a fair shake. I know at times he has had a reputation as a right-wing ideologue, but I think that was exaggerated and for the most part undeserved.

The reception didn't raise a fortune for Pataki, maybe thirty-five thousand dollars. I had enjoyed talking to him, but I didn't give it another thought.

A few days after Cuomo lost the governorship to Pataki, I received a call at my office from Al D'Amato. The senator was holding a private celebration dinner in the city for a small circle of influential Republicans and the governor-elect, and he invited me to attend.

I said, "Since my bypass, Doris doesn't let me stay out late. I'd like to come, but I'll have to get a pass from her."

"I'll handle it," Al said, and phoned Doris to get me my pass.

When I arrived at the restaurant my first thought was—I wonder what my old friends from the Liberal Party would think of me now? I didn't have much time to reflect on that question because as soon as George Pataki saw me he gave me a hug and said he couldn't thank me enough.

"What'd I do?" I asked.

"The money meant a lot," he said.

"It wasn't that much money," I replied.

"But it was early money," he said. "And it meant a great deal to me. And by the way, tell Doris I read her letter and I'm going to do everything I can to help the learning disabled."

Doris and I were pleased that the governor kept his promise. In 1998, the state-funded New York Cares program will provide residences across the state with space for five thousand mentally and physically challenged people.

It must have been a couple of months after Jeffrey had relocated to Long Island that I had an experience I will always remember. My old friend Hank Greenberg passed away, and I attended a memorial service for him at our synagogue in Flushing, Temple Gates of Prayer. In the middle of the service, his grandson stood up and attempted to begin a eulogy for his grandfather. As the young man tried to speak, I realized that, like Jeffrey, he was learning disabled. And when he broke down crying and was unable to start his speech, I also began to sob, wondering who would take care of Jeffrey once I was gone. In my heart I was certain that his sister, Lisa, and her husband, Lon, would be capable of tending to his needs, but I knew how lonely Jeffrey would be because I had been that lonely as a child.

I am fortunate. My apartments in New York and Florida both have wide, glorious views of water, and sometimes, in the early evenings, I sit and watch the sunset, the shining gold and red light fading first to violet and finally to dark blue. It gives you something to think about, this glimmering moment at the end of the day, and occasionally this is what I think: If I spent my life running from the loneliness of the Brooklyn Hebrew Orphan Asylum, the assorted terrors of foster care, my parents' poverty and emotional struggles, with God's help I had run in the right direction—into the arms of Doris and our children and grandchildren.

I am seventy years old now, and I know that my own sunset is inevitable, but I won't watch it alone, and I am comforted by the knowledge that the colors of this sunset will be as warm and beautiful as love.

ACKNOWLEDGMENTS

I could never have written this book without the help of some very special people who shared their experiences, viewpoints and memories with me. However, there are also other people, who while not mentioned on these pages, have been enormously helpful to me during my life, and I want to thank them as well.

Let me begin by thanking Benjamin Frankel, a gentleman I met at the home of the Austrian Ambassador to the United States. During a conversation over lunch, Ben observed that I had lived an interesting life and should write a book about it. He was then kind enough to send me a copy of a book written by Richard Rhodes whose early childhood was similar to mine.

My thanks to Arthur Rubin, accomplished actor and tenor, neighbor and friend, who, when I was recuperating from my by-pass surgery, gave me a record of his songs that was to be a legacy to his family. His gift inspired me to do my own memoirs.

Special thanks to Harvey Roth, my childhood friend and next-door neighbor on Neptune Avenue. Harvey, Murray Getman, Duvie Goldstein and Herb Hirschhorn were my poolroom pals and school-mates, and they generously helped me fill in the background of my youth. Thanks also to Bob Levine, my friend and fellow Boy Scout.

I would like to thank Leona Ferrer of the J.C.C.A. for her help in obtaining my records regarding my stay at the Brooklyn Hebrew Orphan Asylum. The Jewish Historical Society also helped to prod my memory by allowing me to look at BHOA materials from the 1930s.

I am grateful to my partners and friends George Esernio and Jeffrey Schwartz for their loyalty and friendship over the years, and I am especially grateful to all the other members of my firm: Bob Bohner, Anton Borovina, Ed Flint, Stu Gordon, Jack Hall, Sally Keenan, Frank Livoti, Alan Marder, Peter Marullo and Roberta McManus for their willingness to sanction my spending some "bill-able" time in order that I might complete this memoir. Thank you Alan, Sally, and Frank for reviewing the manuscript with keen eyes.

Thanks to my dear friend Franklin Knobel for his recollections of the Bohack case and more important for his faith and confidence in my ability as a lawyer. I also owe Frank a thank you for his special friendship and advice through the years, for without him there would be less of a story to tell.

I am particularly grateful to Joseph Ferrara for his friendship through the years. He has been the one person I can call with any problem at two o'clock in the morning. He is an irreplaceable friend.

A special thanks to Jerry Edelstein, my political mentor and comrade during my Liberal Party days, for his help in filling in the gaps of my memory.

My thanks and appreciation to my secretary, Gerry Cefalu, for her untiring efforts in arranging my schedule to accommodate the work on this book and for her sage advice about these pages.

I must also extend my thanks to Gail Shepey of my office for her assistance in preparing the index of my book.

To Eddie Miller, my cousin and dear friend, I extend my sincere appreciation for his help with the background of my early life and family history, and for providing me with so many pictures that re-energized my memory.

I am indebted to Chris Jeffries, one of the new icons of New York real estate, for helping me with the fine points on the outcome of the Bohack case, and for allowing me to become a part of his team to help develop his future projects. I also owe a debt of gratitude to the late Lou Robustelli and Lou Campanelli for their help in providing further background information on the Bohack settlement.

My further thanks to Jesse Levine for his invaluable assistance in getting through the daily problems of the Bohack Corporation during the bankruptcy proceeding, and most important for his aid and comfort during my illness, which enabled us to see the Bohack matter through the end.

I extend my appreciation to Bankruptcy Judges Dorothy Eisenberg, Connie Duberstein and C. Albert Parente for their help in providing me with the judicial background on the Bohack settlement, and to Judge Re for passing along a copy of my first article in the *New York Law School Law Review*.

I also extend my thanks to Al Baron, an honest, hard-working, straightforward guy, who helped with the background on Community National Bank, and also Herb Feinberg for his help on that chapter.

I am deeply indebted to Josephine Cruz for keeping me together in cardiac rehabilitation, and Anita Ovberg, who recommended me to Dr. Shanies. Many special thanks to Dr. Stanley Shanies and Dr. Maurice Safrin. Thank God for good doctors; otherwise, I would never have been here to write this book.

I must also mention Wilbur Breslin, a friend, client and visionary, whose energy level I would love to have, and Gary Calmenson, who introduced me to Willie. My thanks to Marty Schackner, Beth Alderman and Paul Berger, and the staff of Breslin Realty, who were a major factor in forming the strategy that resulted in the successful conclusion of the Wilbur Breslin dream.

Special mention must be made of some of the people I have grown to respect and admire who merely by their friendship and support have added much to my life: Alan Hevesi, a friend for thirty years, who I hope will become the 108th mayor of New York City; H.Carl McCall, my pick for the next Governor of the State of New York, a good friend and an exceptional human being; Senator Alfonse D'Amato, a friend and a guy who gets things done and always keeps his word; Governor George Pataki, who expedited the process of getting my son, Jeffrey, into his current ACLD placement and who continues to help the mentally challenged.

I would like to thank my good friends, Sam Albicocco and Santa Albicocco, for their confidence in me, which has resulted in many new clients for the office, and to Rocco Rossini for his friendship and faith in my ability as an attorney.

My thanks to Gary Melius, a client who has become a friend and business associate, and to George Dempster, for his kindness, his understanding, and his untiring efforts to help me during my illness.

Many thanks to Frank Schellace for helping me resolve some of my most complex cases.

Thanks to Simone Levitt, wife of the late William Levitt, the renowned developer of suburban America. Simone's friendship and enthusiasm were instrumental in helping conclude this book.

My deep appreciation goes to my late uncle, Frank Shaw, who filled in Louie's background and his relationship with Ida and the children. I am also grateful to my two cousins, Shirley Cheresnick and Florence Goldberg, who provided me with the insight into Louie and Mother's life together.

A special thanks to Rita Smolkin, the daughter of the Greenbergs, who was helpful in remembering my time in my first foster home.

My thanks to the entire Politi family for the friendship they displayed to our son, Jeffrey.

My sincere gratitude to my brother Sol Shaw, who endured so much with me during my early childhood and provided me with the background for this book, and his daughter, Sheila Neier, who helped fill in some other blank spaces.

Sincerest thanks to Lenny and Sandi Meyerowitz. Lenny is truly my adopted brother and together with his wife, Sandi, represent forty years of vacations together, all of them filled with good humor, good family and laughter.

How can I ever truly show my appreciation to my daughter, Lisa, for her support during the writing of this book? I also want to thank her husband, my son-in-law, Lon, for his help. Both of them have given me two of the most beautiful granddaughters anyone could hope for.

My appreciation to my son Jeffrey Scott Shaw, for his courage and his ability to always rise to the occasion.

Thanks to Shoshana Cardin, wife of the late Jerome Cardin, who introduced me to Peter Golden.

Last but not least, my appreciation and thanks to Peter Golden, for his ability to work with a businessman and for helping me extract the important parts of my life and put them into words.

There are many people to whom I owe a debt of gratitude. Many have touched my life in different and special ways and through those experiences helped shape my destiny. If I have left anyone out, please accept my heartfelt apologies.

INDEX

ABOUT THE AUTHORS

J. Stanley Shaw is one of the preeminent bankruptcy attorneys in the United States and the senior partner of the law firm Shaw, Licitra, Bohner, Esernio & Schwartz, in Garden City, New York. He lives with his wife, Doris, in Bayside, New York, and Hallandale, Florida.

Peter Golden is a journalist whose work has appeared in numerous national newspapers and magazines. Winner of several awards for writing excellence, Golden is also the author of *Quiet Diplomat*, a biography of industrialist and political-insider Max M. Fisher. Golden lives in Albany, New York, with his wife, Annis, and son, Benjamin.